Learning in Living Color

Related Titles of Interest

Comprehensive Multicultural Education: Theory and Practice, Fourth Edition
Christine I. Bennett
ISBN: 0-205-28324-1

Global Perspectives for Educators
Carlos F. Diaz, Byron G. Massialas, John A. Xanthopoulos
ISBN: 0-205-26366-6

Connecting with Traditional Literature: Using Folktales, Fables, and Legends to Strengthen Students' Reading and Writing
Kimberly Kimbell-Lopez
ISBN: 0-205-27531-1

Essentials of Children's Literature, Third Edition
Carol Lynch-Brown and Carl M. Tomlinson
ISBN: 0-205-28136-2

Because We Can Change the World: A Practical Guide to Building Cooperative, Inclusive Classroom Communities
Mara Sapon-Shevin
ISBN: 0-205-17489-2

Together and Equal: Fostering Cooperative Play and Promoting Gender Equity in Early Childhood Programs
Carol Hilgartner Schlank and Barbara Metzger
ISBN: 0-205-18155-4

Open Minds to Equality: A Sourcebook of Learning Activities to Affirm Diversity and Promote Equality, Second Edition
Nancy Schniedewind and Ellen Davidson
ISBN: 0-205-16109-X

Multicultural Education: A Handbook of Activities, Information, and Resources, Fifth Edition
Pamela L. Tiedt and Iris M. Tiedt
ISBN: 0-205-27528-1

For more information or to purchase a book, please call 1-800-278-3525.

Learning in Living Color

Using Literature to Incorporate Multicultural Education into the Primary Curriculum

Alora Valdez

Allyn and Bacon

Boston ■ London ■ Toronto ■ Sydney ■ Tokyo ■ Singapore

Series Editor: Virginia Lanigan
Series Editorial Assistant: Bridget Keane
Manufacturing Buyer: Suzanne Lareau
Editorial-Production Service: Omegatype Typography, Inc.
Electronic Composition: Omegatype Typography, Inc.

Library of Congress Cataloging-in-Publication Data

Valdez, Alora
    Learning in living color : using literature to incorporate
multicultural education into the primary curriculum / by Alora
Valdez.
        p.   cm.
    Includes bibliographical references (p.) and indexes.
    ISBN 0-205-27445-5
    1. Children's literature—Study and teaching (Primary)—United
States.   2. Multicultural education—United States.   I. Title.
LB1527V35   1999
372.64—dc21   98–30374
                                                        CIP

Printed in the United States of America

10   9   8   7   6   5   4   3   2   1   02   01   00   99   98

Credits
Line drawings scattered throughout the book courtesy of Jennifer and Rudy Alzua and Damian Davis.

Permissions acknowledgments continue on page 239, which constitutes a continuation of the
copyright page.

This book is dedicated to:
The memory of my mother—my guiding light;
Don—the air beneath my wings;
Jennifer and Rudy—my shining stars;
Damian—my entire universe;
and all the children around the world.

CONTENTS

5 Focusing on Deconstructing Stereotyping   73

6 Focusing on Different Perspectives   90

PREFACE

Students of color already make up more than 30 percent of the school-age students in the United States, and this percentage continues to rise. We live in a multicultural society, and yet we do not live in a pluralistic society. In a truly pluralistic society, all people share equal access to opportunities such as education regardless of their race, ethnicity, culture, age, gender, or social class. Multicultural education is designed to reduce race, ethnicity, class, and gender divisions by helping all students acquire the knowledge, attitudes, and skills they need in order to become active citizens in a democratic society and participate in social change. Because of the changes in our country, an enormous number of teachers are now requesting information concerning multicultural education. This book describes how to use literature in order to incorporate multicultural education into a primary curriculum on a daily basis.

Organization of Book

Learning in Living Color is divided into three parts. Part One (Chapters 1 and 2) uses research and theory to address the underlying assumptions of multicultural education and literacy programs. In Part One I also offer suggestions for setting up balanced multicultural and literacy programs, including program goals, curriculum, environment, materials, teaching approaches, learning strategies, and evaluation processes.

Part Two provides integrated language arts lessons that incorporate multicultural education into the primary curriculum. The lessons are organized into chapters that focus on the following multicultural concepts:

Each lesson includes steps that help teachers integrate literacy learning processes: (1) Introducing the selection by activating prior knowledge and supplying a purpose for reading selection; (2) having students read and respond to the selection; (3) extending the literature; (4) selecting more books that relate to the multicultural objectives. These multicultural activities help students raise their consciousness about other groups in society, consider different perspectives, analyze inequality and oppression in society, and develop skills for social action.

The activities provided in Chapters 3 through 7 were shared with pre- and in-service teachers during staff development processes. One teacher who used the activities in his own classroom said, "I used to think teaching multicultural education meant teaching a whole other subject on top of what we already teach, but it's not." Another teacher talked about how excited she was to see the children become so actively involved in learning about other people and their perspectives. The children from these classrooms shared comments such as "I enjoy reading books about different people who are like me," "My favorite was learning about slavery and how it was wrong," and "I like the activities that help us make things better."

Part Three provides an up-to-date list of quality literature, both primary (P) and intermediate (I), that relates to the goals of teaching children to understand themselves and others; to understand their own and others' cultures, history, and contributions; to deconstruct stereotyping; to understand different perspectives; and to become actively involved in social action. These books are listed in two ways: The Concept Book List organizes the books alphabetically according to concept heading, and the Author Book List organizes the books alphabetically according to author. The books selected are works that present relevant multicultural issues, emphasize human rights, represent a diversity of groups, show sensitivity to a broad range of cultural experiences, have high literary value, have pleasing format and/or illustrations that enrich the text, and are written primarily for elementary-aged children. These books were either selected by professionals on the National Council for Social Studies and the Children's Book Council or personally tested out in primary classrooms.

Acknowledgments

This book would not have been possible without the help of many people. I am deeply grateful to my daughter, son-in-law, and grandson for drawing the decorative sketches. I have also been most fortunate to have three talented women—Carole Peterson, Heather Murray, and Krista Gjertsen—contribute fabulous ideas for the lessons.

I owe a debt of gratitude to the many dedicated Rhode Island teachers and student teachers at Narragansett Elementary School in Narragansett, Narragansett Pier School in Narragansett, Veazie Street School in Providence, and Roberts Elementary in Central Falls who worked with me to make the Urban–Suburban Partnership Project a success. I especially want to thank Carol Batchelder, Virginia Benoit, Denise Bilodeau, Mindy deMelo,

Beverly Deware, Elaine Eisenhaure, Donna Gatinella, Renee Grant-Kane, Betty Gulley, Paula Holland, Ruth Jernigan, Kadina Pena, Carol Prest, Hope Rawlings, Tom Sylvia, Holly Walsh, Pam Westkott, and Lynn Zilly for being a part of the Partnership Project and for giving me feedback concerning some of the multicultural lessons in this book. Thanks also to the administrators at these schools—Geraldine Copotosto, Janice DeFrances, Dave Hayes, Frank Polatta, Jeffrey Sincoski, and John Wedlock—for helping make the Partnership Project a reality.

I am deeply indebted to my best friend and fellow educator, Paula Walker, for allowing me to photograph her classroom at Borton Magnet School while her students were actively involved in lessons from this book. Paula and I have laughed and embraced life together as friends for twenty-five years, and I hope we continue to do the same for another twenty-five. And many thanks to Dr. Robert Wortman, the principal of Borton Magnet School, who has always upheld my visions. I have known Bob from way back. He always makes me feel welcome to Borton, my home away from home. Thanks also to Teri Melendez at Borton Primary Magnet School for ideas that I have incorporated in this book.

I shall always be grateful to my colleagues in the Education Department at the University of Rhode Island, especially Dr. Sandy Jean Hicks and Reba Gould, for all of their help. Dr. Hicks encouraged me to stretch from my specialties in language arts and reading into the field of multicultural education. Reba was always there to help me whenever the occasion arose. I do not want to forget to thank Ted Kellogg, my department chair, for just believing in me. My deep appreciation goes out to Virginia Richardson, a colleague and friend, who inspired me to earn my doctorate and become a professor. Without her help, none of this would have been possible.

I want to send thanks to Allyn and Bacon editor Virginia Lanigan and editorial assistant Kris Lamarre for all of the assistance they have provided. They have gone out of their way to make me feel welcome to their publishing company.

My appreciation goes to the following reviewers for their comments on the manuscript: Jami Craig, Countryside Elementary School; Dr. Stephanie Moretti, Menlo Park School; Mary R. Jalongo, Indiana University of Pennsylvania; and Pamela Monk, Boynton Middle School.

Most of all I send my love and appreciation to my family. My husband, Don, has been there through thick and thin, even when times have been tough. He is the most loving person I know. My daughter and son-in-law, Jennifer and Rudy Alzua, have really put a large part of themselves into this book. Thank you, guys. And even my special grandson, Damian Davis, pitched in. Damian, I love you dearly. I am deeply indebted to my brothers, Jeffrey Cain and Michael Cain, and to my dad, Gerald Cain, for listening to me go on and on about this book. Maybe now they can call me and I will be able to discuss something else. My mom, Mary Lu Soresen, also deserves a lot of gratitude. She always checked up on me concerning the progress of this book. Well, Mom, I did it!

PART ONE

Theoretical Framework for Multicultural Education and Literacy Learning

1 Multicultural Education

Multicultural education is a framework, a way of thinking, a philosophical viewpoint, a value orientation, and a set of criteria for making decisions that serve the educational needs of a culturally diverse population. Let's consider the basic assumptions that undergird this framework.

Underlying Assumptions

Definitions of Multicultural Education

Multicultural education permeates the entire curriculum while it focuses on the kind of knowledge, reflection, and action needed in order to promote social change (Frazier, 1977; Garcia, 1988; Grant, 1977, 1978; Nieto, 1996). Banks (1993a) maintains that

> multicultural education is an idea, an educational reform movement, and an ongoing process whose major goal is to change the structure of educational institutions so that male and female children, exceptional children, and children who are members of diverse racial, ethnic, and cultural groups will have an equal chance to achieve academically in school. (p. 1)

Importance of Multicultural Education

All children need multicultural education in order to learn to challenge and reject racism and other forms of discrimination; to accept and affirm pluralism; and to advance the democratic principles of social justice. Multicultural education is important because ethnic pluralism is now influencing the lives of young people. Young people are acquiring knowledge or beliefs that are sometimes invalid concerning ethnic and cultural groups, and invalid knowledge and beliefs about ethnic and cultural groups are limiting the perspectives that many people have available to them. It is essential that all the members of our society develop multicultural literacy—a solidly based understanding of racial, ethnic, and cultural groups and their significance in U.S. society (Banks, 1991b, 1994; NCSS 1992).

Approaches for Teaching Multicultural Education

Banks (1991b, 1993a, 1995) discusses the following four empirically based approaches used to teach multicultural education in the United States:

1. *The Contribution Approach* attempts to integrate ethnic and multicultural content into the mainstream curriculum by inserting heroes, holidays, and discrete cultural elements into the curriculum. Yet any heroes who challenged dominant society's ideologies, values, or conceptions are not usually chosen for study. The basic structure, goals, and salient characteristics of mainstream curriculum does not change. This approach gives teachers a plan of how to integrate ethnic content into curriculum without focusing on the important concepts and issues related to the victimization and oppression of ethnic groups and their struggles against racism and for power.

2. *The Additive Approach* adds content, concepts, themes, and perspectives to the curriculum without integrating them into the unit of instruction. For example, a teacher adds a book, a unit, or a course without substantially changing the structure of the curriculum. The events, concepts, issues, and problems are selected to reflect mainstream and Eurocentric perspectives. The perspective of the victors is usually what becomes institutionalized within the schools and the mainstream society.

3. *The Transformation Approach* enables children to view concepts, issues, events, and themes from the points of view of the ethnic, racial, and cultural groups that were the most active participants in, or were cogently influenced by, the event, issue, or concept being examined. The approach changes the fundamental goals, structures, and perspectives of the curriculum by infusing perspectives, frames of reference, and content from diverse groups in order to extend children's understanding of the nature, development, and complexity of the United States' society. The main concern is to point out the common U.S. culture that originates in the various cultural, racial, ethnic, and religious groups that make up the United States. This approach leads to a perspective that views ethnic events, literature, music, and art as integral parts of a common, shared U.S. culture.

4. *The Social Action Approach* is based in the transformation approach but also helps children understand the concept, issue, or problem being studied enough to make decisions about appropriate actions to solve the issues. Teachers are change agents who can guide children into becoming reflective social critics, decision makers, and skilled participants in social change. In this way, victimized and excluded ethnic and racial groups have a better chance to become full participants in U.S. society, and the nation can move closer to realizing its democratic ideals. The goal of this approach is to help children become aware of social issues and then become actively involved in finding solutions. Therefore, a teaching unit should include a problem or question requiring decision making; inquiry that provides data related to the problem; value inquiry and moral analysis; and decision making and social action.

In reviewing the multicultural literature, Grant and Sleeter (1993) found that educators use one or more of the following five approaches in order to work with children of color, children from low-income backgrounds, and white female children.

1. *The Teaching the Exceptional and Culturally Different Approach* aims solely at helping members of particular groups such as children from the inner city, bilingual children, mainstreamed special education children, immigrants, children of color, children from low-income families, and/or children with special needs make up for deficiencies at home. Teachers work with children's learning styles, culturally relevant materials, and students' native languages to help children attain success in school and society. This approach emphasizes aspects of Western culture in order to help children assimilate into the dominant culture.

2. *The Human Relations Approach* encourages positive self-concepts and relationships among children. Teachers plan and implement activities that stress cooperative learning and that tend to deconstruct stereotyping. Contributions made by members of other racial, cultural, and ethnic groups are also emphasized. Teachers who use this approach do not view any of these groups as oppressed or victimized.

3. *The Single-Group-Studies Approach* promotes raising students' consciousness about oppressed groups such as ethnic, minorities, people in the labor movement, women, or people with disabilities. This approach uses activities that teach about a particular group's history, culture, and contributions as well as how that group has been oppressed by the dominant society. But teachers may replicate distortions or inaccuracies, without realizing it, when they attempt to teach a well-meaning lesson or unit about a given group; they may not have studied an oppressed group in enough depth to realize the degree to which single-group-studies departments replicate the traditional perspectives of the dominant group. They may also be using textbooks that appear to be multicultural but are still dominated by a white male viewpoint and treat other groups in a fragmented fashion. Yet there is plenty of material available to educate oneself, and a fair amount available to educate one's students, about various groups in society.

4. *The Multicultural Education Approach* uses the goals of the first three approaches but transforms the entire educational process in order to reflect diversity, promote equality, and encourage cultural pluralism. This approach builds on learning styles, adapts to skill levels, and involves children actively thinking and exploring life situations, while assisting in the maintenance of first language and multilingual acquisition for all children. Curriculum content is reorganized around perspectives on and knowledge about various racial, ethnic, sociocultural, disability, and gender groups while drawing on the content developed through single-group studies. This approach rejects tracking and ability grouping on the grounds that they institutionalize differential achievement and unequal learning opportunities. Activities used in this approach encourage children to consider different perspectives.

5. *The Education That Is Multicultural and Social Reconstructivist Approach* builds on the first four approaches, especially the single-group-studies and multicultural education approaches. This approach begins with contemporary social justice issues that cut across various groups. It uses disciplinary knowledge to examine these issues and create means of effecting change. Activities in this approach aim to help students analyze inequality and oppression in society and acquire skills in order to become change agents.

Banks's (1991b, 1993a, 1995) analysis of the four approaches used to teach multicultural education and Grant and Sleeter's (1993) description of five approaches teachers use in working with children of color, children from low-income backgrounds, and white female children guided the theoretical framework for the lessons presented in Chapters 3 through 7 of this book.

A Balanced Multicultural Education Program

For multicultural education to be successfully implemented, educational changes must be made in the schools' goals; curriculum; environment (atmosphere and teaching materials); instructional methods (motivation, teaching strategies, and assessment); student learning strategies; goals, norms, and culture; teacher training and ongoing staff development; and program assessment.

Multicultural Goals

In order to ensure that all children will survive and function in a future U.S. society in which one out of every three people will be a person of color, educators need to:

1. Enable all children to achieve success academically (Banks, 1993a, 1993b; Nieto, 1996; Sleeter, 1992; Sleeter & Grant, 1988);
2. Help children develop empathy, sensitivity, and respect for members of various racial, ethnic, cultural, gender, and social class groups (NCSS, 1992);
3. Utilize activities that teach children to understand the different perspectives of various groups (Grant & Sleeter, 1993);
4. Assist children in becoming multiculturally literate so they possess the knowledge, skills, and attitudes they will need in a diverse U.S. society (Banks, 1991b, 1994; NCSS, 1992);
5. Further a democratic society in which children of all groups experience cultural democracy and empowerment (Banks, 1991c; Gay, 1993); and
6. Encourage cross-cultural competency in cultures beyond our national boundaries and the knowledge and comprehension we need to understand how all people living on earth are interconnected (Becker, 1979).

Multicultural Curriculum

Blackman (1992) contends that a multicultural curriculum should be an integrated part of the total curriculum. Teachers should use interdisciplinary and multidisciplinary methods to organize, implement, and transform the curriculum. The goals are to:

1. Make sure children view concepts, events, and perspectives in light of the experiences and points of view of diverse ethnic and cultural groups (Banks, 1991a; Sleeter & Grant, 1989);
2. Incorporate activities into the curriculum to help all children develop an awareness of social issues that involve unequal distribution of power, oppression, and opportunity (Blackman, 1992; Sleeter, 1992);

3. Support children's development of decision-making and social action skills that will enable them to become operative change agents in our society (Banks, 1991c, 1997; Grant & Sleeter, 1993; Sleeter, 1992);
4. Ensure that all children are introduced to or become literate in at least two different languages (NCSS, 1992; Ovando, 1993);
5. Attain the kind of instructional content that spreads ethnic and cultural diversity throughout the school environment (NCSS Task Force, 1992);
6. Support ethnic and cultural diversity by encouraging certain values, attitudes, and behaviors (NCSS, 1992);
7. Assist children in interpreting events, situations, and conflict from diverse ethnic and cultural perspectives and points of view (Banks, 1991c; Blackman, 1992; NCSS, 1992);
8. Help children recognize and comprehend the ever present struggle between ideals and realities in human societies (Blackman, 1992; NCSS, 1992);
9. Support the acquisition of the decision-making abilities, social participation skills, and sense of political efficacy that are necessary for effective citizenship (NCSS, 1992);
10. Extensively explore the cultures, historical experiences, social realities, and existential conditions of the various ethnic, racial, cultural, gender, and social class groups in the United States (NCSS Task Force, 1992); and
11. Provide alternatives and options for members of various cultural, racial, ethnic, gender, and social class groups (NCSS, 1992; Nieto, 1996).

A Multicultural Environment

Atmosphere. Effective multicultural teaching can take place within an educational setting that encourages diversity. To attain this atmosphere, schools should reform the entire environment by:

- Understanding, respecting, and valuing the differences among members of various cultural, racial, ethnic, gender, and social class groups (NCSS, 1992; Nieto, 1996);
- Encouraging positive multicultural interactions among students, teachers, and support staff from various racial, ethnic, and cultural groups (Banks, 1991c; NCSS, 1992);
- Assisting children in gaining the skills necessary for positive interpersonal and intercultural group interactions (NCSS, 1992); and
- Cultivating a multiethnic and multiracial school staff consisting of high-quality teachers (Ferguson, 1991; NCSS, 1992).

Materials. In order to permeate the total environment with ethnic and cultural diversity, schools must make the following readily available to students:

- Instructional materials that "treat racial and ethnic differences and groups honestly, realistically, sensitively" (NCSS, 1992, 141);
- Instructional materials and resources that accurately reflect the experiences of people of color, women, people with disabilities, and people living in poverty (Gay, 1993; Grant & Tate, 1995; NCSS, 1992);

- Instructional materials and resources that reflect the histories, cultures, and contributions of many racial, ethnic, and cultural groups from their point of view (Gay, 1993; NCSS Task Force, 1992);
- Materials and resources written by and about members of various cultural, racial, ethnic, gender, and social class groups (NCSS, 1992);
- Materials and resources that promote examination, understanding, and empathy for people from various ethnic and cultural groups (NCSS, 1992);
- Literature such as poetry, short stories, novels, folklore, plays, essays, and autobiographies of people from various ethnic and cultural groups (NCSS, 1992); and
- A variety of the arts—music, art, architecture, and dance—expressing the perspectives of various ethnic and cultural groups (NCSS, 1992).

Multicultural Instruction

Motivation.   The social dimensions of the classroom are important in motivating many children to engage in learning. Therefore, invite children to get actively involved with multicultural education by:

- Reflecting a positive attitude toward multicultural literacy (Banks, 1988a; NCSS Task Force, 1992);
- Having high expectations for children; specifying the knowledge, skills, and understandings you wish them to learn, and teaching the children that knowledge, those skills, and those understandings (Brookover & Erickson, 1975; Gay, 1993; NCSS, 1992; Nieto, 1996; Persell, 1993; Sleeter, 1992);
- Protecting children's right to cultivate and maintain a positive self-concept and sense of self-worth (Donaldson, 1994; Gay, 1993; NCSS Task Force, 1992; Nieto, 1996); and
- Making maximum use of the social and cultural practices of the community for instructional purposes in the classroom (Moll, 1992; NCSS Task Force, 1992).

Teaching Strategies.   Multicultural education is a broad concept with several different and important dimensions. In order for teachers to respond to multicultural issues, Banks (1991b, 1992, 1993a, 1993b) contends they need to:

- Change instruction in ways that will equalize the potential for academic achievement of children from diverse racial, cultural, gender, and social class groups;
- Utilize examples and content from various cultures and groups to portray key concepts, principles, generalizations, and theories from all instructional disciplines;
- Assist children in exploring and comprehending the implicit cultural assumptions, frames of reference, perspectives, and biases that influence the construction of knowledge within each instructional discipline (Gould, 1981).

Other strategies teachers can use to provide children with an equal opportunity to learn include:

- Eliminating tracking, as well as providing other strategies such as cooperative learning, to improve learning and intergroup relations in various instructional disciplines

(Aronson & Gonzales, 1988; Gay, 1993; NCSS, 1992; Oakes, 1985, 1992; Persell, 1993; Sleeter, 1992);

- Providing culturally compatible, congruent, appropriate, responsive, and/or relevant instruction to improve children's academic success (Au & Kawakami in Nieto, 1996);
- Using comparative instructional approaches that focus on the similarities and differences among and between children of different racial, ethnic, and cultural groups (Blackman, 1992; NCSS, 1992);
- Constructing active instructional opportunities that promote children's using various modes of oral and written language in order to interact with members of other racial, ethnic, and cultural groups (Cohen, 1986; Cooper & Sherk, 1989; Garcia, 1993);
- Structuring instructional tasks so children can acquire or activate the prior knowledge needed to enhance learning, especially in the area of literacy (Smith, 1965);
- Providing instructional tasks that require children to use higher-order thinking skills such as hypothesizing, predicting, evaluating, and synthesizing ideas (Bowman, 1993; Braddock & McParland, 1993; Darling-Hammond, 1995; Resnick, 1987);
- Utilizing small group projects, speakers, discussions in which the children do most of the talking, interviews, and experiments in order to provide for different ethnic and cultural communication styles (Au & Kawakami, 1994; NCSS, 1992; Nieto, 1996; Sleeter & Grant, 1989);
- Planning events in which children participate in the aesthetic experiences of various ethnic and cultural groups (NCSS Task Force, 1992); and
- Providing children with opportunities to write their own literature and create their own fine arts (NCSS, 1992).

Student Assessment.   To make the school a truly multicultural institution, educators need to make major changes in the ways children are assessed and evaluated. For example, schools should

- Apply the kind of assessment devices that provide multidimensional views of performance and help inform ever changing approaches to instruction (Darling-Hammond, 1995; Mercer, 1989);
- Utilize long-term assessment procedures that reflect the ethnic and cultural diversity of the children (Gay, 1993; NCSS, 1992; Nieto, 1996);
- Use day-to-day assessment techniques that take into account the ethnic and cultural diversity of the children (NCSS, 1992); and
- Employ alternative ways to assess students' learning, such as performance-based or authentic assessments that engage students in the real world (Wiggins, 1989).

Students' Learning Styles

In order that intergroup relations and achievement for children of different ethnicities and backgrounds be improved, a school's instructional program—goals, curriculum, environment, objectives, strategies, and learning materials—should do the following:

1. Build on children's cultural and ethnic learning styles (Banks, 1988b; NCSS, 1992; Nieto, 1996; Shade & New, 1993);

2. Tap into the children's multiple intelligences and employ their multiple pathways to learning (Gardner, 1983, 1991);
3. Accommodate the cognitive styles, language, and communication of the various ethnic and cultural groups within a classroom (Heath, 1983; NCSS, 1992); and
4. Stress cooperative rather than competitive learning (NCSS, 1992; Nieto, 1996; Slavin, 1983, 1990).

Restructuring the Goals, Norms, and Culture of School

In order that children from diverse racial, ethnic, and social-class groups will experience educational equality and cultural empowerment (Cummins, 1986), schools' goals, norms, and culture need to be restructured. Schools should

1. Reflect the various cultures and learning styles of the children (Banks & Banks, 1989);
2. Radically change some of the major assumptions, beliefs, and structures within school (NCSS, 1992);
3. Alter the nature of teaching work and knowledge (Darling-Hammond, 1995);
4. Create a more active, integrated, and intellectually challenging curriculum (Darling-Hammond, 1995);
5. Make teachers more active in developing curriculum and assessing student performance (Darling-Hammond, 1995);
6. Transform the nature of teacher coaching and mentoring (Darling-Hammond, 1995); and
7. Work more closely with families and community agencies (Darling-Hammond, 1995).

Teacher Training and Ongoing Staff Development

The report of the NCSS Task Force on Ethnic Studies Curriculum Guide (1992) contends that schools should require pre- and in-service teachers, librarians, administrators, and support staff to attend continuing, extensive, and systematic multicultural teacher training and ongoing staff development. The goals for this type of training would include:

1. Providing all participants with time to explore their attitudes and feelings about their own and others' ethnicity (NCSS, 1992);
2. Enabling participants to learn how to create and select multiethnic instructional materials (Banks, 1997; Grant, 1995; NCSS Task Force, 1992);
3. Helping all participants to gain understanding, sensitivity, and knowledge about various racial, ethnic, and cultural groups (Bullivant, 1993; NCSS, 1992);
4. Having all participants examine the verbal and nonverbal pattern of interethnic group interactions (Grant & Sleeter, 1989; NCSS Task Force, 1992);
5. Helping all participants to incorporate multicultural content into the curriculum (NCSS, 1992);
6. Encouraging all participants to analyze their teaching procedures and styles to determine the extent to which they reflect multicultural issues and concerns (Banks, 1993a);

7. Helping all participants gain a strong knowledge base on how children learn and develop (Darling-Hammond, 1995);
8. Assisting all participants in acquiring a strong knowledge base on how curricular and instructional strategies can address children's needs (Darling-Hammond, 1995); and
9. Furnishing all participants with a strong knowledge base on how changes in school and classroom organization can support children's growth and achievement (Darling-Hammond, 1995).

Program Assessment

Gay (1993) and the NCSS (1992) maintain that schools should provide an ongoing evaluation of their program in terms of the following:

1. Multicultural goals
2. Multicultural curriculum
3. Multicultural environment—atmosphere and teaching materials
4. Multicultural instructional methods—motivation, teaching strategies, and assessment
5. Multicultural children's learning strategies
6. Multicultural school culture
7. Multicultural teacher training and staff development

Teachers should also reflect on Banks's (1991b, 1992) three dimensions of instruction —content integration, the knowledge construction process, and an equity pedagogy—when trying to respond to their own issues of multicultural education.

REFERENCES

Aronson, E., & Gonzales, A. 1988. Desegregation, jigsaw, and the Mexican–American experience. In P. A. Katz & D. A. Taylor, eds., *Eliminating racism: Profiles in controversy,* pp. 301–314. New York: Plenum.

Au, K. H., & Kawakami, A. J. 1994. Cultural congruence in instruction. In E. R. Hollins, J. E. King, & W. C. Hayman, eds., *Teaching diverse populations: Formulating a knowledge base.* Albany: State University of New York Press.

Banks, J. A. 1988a. *Multiethnic education: Theory and practice,* 2nd edition. Boston: Allyn and Bacon.

Banks, J. A. 1988b. Ethnicity, class, cognitive, and motivational styles: Research and teaching implications. *Journal of Negro Education, 57,* 452–466.

Banks, J. A. 1991a. Multicultural literacy and curriculum reform. *Educational Horizons, 69,* 135–140.

Banks, J. A. 1991b. The dimensions of multicultural education. *Multicultural Leader, 4(1),* 3–4.

Banks, J. A. 1991c. Multicultural education: Its effects on children's racial and gender role attitudes. In J. P. Shaver, ed., *Handbook of research on social studies teaching and learning,* pp. 459–469. New York: Macmillan.

Banks, J. A. 1992. Multicultural education: Approaches, developments, and dimensions. In J. Lynch, C. Modgil, & S. Modgil, eds., *Cultural diversity and the schools: Vol. 1. Education for cultural diversity: Convergence and divergence,* pp. 83–94. London: Falmer Press.

Banks, J. A. 1993a. Multicultural education: Characteristics and goals. In J. A. Banks & C. A. M. Banks, eds., *Multicultural education: Issues and perspectives,* 2nd edition. Boston: Allyn and Bacon.

Banks, J. A. 1993b. The cannon debate, knowledge construction, and multicultural education. *Educational Researcher, 22(5),* 4–14.

Banks, J. A. 1994. *An introduction to multicultural education.* Boston: Allyn and Bacon.

Banks, J. A. 1995. Multicultural education: Historical development, dimensions, and practice. In J. A. Banks & C. A. M. Banks, eds., *Handbook of research on multicultural education,* pp. 3–24. New York: Macmillan.

Banks, J. A. 1997. *Teaching strategies for ethnic studies,* 6th edition. Boston: Allyn and Bacon.

Banks, J. A., and Banks, C. A. M. 1989. *Multicultural education: Issues and perspectives.* Boston: Allyn and Bacon.

Becker, J. M., ed. 1979. *Schooling for a global age.* New York: McGraw-Hill.

Blackman, J. A. 1992, Nov. Confronting Thomas Jefferson, slave owner. *Phi Delta Kappan,* pp. 220–222.

Bowman, B. 1993. Early childhood education. In L. Darling-Hammond, ed., *Review of research in education: Vol. 19,* pp. 101–134. Washington, DC: American Education Research Association.

Braddock, J., & McParland, J. M. 1993. Education of early adolescents. In L. Darling-Hammond, ed., *Review of research in education: Vol. 19,* pp. 135–170. Washington, DC: American Education Research Association.

Brookover, W. B., & Erickson, E. 1975. *Sociology of education.* Homewood, IL: Dorsey.

Bullivant, B. M. 1993. Culture: Its nature and meaning for educators. In J. A. Banks & C. A. M. Banks, eds., *Multicultural education: Issues and perspectives,* 2nd edition. Boston: Allyn and Bacon.

Cohen, E. G. 1986. *Designing group work: Strategies for the heterogeneous classroom.* New York: Teachers College Press.

Cooper, E., & Sherk, J. 1989. Addressing urban school reform: Issues and alliances. *Journal of Negro Education, 58(3),* 315–331.

Cummins, J. 1986. Empowering minority students: A framework for intervention. *Harvard Educational Review, 56,* 18–36.

Darling-Hammond, L. 1995. Inequality and access to knowledge. In J. A. Banks & C. A. M. Banks, eds., *Handbook of research on multicultural education,* pp. 465–483. New York: Macmillan.

Donaldson, K. 1994, Dec. Through students' eyes. *Multicultural Education,* pp. 26–28.

Ferguson, R. F. 1991. Paying for public education: New evidence in how and why money matters. *Harvard Journal on Legislation, 28(2),* 465–498.

Frazier, L. 1977. Multicultural facet of education. *Journal of Research and Development in Education, 11,* 10–16.

Garcia, R. I. 1988. *Teaching for a pluralistic society: Concepts, models, strategies.* New York: Harper and Row.

Garcia, E. 1993. Language, culture, and education. In L. Darling-Hammond, ed., *Review of research in education: Vol. 19,* pp. 51–98. Washington, DC: American Education Research Association.

Gardner, H. 1983. *Frames of the mind: The theory of multiple intelligences.* New York: Basic Books.

Gardner, H. 1991. *The unschooled mind.* New York: Basic Books.

Gay, G. 1993. Ethnic minorities and educational equality. In J. A. Banks & C. A. M. Banks, eds., *Multicultural education: Issues and perspectives,* 2nd edition. Boston: Allyn and Bacon.

Gould, S. J. 1981. *The mismeasurement of man.* New York: Norton.

Grant, C. A. 1977. Education that is multicultural and P/CBTE: Discussion and recommendations for teacher education. In F. H. Klan & D. M., eds., *Pluralism and the American teacher: Issues and case studies,* pp. 63–80. Washington, DC: Ethnic Heritage Center for Teacher Education of the American Association of Colleges for Teacher Education.

Grant, C. A. 1978. Education that is multicultural—isn't that what we mean? *Journal of Teacher Education, 29,* 45–49.

Grant, C. A., ed. 1995. *Educating for diversity: An anthology of multicultural voices.* Boston: Allyn and Bacon.

Grant, C. A., & Sleeter, C. E. 1989. *Turning on learning: Five approaches for multicultural teaching plans for race, class, gender, and disability.* Englewoods Cliffs, NJ: Merlin.

Grant, C. A., & Sleeter, C. E. 1993. Race, class, gender, and disability in the classroom. In J. A. Banks & C. A. M. Banks, eds., *Multicultural education: Issues and perspectives,* 2nd edition. Boston: Allyn and Bacon.

Grant, C. A. & Tate, W. F. 1995. Multicultural education through the lens of multicultural education research literature. In J. A. Banks & C. A. M. Banks, eds., *Handbook of research on multicultural education,* pp. 145–168. New York: Macmillan.

Mercer, J. R. 1989. Alternative paradigms for assessment in a pluralistic society. In J. A. Banks & C. A. M. Banks, eds., *Multicultural education,* pp. 289–304. Boston: Allyn and Bacon.

Moll, L. C., 1992. Bilingual classroom studies and community analysis: Some research trends. *Educational Researcher, 21*(2), 20–24.

NCSS Task Force on Ethnic Studies Curriculum Guide. 1992, Sept. Curriculum guidelines for multicultural education. *Social Education,* pp. 274–294.

Nieto, S. 1996. *Affirming diversity: The sociopolitical context of multicultural education,* 2nd edition. New York: Longman.

Oakes, J. 1985. *Keeping track: How schools structure inequality.* New Haven, CT: Yale University Press.

Oakes, J. 1992. Can tracking research inform practice? Technical, normative, and political considerations. *Educational Researcher, 2(4),* 12–21.

Ovando, C. J. 1993. Language diversity and education. In J. A. Banks & C. A. M. Banks, eds., *Multicultural education: Issues and perspectives,* 2nd edition. Boston: Allyn and Bacon.

Persell, C. H. 1993. Social class and educational equality. In J. A. Banks & C. A. M. Banks, eds., *Multicultural education: Issues and perspectives,* 2nd edition. Boston: Allyn and Bacon.

Resnick, L. B. 1987. *Education and learning to think.* Washington, DC: National Academy Press.

Shade, B. J., & New, C. A. 1993. Cultural influence on learning: Teaching implications. In J. A. Banks & C. A. M. Banks, eds., *Multicultural education: Issues and perspectives,* 2nd edition. Boston: Allyn and Bacon.

Slavin, R. E. 1983. *Cooperative learning.* New York: Longman.

Slavin, R. E. 1990. *Cooperative learning: Theory, research, and practice.* Englewood Cliffs, NJ: Prentice-Hall.

Sleeter, C. E. 1992. Multicultural education: Five views. *Kappa Delta Pi Record, 29,* 4–8.

Sleeter, C. E., & Grant, C. A. 1988. *Making choices for multicultural education: Five approaches to race, class, and gender.* Columbus, OH: Merlin.

Sleeter, C. E., & Grant, C. A. 1989. An analysis of multicultural education in the United States. *Harvard Educational Review, 57(4),* 421–444.

Smith, N. B. 1965. *American reading instruction.* Newark, DE: International Reading Association.

Wiggins, G. 1989. Teaching to the (authentic) test. *Educational Leadership, 46(7),* 41–47.

2 Literacy Learning

The use of literature to promote multicultural education is the theme of all the lesson plans and book lists in this book. Fundamental to the use of literature is literacy learning itself.

Underlying Assumptions

The Goal of Literacy Learning

The ultimate goal of literacy learning, often viewed as acquisition of the ability to read and write, is to comprehend/construct meaning (Halliday, 1975; Teale & Sulzby, 1986). Comprehension/construction of meaning is the process of relating ideas from the text to one's prior knowledge and background (Anderson & Pearson, 1984; Goodman, 1986; Rosenblatt, 1938/1983; Rumelhart, 1980).

Motivation

Children learn more readily when they are highly motivated (Holdaway, 1979). Parents and teachers help motivate children for language and literacy learning if they (1) show a positive attitude towards literacy (Fader, 1982; Routman, 1988; Wigfield & Asher, 1984); (2) have high expectations for all children (Hennings, 1997; Wigfield & Asher, 1984); (3) surround children with real literature (Rosenblatt, 1938/1983; Sanders, 1987); (4) assist children in developing language/literacy holistically (Goodman, 1986; Halliday, 1975); (5) read aloud to children every day and provide opportunities for children to share every day (Dressel, 1990; Feitelson, Kita, & Goldstein, 1986; Goodman, 1986; Hennings, 1997; McCormick, 1977; Strickland & Taylor, 1989); and (6) establish a cooperative classroom environment (Berghoff & Egawa, 1991; Hennings, 1997).

Emergent Literacy

Emergent literacy, the continuous and unending process of acquiring language through interactions and experiences, is an important factor in literacy learning (Whitmore & Goodman, 1993). When children have real literacy experiences for their own social, technical, and aesthetic purposes and are supported by a more experienced individual, they become independent readers and writers (Sanders, 1987; Strickland, 1990; Taylor & Dorsey-Gaines, 1988).

A Literate Classroom

A literate classroom is vital in promoting language and literacy learning. Teachers should encourage language and literacy learning by making optimal use of available space, selecting and promoting quality literature, providing children with a wide range of literacy materials, and cultivating a cooperative classroom community (Berghoff & Egawa, 1991; Cooper, 1997; Goodman & Goodman, 1991; Hennings, 1997; Huck, Helper, & Hickman, 1993; Norton, 1991; Wortman & Haussler, 1989).

Integration of Language Use

Children learn to read, write, speak, listen, and think simultaneously as they become literate. Speaking, listening, reading, writing, and thinking are integrated because they are integrated in real language use; they are all happening in the context of real experiences and are the tools to support learning across the curriculum (Cooper, 1997; Goodman, 1986; Pappas & Brown, 1987; Routman, 1994; Strickland, 1990).

Reading and Writing As Mutually Supportive

Reading and writing are both constructive processes that are mutually supportive (Pearson & Tierney, 1984). Readers learn to read by reading, and writers learn to write by writing and responding in supportive contexts to their reading and writing—a "skills-through-application approach" (Goodman, 1986; Pappas & Brown, 1987; Walmsley & Walp, 1990, p. 258). Therefore, reading and writing assignments should always be interrelated (Atwell, 1987, 1991; Pearson & Tierney, 1984).

A Balanced Literacy Program

Successful implementation of a literacy program requires changes in many aspects of education: motivational techniques, the classroom environment, instructional methods, methods used to plan for literacy learning, evaluation processes, and ways to connect the home and school.

Motivational Techniques for Literacy Learning

Show a Positive Attitude toward Literacy.   Teachers should cultivate a love for learning and make learning to read and write easy, desirable, and pleasurable (Fader, 1982; Routman, 1988; Wigfield & Asher, 1984).

Have High Expectations for All Children.   All children are capable of learning, so it is important that teachers set high expectations for success for all students (Hennings, 1997; Wigfield & Asher, 1984).

Surround Children with Real Literature.   Surround children with real literature in order to promote daily, self-selected reading and writing (Rosenblatt, 1938/1983; Sanders,

1987). Real literature programs encourage children to read/listen to stories again and again with "passionate attention" (Cullinan & Galda, 1994; Huck, 1989; Sanders, 1987).

Danielson and LaBonty (1994) contend that the use of real literature in the classroom helps teachers to (*a*) celebrate artistry; (*b*) teach vocabulary and concept development; (*c*) give early readers confidence in their reading ability; (*d*) promote understanding of cultural diversity; (*e*) generate an interest in the real world; (*f*) involve readers in the infectious nature of language; (*g*) motivate children to read for enjoyment; (*h*) provide positive models for writing; (*i*) integrate the entire curriculum; (*j*) allow children not just to read a story but to nurture their dreams and imagination.

Assist Children in Developing Language/Literacy Holistically.   Children become more effective language learners when language learning is "whole, real and relevant; sensible and functional; encountered in the context of its use; and chosen by the learner" (Goodman, 1986, p. 26). That is, children should learn language holistically rather than in bits and pieces (Goodman, 1986; Halliday, 1975). In order to assist children in constructing meaning, teachers should focus on phonics only in the context of the text (Goodman, 1986).

In a whole language program, children should (*a*) use language, in all its varieties, for their own purposes because merely learning a sequence of skills will not facilitate the use of language (Goodman, 1986); (*b*) be immersed in the world of print and learn to read and write through natural interaction with that world (Whitmore & Goodman, 1993); (*c*) learn to read by interacting with authentic texts and making meaning in reference to them (Goodman, 1986); and (*d*) learn to focus on the meaning of the stories, not on the parts of the words.

Read Aloud to Children Every Day and Provide Opportunities for Children to Share Every Day.   Reading aloud and providing opportunities for speaking/sharing daily motivates children to read and write while providing a basis for expanding oral language and drawing upon prior knowledge (Dressel, 1990; Goodman, 1986; Feitelson, Kita, & Goldstein, 1986; Hennings, 1997; McCormick, 1977; Strickland & Taylor, 1989).

Guidelines for reading aloud to children every day in your classroom: (1) find a comfortable environment; (2) become a storyteller; and (3) allow for discussion (Cooper, 1997; Goodman, 1986). Also, make sure to provide a special time in which children can share or present their finished writing projects. You can accomplish this through show-and-tell time, by establishing "author's chair," or by displaying children's works (Cooper, 1997).

Establish a Cooperative Classroom Community.   Language and literacy learning are cultivated when children belong to a cooperative classroom community in which they interact and collaborate naturally with each other on a daily basis (Berghoff & Egawa, 1991; Hennings, 1997). Children should work together in pairs, in small groups, in large groups, and independently within classroom communities (Hennings, 1997).

A Literate Classroom Environment

Classroom Setup.   To create a literate environment, make sure to include the following areas in the classroom:

library area; writing/publishing area; listening, speaking, viewing areas; conference area; research area; creative arts area; math, science, and social studies areas; group meeting/ sharing area; computer/technology area; and display area (Cooper, 1997).

Literacy Materials.   To promote literacy learning, include the following materials in the classroom:

Kinds of Literature.   Participation books, Big Books, finger rhymes, nursery songs, ABC books, counting books, concept books, wordless books, books for beginning readers, picture books, folktales, fables, myths, epics, modern fairy tales, modern fantasy, science fiction, poetry, realistic fiction, historical fiction, biography, nonfiction, newspapers, magazines, computer software, reference books, dictionaries, thesauruses, content area books, and basal readers (Huck, Helper, & Hickman, 1993).

Writing Utensils.   Pencils, pens, colored pencils, crayons, Magic Markers, paint brushes.

Paper.   Lined, unlined, storybook, and drawing paper; stationery; postcards; graph and computer paper.

Additional Supplies.   Stapler, staple remover, erasers, rulers, scissors, glue, tape, paper clips, paper punches, paper fasteners, date stamp and pad, "Unedited" stamp.

Materials for Publishing.   Computers, typewriters, and tape recorders.

Selection Criteria.   Chose literature according to the following criteria: its worth, students' needs and interests, curriculum requirements, developmental appropriateness, student attraction, literary appeal, and cultural and social authenticity (Goodman & Goodman, 1991; Huck, Helper, & Hickman, 1993; Norton, 1991).

Instructional Methods

Important elements of instruction in a balanced literacy program are setting goals, supporting emergent readers, and helping children construct meaning.

Setting Instructional Goals.   Two key goals are a focus on meaning and the integration of listening, speaking, reading, writing, and thinking.

Focus on Meaning.   Comprehension involves both construction of meaning and a strategic process (Cooper, 1997). In construction of meaning, readers relate new information presented by the author to old information stored in their minds—schemata, prior knowledge, and background knowledge (Anderson & Pearson, 1984; Goodman, 1986; Rosenblatt, 1938/ 1983; Rumelhart, 1980). Many studies have shown that schemata, prior knowledge, and background knowledge, which children develop through real experiences, greatly influence comprehension (Pearson, Hansen, & Gordon, 1979).

In comprehension as a strategic process, readers use metacognition to adjust their reading according to the purpose of their reading and the type of text they are reading (Anderson, Hiebert, Scott, & Wilkinson, 1985). Metacognition is the knowledge and control students have over their own thinking and learning (Brown, 1980).

In order to help children comprehend/construct meaning, help them to interact meaningfully with the text and each other through authentic speech and literacy events (Goodman, 1986; Routman, 1988). Provide the children with metacognitive strategies; for example, teach them to focus on relevant features of the text in relation to their prior experiences (Cooper, 1997; Dalrymple, 1991a; Goodman, 1986; Hennings, 1997). Also, make sure to emphasize semantics and syntax before phonics; strategies for reading and writing should focus primarily on meaning (Routman, 1988).

Integration of Listening, Speaking, Reading, Writing, and Thinking.   Listening, speaking, reading, writing, and thinking are interrelated parts of a literary curriculum (Fredericks, Meinbach, & Rothen, 1993). Therefore, a major focus of instruction should be the development of socially interactive activities that encourage children to authentically create and communicate meanings and to use language in all its forms—through listening, speaking, reading, writing, and thinking (Cooper, 1997; Hennings, 1997; Pappas, Kiefer, & Levstik, 1990).

Supporting Emergent Readers.   Ways to support beginning readers include encouraging language acquisition, fostering awareness of written language, and promoting shared/repeated reading of enjoyable texts.

Language Acquisition.   Children acquire language by trying out and making approximations of real language. Therefore, accept errors during literacy development; children gradually perfect their use of language through approximations (Halliday, 1975). Provide opportunities in which children create and communicate meanings through social interaction and use language in all its forms in order to become more effective language users (Goodman, 1986; Wells, 1990).

Print, Sight Vocabulary, and Phonemic Awareness.   Children learn phonics and other aspects of word identification by being immersed in meaningful texts and through such activities as shared readings (Adams, 1990). It is important that educators do not support the teaching of isolated phonics, which is contrary to what we know about how children develop literacy (Adams, 1990; Whitmore & Goodman, 1993).

Build and support an awareness of the concepts of print and sight vocabulary through various kinds of literacy events. Create a literate environment; label everything in the classroom with functional print; encourage children to be aware of and use functional print; encourage children to handle books; provide activities that expand on children's sense of the style and form of written language; encourage children to compose through dictation to more capable others and through personal writing (Goodman 1986).

Shared/Repeated Reading.   Shared reading and repeated reading of meaningful texts provide support for beginning readers (Freppon, 1991). "Children learn most effectively through participation in meaningful, joint activities in which their performance is assisted and guided by a more competent member of the culture" (Wells, 1990, p. 15). Lev Vygotsky (1978) contends that children learn in the zone of proximal development—the range in which a child can perform a task by first being supported by more experienced adults and peers (Vygotsky, 1978; Wells, 1990).

The purposes of shared reading include reading for pleasure, to develop meaning, to develop concepts about print, to explore language, and to decode words within the context of the text (Cooper, 1997). Books that are highly predictable—in terms of rhyme and sound patterns and plot—and highly motivating should be used for shared reading. Children can use the patterns provided in the highly predictable books also to assist them in writing (Holdaway, 1979). During repeated readings, sound elements are modeled; you can then encourage the children to spell words as they think they are spelled (invented spelling).

A lesson plan for shared reading can look like this: (1) Warm up. (2) Reread a favorite story. (3) Extend the book or have a language study. (4) Read a new book. (5) Have individual reading. (6) Include creative activities. (7) Allow children to share (Cooper, 1997).

A lesson plan for repeated reading can look like this: (1) Teacher reads aloud. (2) Children read along. (3) Children read alone. During read-alongs the adult reads aloud and stops periodically to allow the children to take over. Read-alongs include listening post centers, Big Books, sing-along charts, and choral reading of poems (Cooper, 1997).

Helping Children Construct Meaning. The ultimate goal in developing literacy is to help students comprehend/construct meanings. The following methods can assist the children in becoming independent readers and writers.

Activating Prior Knowledge. Rosenblatt (1991) was the first researcher to suggest that reading is a transaction between the reader and the text. She believed that readers have the right to, and do, establish or construct texts' meanings. In order to further the children's ability to construct meaning/comprehend, teachers should help children learn to activate their own prior knowledge and experience (Cooper, 1997; Hennings, 1997). Activating prior knowledge also helps children set their own purposes for reading (Rumelhart, 1980).

Developing Vocabulary. Research has established a strong relationship between knowledge of word meaning and construction of text meaning (Anderson & Freebody, 1981). Two ways in which children acquire vocabulary are through wide reading and through direct instruction in word meaning (Beck & McKeown, 1991). Most vocabulary learning should take place through independent reading (Cooper, 1997). When direct instruction is necessary, vocabulary should be taught in context before, during, and/or after reading (Beck & McKeown, 1991; Cooper, 1997; Graves, 1987; Routman, 1988). Children can also be made aware of word meanings by using vocabulary journals and through read-alouds, discussion circles, word banks, the writing process, and word walls (see Cooper, 1997).

Encouraging Response to Literature. Children develop a sense of ownership, pride, and respect for learning in a classroom when they listen to, read, and respond to everything they read, write, and hear daily (Parsons, 1990). Children use what they observe in reading and listening to stories in the writing process (Cooper, 1977; Goodman, 1986). Children can respond personally to literature through retellings, summarizing, analyzing, and generalizing.

Children can respond creatively to literature through journals (diaries, response journals, dialogue journals, and double-entry journals), response options (see list under "Connecting Reading and Writing" below), literature discussion groups, and reader's theater (Calkins, 1986; Cooper, 1997; Graves, 1983; Harste & Short, 1991; Pappas, Kiefer, & Levstik, 1990).

Modeling Strategies.   Children need to learn strategies in order to become independent readers and writers (Anderson, Hiebert, Scott, & Wilkinson, 1985; Brown, 1980; Paris, Lipson, & Turner, 1991). Teachers should encourage, model, and provide opportunities for children to practice specific reading and writing strategies that will help readers make sense of print and writers express meaning. These strategies include brainstorming, predicting, selecting, divergent and evaluative questioning, and confirming and self-correcting strategies (Cooper, 1997; Goodman, 1986; Routman, 1988).

Connecting Reading and Writing.   Integrating reading and writing is important for several reasons:

- Reading and writing are closely related;
- Reading and writing develop together naturally;
- Reading and writing use identical cognitive processes;
- Connecting reading and writing produces outcomes not attributable to either process alone;
- Reading improves writing achievement and vice versa;
- Communication is fostered by both reading and writing;
- Both readers and writers use their experiences and purposes to construct meaning; and
- Children take charge of their own reading and writing through the writing process (Calkins, 1986; Graves, 1991; Karelitz, 1993).

Ways to connect reading and writing can be grouped in two main categories: response to literature and practice of the writing process.

Children can respond to literature by keeping diaries, response journals, dialogue journals, or double-entry journals; by writing Big Books, pop-up books, or rebus stories; by reading related books, magazine articles, or poetry; by creating a slide show, a series of cartoons, or transparencies from different parts of the book; by writing a letter to the author, to a character in the book, or to the illustrator; by rewriting the story as a folktale, fairy tale, or tall tale; or by creating another beginning or ending to the story (Cooper, 1997; Pappas, Kiefer, & Levstik, 1990; Hennings, 1997).

Utilizing the writing process begins with choosing a topic to write about. Help children compose meaning so as to convey it to the reader, think about what they have written, reread it, and revise it to make it clearer (Pearson & Tierney, 1984). Model good techniques for *prewriting, drafting, revising, editing, "publishing,"* and *conferencing* in order to help children work toward independent writing (Goodman, 1986; Hennings, 1997).

Children *prewrite* in order to activate their own prior knowledge and choose their topic. Prewriting activities include brainstorming, clustering, mapping, listening, reading, being read to, talking, engaging in conferences, writing in journals, drawing pictures, writing titles, dramatizing, and participating in daily literacy events.

Children use *drafting* in order to develop their topic without worrying about revising and/or editing. Emphasize writing for meaning and communication; stress ideas over form; promote the consideration of voice and audience; and provide drafting time, strategies, and opportunities.

Children *revise* in order to improve upon the quality of what they have written. At this stage emphasize unity development, clarity, emphasis, word choice, and organization. Also, have children consider whether they need to add reasons, examples, other supporting evidence, further supporting information, qualifying details, concrete examples, and/or sensory details.

Children *edit* to check their spelling, writing mechanics, and sentence structure. Let children be their own and others' editors for pieces of writing that they want to publish. Editing helps children increase their vocabulary and improve their handwriting, spelling, grammar, punctuation, and capitalization skills.

Children's works are *"published"* in the form of a final copy that can be shared with others. Ways in which you can publish children's work include reading students' work aloud to the class; publishing a classroom newspaper; furnishing collections of children's pieces; mailing works to a local newspaper; allowing children to choose favorite pieces to publish each semester; producing transparencies of children's papers; sharing children's work with other adults.

Conferencing enables you and the students to focus on any stage of the writing process. When you have a teacher–child conference, play a low-key role. Do not dominate the conversation but develop the art of questioning instead of telling what to do, use questions to move the child along, and show an interest in what the child is trying to express. Get to know as many of the child's interests as possible, be aware of the child's strengths and weaknesses in writing, and be positive at all times. Children can also learn peer conferencing techniques from conferencing with their teacher. For example, the teacher can share a transparency of a piece of writing with students, guide a class discussion about the piece of writing and model questioning techniques that would be appropriate in peer conferencing, and engage children in read-around groups so children can hear several readings of and responses to their papers.

Children may explore a wide variety of types of writing. Possibilities include patterned stories, interviews, instructions, lists, informational texts, recipes, newspaper articles, thank-you letters, notes, postcards, scripts, poetry (free thoughts, haiku, tanka, acrostics, rhyming, narratives), accounts, biographies, autobiographies, historical fiction, realistic fiction, mystery fiction, talking-beast tales, and *pourquoi* tales (Hennings, 1997).

Accepting Approximations in Reading and Writing.   Children go through approximations as they strive to develop their own literacy; therefore, they should be encouraged and praised for taking risks (Cambourne, 1988; Goodman, 1986; Routman, 1988; Wells, 1990). Children naturally try out new functions and strategies through extensive reading by focusing on meaning. Therefore, reading miscues should be celebrated if they contribute to constructing meaning. During writing, children first use invented spelling as needed in writing. Spelling then develops naturally through writing for real purposes. Therefore, provide authentic purposes for reading and writing in the classroom, and accept reading miscues and invented spellings while at the same time teaching conventional reading and spelling strategies (Routman, 1988; Wilde, 1989).

Promoting Independent Reading and Writing.   Children learn to read and write by reading and writing (Cooper, 1986). Support children in becoming independent readers and writers by planning some of the following activities: journals, records of books read/time spent reading, author's chair/reader's chair (Graves & Hansen, 1983), home reading and writing.

The following approaches to reading and writing are used according to how much support children need. Remember that the ultimate goal is to assist children in becoming independent readers and writers.

Reading approaches include *independent, cooperative, guided,* and *shared* reading as well as reading aloud.

In *independent* reading children read by themselves. Time should be provided for independent reading daily, because in-school independent reading time may be more important than out-of-school time (Anderson, Wilson, & Fielding, 1988; Taylor, Frye, & Maruyama, 1990;

Cooperative reading uses the principles of cooperative learning (Slavin, 1990). Children take turns reading a piece of the text to each other.

In *guided* reading the teacher carefully guides the children through silent reading by encouraging children to make predictions and asking directed questions (Beck, 1984). In this method the teacher should be aware of the role of the questions and prompts because simply asking children about what they have read is not going to teach them how to construct meaning (Durkin, 1978).

Holdaway (1979) developed the *"shared* storybook experience." The teacher reads the children's favorite stories, rhymes, and poems and asks the children to read along when they are ready.

In *reading aloud* the teacher reads the text out loud to the children.

Writing approaches (Hall, 1989) include *independent, guided,* and *shared or language experience* approaches.

In *independent* writing children write by themselves. Provide time each day for independent writing (Anderson, Wilson, & Fielding, 1988; Goodman, 1986; Graves, 1994).

In *cooperative* writing children take turns writing a piece (Greaves, 1989).

In *guided* writing the teacher supports children during their writing of a piece (Routman, 1991). Use conferences during the writing process as times when the teacher can support children or the children can support other children (Herring, 1989).

In the *shared or language experience approach,* the whole class or individuals dictate an experience that the teacher writes on chart paper, or chalkboard (Cooper, 1997; McKenzie, 1985).

Planning for Literacy Learning

Thematic Units.   Teachers use thematic units to establish connections across all subject areas; provide breath and depth to the curriculum; expose children to various learning experiences; provide various reasons for learning; show relationships among content areas; integrate language across the curriculum; give children choices; accept various answers; promote cooperative learning; integrate speaking, listening, reading, writing, and thinking; invite authentic language for meaningful purposes; promote meaning making; nurture problem solving and risk taking; acknowledge approximations in children's language and learning;

encourage ownership and choices; promote autonomy and control of learning; facilitate self-regulation; and accommodate reflective thinking through sustained time (Dalrymple, 1991b; Fredericks, Meinback, & Rothen, 1993; Hennings, 1997; Pappas, Kiefer, & Levstik, 1990).

Literacy Lesson Plan Format.   The following lesson plan format is shown in J. D. Cooper's 1997 book *Literacy: Helping Children Construct Meaning*. It is the basis for the format I present in Chapter 3 through 7 of this book.

Introduction to Literature

> *Activating Prior Knowledge*

> *Setting Purpose for Reading Selection*

Reading and Responding to Literature

> *Read Selection*

> Selection should be read either independently, cooperatively, guided, shared, or aloud.

> *Respond to Selection*

Extending the Literature

1. Independent work should be meaningful and relevant;
2. Literature extension activities should include the creative arts (Clay, 1979); and
3. Related math, science, and social studies activities should be included (Routman, 1988).

Evaluating Literacy Learning through Portfolios

Portfolios offer a child-centered way for a teacher to assess and evaluate children's progress in literacy learning over a period of time. Assessment through portfolios becomes collaborative rather than competitive. Portfolios help parents become engaged in seeing firsthand what their child is achieving (Goodman, 1986; Jenkins, 1996; Milliken, 1992; Serger, 1992; Tierney, Carter, & Desai, 1991).

Items are placed in portfolios in order to indicate students' ability to own their own learning, comprehend in reading, express themselves in writing, use the writing process, identify words, develop language and vocabulary, and read voluntarily. Portfolio items may include projects, surveys, reports, and units from reading and writing; finished samples that illustrate wide writing; samples of writing across the curriculum; literature extensions; a record of books read; audiotapes of reading; responses to literature; evidence of literature circle discussions; writing that illustrates critical thinking about reading; notes from individual reading and writing conferences; items that are evidence of developmental style; writing that shows growth in usage of traits; first draft to final product samples; writing that illustrates topic generation; evidence of effort; self-evaluations; anecdotal records; checklists; and interest inventories (Au, Scheu, Kawakami, & Herman, 1990; Tierney, Carter, & Desai, 1991).

Portfolios help children set their own goals; choose reading material and writing topics; organize, maintain, and accept responsibility for portfolios; develop, share, and reflect upon their portfolios; select writing and reading samples; collaborate with others; understand their own personal strengths and weaknesses in process, effort, progress, and achievement, as well as in products being assessed; have a better sense of their own reading and writing processes across time; collect, analyze, and compare writing and reading samples; be involved in self- and peer assessment (Graves, 1992; Tierney, Carter, & Desai, 1991).

Portfolios help teachers become directly involved in the assessment process by collecting student work samples; encouraging student involvement and interaction; helping students manage portfolios; developing an interactive style of teaching; having firsthand records of what students are actually doing; gathering information from interactions with each child about his/her portfolio so as to plan instruction; making assignments that encourage decision making, drafting, reflecting, discussing, reading, and responding; providing modeling of expectations; analyzing student work samples; obtaining a richer, clearer view of students across time; negotiating a view of the student that is more fully informed in terms of what each individual child has achieved; having a vehicle for child-centered assessment practices that focus on helping the learner (Tierney, Carter, & Desai, 1991; Voss, 1992).

Home–School Connection

Research shows that a close home–school connection that involves parents in their children's education enhances literacy learning and motivates students (Boyer, 1995; Vukelich, 1984; Whitmore & Goodman, 1993). In order to establish and maintain such a home–school connection, invite parents to be a part of their children's education (Routman, 1988). Meet with the parents or send out periodical newsletters in order to encourage the parents to get more involved. Some suggestions for what parents can do include modeling reading for different purposes; encouraging their child to read for a purpose; surrounding their child with various types of print and quality literature; taking their child to the library; having their child sign his or her own name to check out library books; letting their child choose books; reading aloud to their child every day; encouraging their child to read along; encouraging their child to read to them; taking turns reading aloud and having the child read aloud; making connections between reading and writing; sharing letters, advertisements, magazines, signs, packages, and other literacy events with their child; supplying their child with various writing supplies; modeling writing for different purposes; encouraging their child to write for a purpose; listening to their child read his or her writing aloud to them; and encouraging and praising their child for all efforts (Fredericks, Meinbach, & Rothen, 1993; Herring, 1989; Strickland & Taylor, 1989).

REFERENCES

Adams, M. 1990. *Beginning to read: Thinking and learning about print.* Cambridge, MA: MIT Press.
Anderson, R. C., & Freebody, P. 1981. Vocabulary knowledge. In J. T. Guthrie, ed., *Comprehension and teaching: Research reviews.* Newark, DE: International Reading Association.
Anderson, R. C., Hiebert, E. H., Scott, J. A., & Wilkinson, I. A. G. 1985. *Becoming a nation of readers: The report of the Commission of Reading.* Washington, DC: National Institute of Education.

Anderson, R. C., & Pearson, P. D. 1984. A schema-theoretic view of the basic processes in reading comprehension. In P. D. Pearson, ed., *Handbook of reading research,* pp. 255–291. New York: Longman.

Anderson, R. C., Wilson, P. T., & Fielding, L. G. 1988. Growth in reading and how children spend their time outside of school. *Reading Research Quarterly, 23(3),* 285–303.

Atwell, N. 1987. *In the middle: Writing, reading, and learning with adolescents.* Portsmouth, NH: Heinemann.

Atwell, N. 1991. *Side by side: Essays on teaching to learn.* Portsmouth, NH: Heinemann.

Au, K. H., Scheu, J. A., Kawakami, A. J., & Herman, P. A. 1990. Assessment and accountability in a whole language curriculum. *Reading Teacher, 43,* 574–578.

Beck, I. L. 1984. Developing comprehension: The impact of the directed reading lesson. In R. C. Anderson, J. Osborn, & R. J. Tierney, eds., *Learning to read American schools: Basal readers and content texts,* pp. 3–20. Hillsdale, NJ: Erlbaum.

Beck, I. L., & McKeown, M. 1991. Conditions of vocabulary acquisition. In R. Barr, M. L. Kamil, P. Mosenthal, & P. D. Pearson, eds., *Handbook of reading research,* vol. 2, pp. 789–814. New York: Longman.

Berghoff, B., & Egawa, K. 1991. "No more rocks": Grouping to give students control of their learning. *Reading Teacher, 44,* 536–541.

Boyer, E. L. 1995. *The basic school.* Princeton, NJ: Carnegie Foundation for the Advancement of Teaching.

Brown, A. L. 1980. Metacognitive development and reading. In R. J. Spiro, B. C. Bruce, & W. F. Brewer, eds., *Theoretical issues in reading comprehension,* pp. 453–481. Hillsdale, NJ: Erlbaum.

Calkins, L. M. 1986. *The art of teaching writing.* Portsmouth, NH: Heinemann.

Cambourne, B. 1988. *The whole story: Natural learning and the acquisition of literacy in the classroom.* New York: Ashton–Scholastic.

Clay, M. M. 1979. *Reading: The patterning of complex behavior,* 2nd edition. Auckland, New Zealand: Heinemann Education.

Cooper, J. D. 1997. *Literacy: Helping children construct meaning.* Boston: Houghton Mifflin.

Cullinan, B., & Galda, L. 1994. *Literature and the child.* Fort Worth: Harcourt Brace.

Dalrymple, J. D. 1991a. The chicken study: Third graders prepare for independent study of animals. In Y. Goodman, W. Hood, & K. Goodman, eds., *Organizing for whole language.* Portsmouth, NH: Heinemann.

Dalrymple, J. D. 1991b. Comprehension: Framework for thematic unit studies. In Y. Goodman, W. Hood, & K. Goodman, eds., *Organizing for whole language.* Portsmouth, NH: Heinemann.

Danielson, K. E., & LaBonty, J. 1994. *Integrating reading and writing through children's literature.* Boston: Allyn and Bacon.

Dressed, J. H. 1990. The effects of listening to and discussing different qualities of children's literature on the narrative writing of fifth graders. *Research on the Teaching of English, 24,* 397–414.

Durkin, D. 1978. What classroom observations reveal about reading comprehension instruction. *Reading Research Quarterly, 14(4),* 481–533.

Fader, D. 1982. *The new hooked on books.* New York: Berkley.

Feitelson, L. G., Kita, B., & Goldstein, R. C. 1986. Effects of listening to stories on first graders' comprehension and use of language. *Reading in the Teaching of English, 20,* 339–356.

Fredericks, A. D., Meinbach, A. M., & Rothen, L. 1993. *Thematic units: An integrated approach to teaching science and social studies.* New York: HarperCollins.

Freppon, P. 1991. Children's concept of the nature and purpose of reading in different instructional settings. *Journal of Reading Behavior, 23(2),* 139–163.

Goodman, K. 1986. *What's whole in whole language.* Portsmouth, NH: Heinemann.

Goodman, K. S., & Goodman, Y. M. 1991. Consumer beware! Selecting materials for whole language readers. In K. S. Goodman, L. B. Byrd, & Y. M. Goodman, eds., *The whole language catalog,* p. 119. Santa Rosa, CA: American School Publisher.

Graves, D. H. 1983. *Writing: Teachers and children at work.* Exeter, NH: Heinemann.

Graves, D. H. 1987. The role of instruction in fostering vocabulary development. In M. G. McKeown & M. E. Curtis, eds., *The nature of vocabulary acquisition,* pp. 165–184. Hillsdale, NJ: Erlbaum.

Graves, D. H. 1991. *Build a literate classroom.* Portsmouth, NH: Heinemann.

Graves, D. H. 1992. Help students read their portfolios. In D. Graves & B. S. Sunstein, eds., *Portfolios portraits.* Portsmouth, NH: Heinemann.

Graves, D. H. 1994. *A fresh look at writing.* Portsmouth, NH: Heinemann.

Graves, D. H., & Hansen, J. 1983. The author's chair. *Language Arts, 60,* 176–182.

Greaves, M. 1989. Collaborative authorship. In N. Hall, ed., *Writing with a reason: The emergence of authorship in young children.* Portsmouth, NH: Heinemann.

Halliday, M. A. K. 1975. *Learning how to mean.* New York: Elsevier Nort-Holland.

Harste, J., & Short, K. G. 1991. Literature circle and literature responses. In B. M. Power & R. Hubbard, eds., *The Heinemann reader: Literacy in process.* Portsmouth, NH: Heinemann.

Hennings, D. G. 1997. *Communication in action: Teaching the language arts.* Geneva, IL: Houghton Mifflin.

Herring, G. 1989. Shared writing. In N. Hall, ed., *Writing with a reason: The emergence of authorship in young children.* Portsmouth, NH: Heinemann.

Holdaway, D. 1979. *The foundations of literacy.* Portsmouth, NH: Heinemann.

Huck, C. S. 1989. No wider than the heart is wide. In J. Hickman & B. E. Cullinan, eds., *Children's literature in the classroom: Weaving Charlotte's web,* pp. 252–262. Needham Heights, MA: Christopher Gordon.

Huck, C. S., Helper, S., & Hickman, J. 1993. *Children's literature in elementary school,* 5th edition. Fort Worth: Harcourt Brace.

Jenkins, C. B. 1996. *Inside the writing portfolio: What we need to know to assess children's writings.* Portsmouth, NH: Heinemann.

Karelitz, E. B. 1993. *The author's chair and beyond: Literacy in a primary classroom.* Portsmouth, NH: Heinemann.

McCormick, S. 1977. Should you read aloud to your children? *Language Arts, 54,* 139–143.

McKenzie, M. 1985. *Shared writing: Language matters.* London: Inner London Educational Authority.

Milliken, M. 1992. A fifth-grade class uses portfolios. In D. Graves & B. S. Sunstein, eds., *Portfolios portraits.* Portsmouth, NH: Heinemann.

Norton, D. E. 1991. *Through the eyes of a child: An introduction to children's literature,* 3rd edition. New York: Macmillan.

Pappas, C. C., & Brown, E. 1987. Learning how to read by reading: Learning how to extend the functional potential of language. *Research in the Teaching of English, 21,* 160–184.

Pappas, C. C., Kiefer, B. Z., & Levstik, L. S. 1990. *An integrated language perspective in elementary school: Theory into action.* New York: Longman.

Paris, S. G., Lipson, M. Y., & Turner, J. C. 1991. The development of strategic readers. In R. Barr, M. L. Kamil, P. Monsenthal, & P. D. Pearson, eds., *Handbook of reading research,* vol. 2, pp. 609–640. New York: Longman.

Parsons, L. 1990. *Response journals.* Portsmouth, NH: Heinemann.

Pearson, P. D., Hansen, J., & Gordon, C. 1979. *The effect of background knowledge on young children's comprehension of explicit and implicit information.* Champaign, IL: Center for the Study of Reading, University of Illinois.

Pearson, P. D., & Tierney, R. J. 1984. On becoming a thoughtful reader: Learning to read like a writer. In A. Purves & O. Niles, eds., *Becoming readers in a complex society: Eighty-third Yearbook of the National Society of the Study of Education,* pp. 144–173. Chicago: University of Chicago Press.

Rosenblatt, L. 1938/1983. *Literature as exploration.* New York: Modern Language Association.

Rosenblatt, L. 1991. The reading transaction. In B. M. Power & R. Hubbard, eds., *The Heinemann reader: Literacy in process.* Portsmouth, NH: Heinemann.

Routman, R. 1988. *Transitions: From literature to literacy.* Portsmouth, NH: Heinemann.

Routman, R. 1994. *Invitations: Changing as teacher and learners K–12.* Portsmouth, NH: Heinemann.

Rumelhart, D. E. 1980. Schemata: The building blocks of cognition. In R. J. Spiro et al., ed., *Theoretical issues in reading comprehension,* pp. 33–58. Hillsdale, NJ: Erlbaum.

Sanders, M. 1987. Literacy as "passionate attention." *Language Arts, 64(1),* 33–39.

Serger, D. F. 1992. Portfolio definitions: Towards a shared notion. In D. Graves & B. S. Sunstein, eds. *Portfolios portraits.* Portsmouth, NH: Heinemann.

Slavin, R. E. 1990. *Cooperative learning: Theory, research, and practice.* Englewood Cliffs, NJ: Prentice-Hall.

Strickland, D. S. 1990. Emergent literacy: How young children learn to read and write. *Educational Leadership, 47(6),* 18–23.

Strickland, D. S., & Taylor, D. 1989. Family storybook reading: Implications for children, families, and curriculum. In D. S. Strickland & L. M. Morrow, eds., *Emerging literacy: Young children learn to read and write,* pp. 27–34. Newark, DE: International Reading Association.

Taylor, B. M., Frye, B. J., & Maruyama, G. M. 1990. Time spent reading and reading growth. *American Educational Research Journal, 27(2),* 351–362.

Taylor, D., & Dorsey-Gaines, C. 1988. *Growing up literate.* Portsmouth, NH: Heinemann.

Teale, W. H., & Sulzby, E. 1986. *Emergent literacy: Writing and reading.* Norwood, NJ: Ablex.

Tierney, R., Carter, M., & Desai, L. 1991. *Portfolio assessment in the reading-writing classroom.* Norwood, MA: Christopher Gordon.

Voss, M. M. 1992. Portfolios in first-grade: A teacher's discoveries. In D. Graves & B. S. Sunstein, eds., *Portfolios portraits.* Portsmouth, NH: Heinemann.

Vukelich, C. 1984. Parents' role in the reading process: A review of practical suggestions and ways to communicate with parents. *Reading Teacher, 37,* 472–477.

Vygotsky, L. S. 1978. *Mind in society.* Cambridge, MA: Harvard University Press.

Walmsley, S. A., & Walp, T. P. 1990. Integrating literature and composing into the language arts curriculum: Philosophy and practice. *Elementary School Journal, 90(30),* 251–274.

Wells, G. 1990. Creating the conditions to encourage literate thinking. *Educational Leadership, 47(6)* 13–17.

Whitmore, K. F., & Goodman, Y. M. 1993. Inside the whole language classroom: Students delight in taking charge of their learning. In SDE sourcebook, *Whole teaching: Keeping children in the center of curriculum and instruction.* Peterborough, NH: Society for Developmental Education.

Wigfield, A., & Asher, S. P. 1984. Social and motivational influences on reading. In P. D. Pearson, ed., *Handbook of reading research,* pp. 423–452. New York: Longman.

Wilde, S. 1989. Looking at invented spelling: A kidwatcher's guide to spelling. In K. Goodman, Y. Goodman, & W. Hood, eds., *The whole language evaluation book.* Portsmouth, NH: Heinemann.

Wortman, R., & Haussler, M. M. 1989. Evaluation in a classroom designed for whole language. In K. Goodman, Y. Goodman, & W. Hood, eds., *The whole language evaluation book.* Portsmouth, NH: Heinemann.

PART TWO

Lessons for the Primary Curriculum

CHAPTER 3

Focusing on Self-Concept and Understanding Individual Differences and Likenesses

Lesson 3.1: Differences and Likenesses

Books

Being with You This Way by W. Nikola-Lisa

All the Colors of the Earth by S. Hamanaka

Other suggested books about differences and likenesses

Purposes

- To encourage children to appreciate ways in which we are all alike.
- To encourage children to appreciate ways in which we are all different.
- To encourage children to appreciate how they can be a part of a number of different groups.

Appropriate Age Group

Primary

Thematic Unit Connections

Me; Self-Concept; Friendship; Appreciating Similarities and Differences

Curriculum Connections

Language Arts; Social Studies; Mathematics

Objectives

1. The students will listen to/read a story about how we are all the same and yet we are all different.
2. The students will share information about themselves.

3. The students will graph everyone in the class according to their different attributes, likes, dislikes, and so on.

4. The students will do various kinds of math problems with their class graphs.

5. The students will write and illustrate a page about their favorite thing to contribute to a class book.

6. The students will write a poem that describes themselves.

7. The students will revise, edit, and publish the poems.

Materials

- *Being with You This Way* by W. Nikola-Lisa
- *All the Colors of the Earth* by S. Hamanaka
- Materials to do graphing activities
- Materials to make a book
- Materials for writing poetry
- Materials for publishing students' poetry
- Other suggested books about differences and likenesses

Introducing Selection

Activating Prior Knowledge

Ask students to name different ways in which they can be grouped according to their characteristics (e.g., hair color, eye color, height).

Setting Purpose for Reading Selection

1. Introduce *Being with You This Way* by W. Nikola-Lisa.

2. Ask students to look for ways in which the children in this story could be grouped according to their characteristics (e.g., hair color, eye color, height).

Reading and Responding

Read Selection

Have students read/listen to *Being with You This Way.* Students can snap their fingers and/or clap their hands every time that you read "Uh-huh," "Mm-mmm," or "Ah-hah."

Respond to Selection

Discuss ways in which the children in the book were grouped.

Discuss other ways in which children can be grouped (e.g., by how many siblings they have, how many pets they have, what they like to eat, what they like to play, what their favorite subject in school is, or how they get to school).

Extending the Literature

Activity 1

1. Show students how they belong to different groups by graphing their attributes, family characteristics, and so on. (Possible graph topics include color of hair, color of eyes, number of sisters, number of brothers, way in which they get to school, their favorite game played with a ball, their favorite book.)

2. For a math lesson, ask some of the following questions: How many in each category? Which category has more? Which category has less? Which two categories add up to ten? How many more in the first category than the second category? Which category has none? (Make sure the students understand that more does not mean better.)

Activity 2

Students can make a page for a class book by finishing the following phrase "My favorite thing is _____." Ask the students to illustrate their page. The pages can be put together into a class book.

Activity 3

Read Sheila Hamanaka's book *All the Colors of the World* aloud to the students or have the students cooperatively read the book in groups of two.

Ask the students to use the writing process to write a poem.

1. Rehearsing stage: Discuss the descriptive words Hamanaka used to talk about the children in her book. Brainstorm other words that could be used to describe children.

2. Drafting stage: Ask students to write a first draft. The students should not be worried about spelling, and so on in the first draft. The emphasis should be on creativity.

Kindergarteners and first graders can write a poem about themselves using similies. For example:

> My eyes are like _____.
> My hair is like _____.
> My skin is like _____.
> And I am like _____.

Second and third graders can write a cinquian poem (a five-line descriptive poem):

> Line 1. A word for the subject
> Line 2. Four syllables describing the subject
> Line 3. Six syllables showing action
> Line 4. Eight syllables expressing a feeling or an observation about the subject
> Line 5. Two syllables describing or renaming the subject

Revise and edit poems according to suggestions offered in the subsection on "Connecting Reading and Writing" in Chapter 2. Display student poetry by making a "poet tree": stretch a piece of butcher paper from the ceiling to the floor and attach the poems to it.

Related Books

Refer to books about Differences and Likenesses in the Concept Book List.

Lesson 3.2: I Like Me

Books

Cleversticks by B. Ashley

Other suggested books about Asians/Asian Americans

Other suggested books about self-concept

Purposes

- To help children understand that we are all good at different things.
- To introduce children to Asian/Asian American history, culture, and contributions.

Appropriate Age Group

Primary

Thematic Unit Connections

Me; Self-Concept; Appreciating Similarities and Differences

Curriculum Connections

Social Studies; Language Arts

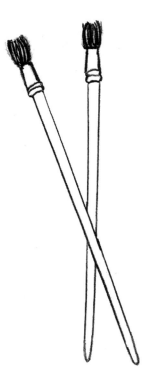

Objectives

1. The students will use their journal to do a quick write or quick illustration to depict what they are good at doing.
2. The students will read/listen to *Cleversticks* by B. Ashley to find out what the little boy in the story is good at doing.
3. The students will retell the story to partners.
4. The students will pantomime a part of the story.
5. The students will read other books about self-concept in order to illustrate and write about what they do best.
6. The students will make a class book or bulletin board titled "What We Do Best."
7. The student will use chopsticks to eat snacks.
8. The students will read/listen to books about Asian/Asian American history, culture, and contributions.

Materials

- *Cleversticks* by B. Ashley
- Materials for conducting quick write or quick illustration
- Materials for pantomiming
- Materials for making a class book
- Different art media
- Chopsticks/snacks
- Other suggested books about Asians/Asian Americans
- Other suggested books about self-concept

Introducing Selection

Activating Prior Knowledge

Ask students to use their pencils and journals to quickly write or illustrate something they feel they are very good at doing. Let each child quickly share what they are good at doing with the rest of the class.

Setting Purpose for Reading Selection

Have students listen to the story to find out (1) Why Ling Sung decided he didn't want to go to school any more and (2) Why Ling Sung's father called him Cleversticks.

Reading and Responding to Selection

Read Selection

Have students read/listen to *Cleversticks*.

Respond to Selection

Have the students get in pairs and retell the story to their partners.

Extending the Literature

Activity 1

Break students into small groups. Have each child in the group be a different character from *Cleversticks*. Let them take turns pantomiming their characters' actions.

Activity 2

Have students read other books that stress self-concept (refer to Self-Concept section of Concept Book List). Then ask them to use different kinds of art media to illustrate what they do best. Then they may write a sentence or two below the illustration describing it. Younger children can dictate what it is that they do best. Collect all the pictures to make a class book or bulletin board. Have the students title the book or bulletin board (e.g., *What We Do Best*). Share class book or bulletin board with other students in your class, parents, students in other classrooms, and so on.

Activity 3

Have students try to use chopsticks to eat various snacks such as crackers, pieces of cheese, rice, and so forth.

Activity 4

Have students read/listen to a book relating to Asian/Asian American history, culture, and contributions from the following list. Ask older students what questions they come up with as they read and what questions they answer as they read. (P = primary; I = intermediate.)

P   Bannerman, H. 1996. *The Story of Little Babaji.* HarperCollins. (Indian history, culture, and/or contributions)

P, I Bash, B. 1996. *In the Heart of the Village: The World of the Indian Banyan Tree.* Little, Brown. (Tale from India)

P, I Bond, R. 1995. *Binja's Blue Umbrella.* Boyd's Mills Press. (Indian history, culture, and/or contributions)

P   Bond, R. 1996. *Cherry Tree.* Boyds Mills Press. (Indian history, culture, and/or contributions)

P   Chin, K. 1995. *Sam and the Lucky Money.* Lee & Low. (Chinese New Year)

P   Claire, E. 1995. *The Little Brown Jay.* Mondo Publications. (Tale from India)

P, I Coeer, E. 1993. *Sadako.* Putnam. (Hiroshima, Japanese history)

P   Coeer, E. 1977. *Sadako and the Thousand Cranes.* Putnam. (Hiroshima, Japanese history)

P   Demi. 1997. *One Grain of Rice: A Mathematical Folktale.* Scholastic. (Tale from India)

P, I Ginsburg, M. 1988. *The Chinese Mirror.* Harcourt Brace Jovanovich. (Chinese tales)

P   Godden, R. 1997. *Premlata and the Festival of Lights.* Greenwillow. (Indian holiday)

P, I Hamanaka, S. 1994. *Peace Crane.* Morrow. (Japanese history, Hiroshima)

P, I Hull, R.; Bateman, E.; & Robinson, C. 1994. *Indian Stories from around the World.* Thomson Learning. (Tales from India)

P, I Jacobs, J., ed. 1994. *Indian Fairy.* Dover. (Tales from India)

P   Jaffrey, M. 1997. *Robi Dobi: The Marvelous Adventures of an Indian Elephant.* Dial. (Indian history, culture, and/or contributions)

P   Kalman, M. 1995. *Swami on Rye: Max in India.* Viking. (Indian history, culture, and/or contributions)

P, I Kipling, R. 1987. *The Jungle Book.* Puffin. (Tales from India)

P, I Kipling, R. 1995. *The Jungle Book.* Gallery Books. (Tales from India)

P   Kipling, R. 1997. *Rikki-Tikki-Tavi.* Morrow. (Tales from India)

P, I   Kipling, R.; Ashachik, D.; & Hannon, H. 1992. *The Jungle Book.* Troll. (Tales from India)

P   Lee, H. V. 1994. *At the Beach.* Holt. (Mandarin Chinese language)

P   Lewis, T. 1995. *Sacred River.* Clarion. (Indian history, culture, and/or contributions)

P, I   Livingston, M. C. 1996. *Festivals.* Holiday House. (Holidays in India)

P   Mahy, M. 1990. *The Seven Chinese Brothers.* Scholastic. (Chinese history)

P   Margolies, B. A. 1992. *Kanu of Kathmandu: A Journey in Nepal.* Simon & Schuster. (Indian history, culture, and/or contributions)

P   Martin, R. 1997. *The Monkey Bridge.* Knopf. (Tale from India)

P   Martin, R., & Anderson, B. 1998. *The Brave Little Parrot.* Putnam. (Tale from India)

P, I   Maruki, T. 1980. *Hiroshima No Pika.* Lothrop. (Hiroshima, Japanese history)

P, I   Mochizuki, K. 1993. *Baseball Saved Us.* Lee & Low. (Japanese American history, internment camps)

P, I   Mochizuki, K. 1995. *Heroes.* Lee & Low. (Stereotyping, Japanese American history)

P, I   Morimoto, J. 1987. *My Hiroshima.* Puffin. (Hiroshima, Japanese history)

P   Nunes, S. M. 1995. *The Last Dragon.* Clarion. (Chinese American culture)

P   Rajpust, M. 1997. *The Peacock's Pride.* Disney Press. (Tale from India)

P   Reddix, V. 1991. *Dragon Kite of Autumn Moon.* Lothrop, Lee & Shepard. (Elderly, Chinese holiday)

P   Say, A. 1982. *The Bicycle Man.* Scholastic. (World War II, stereotyping)

P   Shepard, A. 1995. *The Gifts of Wali Dad: A Tale of India & Pakistan.* Atheneum. (Tale from India)

P   Shepard, A. 1992. *Savitri: A Tale of Ancient India.* Philomel. (Tale from India)

P   Souhami, J. 1997. *Rama and the Demon King: An Ancient Tale from India.* DK. (Tale from India)

P   Uchida, Y. 1993. *The Bracelet.* Philomel. (Japanese American history, internment camps)

P   Waters, K., & Slvenz-Low, M. 1990. *Lion Dancer: Ernie Wan's Chinese New Year.* Scholastic. (Chinese holiday)

P   Wolf, G. 1996. *The Very Hungry Lion: A Folktale.* Annick Press. (Tale from India)

P   Young, E. 1992. *Seven Blind Mice.* Albert Whitman. (Tale from India)

Related Literature

Refer to other books about Self-Concept in the Concept Book List.

Lesson 3.3: Different Kinds of Families

Books

> *Who's in a Family?*
> by R. Skutch
>
> Other suggested books
> about different kinds
> of families

Purposes

- To expose children to the
  many different kinds of
  families.
- To help children under-
  stand where their family
  fits into the different types
  of families.
- To help children accept
  their classmates' families.

Appropriate Age Group

Primary

Thematic Unit Connections

Self and Others; Families; Self-Concept; Appreciating Similarities and Differences

Curriculum Connections

Language Arts; Social Studies; Mathematics

Objectives

1. The students will read/listen to *Who's in a Family?* by R. Skutch.
2. The students will name many kinds of families.
3. The students will make a family album and present it to the class.
4. The students will graph different information about their family.
5. The students will create an acrostics poem.

Materials

- *Who's in a Family?* by R. Skutch
- Pictures or photographs of different kinds of families
- Materials for making family albums

- Materials for writing an acrostics poem
- Materials for making graphs
- Other suggested books about different kinds of families

Introducing Selection

Activating Prior Knowledge

1. Bring in and show students pictures or photographs of different kinds of families (e.g., lion family; mother and two children; mother, father, and one child, etc.).
2. Ask students to determine whether the subjects in each picture could represent a family. This should lead into a discussion on different types of families.

Setting Purpose for Reading Selection

1. Introduce the selection.
2. Have students find a family in the book that reminds them most of their family.
3. Also, have students be alert to the various kinds of families mentioned in the story.

Reading and Responding

Read Selection

Have the students read/listen to *Who's in a Family?*

Respond to Selection

1. Ask students to name the different kinds of families mentioned in the book.
2. Explain to the class that everyone's family is different, but that love is a common thread in each and every family.

Extending the Literature

Activity 1

Have each student make a family album. Each page should contain a drawn picture of a different family member and a written summary about that person. The students can incorporate technology to scan family pictures into the album and use a word processor to write about the family members. The students can decorate covers for their albums. When the family albums are complete, the students can share them with the class. The albums can also serve as a part of a portfolio used during open house or parent/teacher conferences.

Activity 2

Have first and second graders make 3-D molds of their last names. Each child should (1) use molding clay to form the letters in his or her last name; (2) dip a different-colored tissue in watered-down glue to cover each of the letters in the name; (3) repeat, using black tissue paper to connect the different letters together and to make an outline of the total name; and (4) remove the clay from the mold. Display the names in the room.

Have second and third graders write an acrostics poem using their last name. They should describe something special and/or unique about their family.

Here is an example using the family name Valdez.

Very creative
Are the members in my family
Loving to write books all
Day long
Every member writes as s/he
Zips along his/her merry way

Activity 3

For a math lesson, you can tally up information about the class members' families and graph the data. For example: How many members? How many sisters and brothers? How many girls and boys in the family?

Related Books

Refer to books about Family in the Concept Book List.

Lesson 3.4: Rice, Rice, Rice

Books

Everybody Cooks Rice
by N. Dooley

Other suggested books about different kinds of foods

Purposes

- To encourage children to learn about and respect others' cultural backgrounds.

- To encourage children to appreciate our cultural likenesses and differences through foods.

- To introduce children to the contributions Kipling made to our appreciation of Indian culture.

Appropriate Age Group

Primary

Thematic Unit Connections

Cultures; Self and Others; Families; Self-Concept; Appreciating Similarities and Differences

Curriculum Connections

Social Studies; Language Arts

Objectives

1. The students will listen to a story.
2. The students will retell the story through a circular plot pattern.
3. The students will use map skills to discuss the origins of the families in the story.
4. The students will collect rice recipes to make a Class Cookbook.
5. The students will think about being active in social causes.
6. The students will read/listen to some of Kipling's works.

Materials

- *Everybody Cooks Rice* by N. Dooley
- Chalkboard and chalk
- Butcher paper
- Circular plot pattern form
- A map of the world
- Materials for making a Class Cookbook
- Other suggested books about different kinds of foods

Introducing Selection

Activating Prior Knowledge

Explain to the children that they are going to read/listen to a story about families from different countries. Ask the children what a good reader may do to understand what is being read.

Explain that a good reader can read the title to predict what the story is going to be about. Have the students make predictions about what the story may be about by reading the title. Record their responses on the chalkboard and discuss them.

Setting Purpose for Reading Selection

1. Introduce *Everybody Cooks Rice* by N. Dooley.
2. Tell the children that the main character of the story is named Carrie and that Carrie has to search around her neighborhood for her brother.
3. Have the students pay close attention to the different nationalities of the families Carrie encounters on her search for her brother.

Reading and Responding

Read Selection

Have students read/listen to *Everybody Cooks Rice.*

Respond to Selection

1. Ask students to help you map out the places Carrie visited when she searched for her brother. Use a circular plot pattern to map out Carrie's adventures (see Figure 3.1). When a place is mentioned that Carrie visited, have the students record the name, nationality, and origin of the family. Carrie went to many houses, so let the students refer back to the book if they have trouble remembering.

Extending the Literature

Activity 1

1. Display a map of the world in front of the class. In the book *Everybody Cooks Rice,* each family's nationality is mentioned. On the map, mark the city and the country of each family's origins.

2. You could do a lot with this information. Examples:

    a. Introduce the directions—north, south, east, west. Then ask questions, such as is Vietnam north, south, east, or west of China?

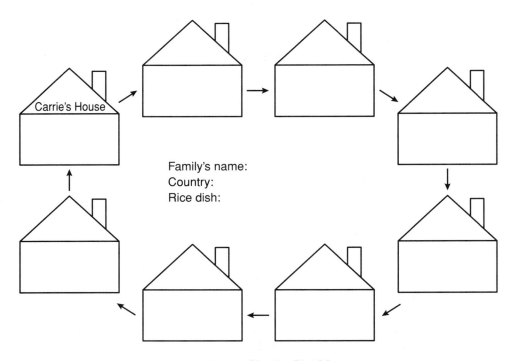

FIGURE 3.1   Circular Plot Map

b. Introduce longitude and latitude. Then have students find the longitude and latitude of each country mentioned in *Everybody Cooks Rice*.

Activity 2

Have students collect rice recipes from their parents. Make a Class Cookbook with all the various rice dishes.

Activity 3

The students can sell their cookbook to parents in the school with the intention of donating the funds to a good cause. A suggestion is to use the money to buy trees and flowers to plant at school or in a nearby town park as suggested in Lesson 7.3 in this book.

Activity 4

Draw attention to the family from India and how they cooked rice. Have the students learn more about India by listening to/reading one or more of Rudyard Kipling's works:

P, I   Kipling, R. 1987. *The Jungle Book.* Puffin. (Tales from India)

P, I   Kipling, R. 1995. *The Jungle Book.* Gallery Books. (Tales from India)

P, I   Kipling, R.; Ashachik, D.; & Hannon, H. 1992. *The Jungle Book.* Troll. (Tales from India)

P   Kipling, R. 1997. *Rikki-Tikki-Tavi.* Morrow. (Tales from India)

Related Books

Refer to books about Foods in the Concept Book List.

Lesson 3.5: The Challenged

Books

Be Good to Eddie Lee by V. Fleming

Other suggested books about the Challenged

Purposes

- To help children understand the amazing and wonderful differences among human beings.
- To help children understand how all children are different and alike.
- To help children understand what they all have in common.

Appropriate Age Group

Primary

Thematic Unit Connections

Cycles; Pond Life; Appreciating Similarities and Differences

Curriculum Connections

Social Studies; Language Arts

Objectives

1. The students will listen to/read a story.
2. The students will participate in a book discussion.
3. The students will discover the life cycle of a frog.
4. The students will create a poster to entice other children to read a book.
5. The students will cooperate in creating a life-size mural of a pond scene.

Materials

- *Be Good to Eddie Lee* by V. Fleming
- Journals
- Materials to set up aquarium
- Magnifying glasses
- Other books about frogs' life cycles
- Materials to make a poster
- Materials to make life-size mural
- Other suggested books about the challenged

Introducing Selection

Activating Prior Knowledge

Ask students if there has ever been a time in their life that they didn't want another child to play with them for no good reason. Discuss.

Setting Purpose for Reading Selection:

Divide the class into eight groups of three or four. Ask each group to listen to/read *Be Good to Eddie Lee* and to be able to discuss one of the following:

a. How is Eddie Lee amazingly and wonderfully different from Christy and Jim Bud?

b. What does Christy do to help Jim Bud be good to Eddie Lee?

c. What does Eddie Lee discover in the pond, and how does Christy share in the discovery?

d. How do we know that Eddie Lee is just like other children?

Reading and Responding

Read Selection

Have students listen to/read *Be Good to Eddie Lee* by V. Fleming.

Respond to Selection

1. Younger children can discuss their responses to their assigned question (as shown above) within their small groups of three or four. Older children can write down their

ideas in their journals and then come together within their small groups to discuss their findings.

2. Children can come together as a whole to discuss their findings

Extending the Literature

Activity 1

In a special place in your room, set up an aquarium with frog eggs where children can discover the life cycle of the frog. Provide magnifying glasses and factual books about frogs and other living things that go through cycles. A few possibilities:

> *Frogs* by G. Tarrant
> *A Frog's Body* by J. Cole
> *Jump, Frog, Jump* by R. Kalan
> *Discovering Cycles* by G. O. Blough
> *Once There Were Giants* by M. Waddell
> *Can't Sit Still* by K. E. Lotz
> *Anna's Athabaskan Summer* by A. Griese
> *In for the Winter, Out for the Spring* by A. Adoff & J. Pinkney

Activity 2

Have students read another book about the challenged; see The Challenged in the Concept Book List. Ask students to create a poster that invites children from other classrooms to enjoy the same books.

Activity 3

As a class, research pond life. Have everyone in the class contribute in a cooperative manner to a life-size mural of a pond.

Related Books

Refer to books about the Challenged in the Concept Book List.

Lesson 3.6: We Speak Different Languages

Books

> *Margaret and Margarita* by Lynn Reiser
> Other suggested books about different languages
> Other suggested books about Hispanic people

Purposes

- To introduce children to the relationship between Spanish and English.

- To encourage children to learn words in languages other than their native tongue.

- To introduce children to Hispanic history, culture, and contributions.

Appropriate Age Group

> Primary

Thematic Unit Connections

> Languages; Self-Concept; Appreciating Similarities and Differences

"Hello"

Curriculum Connections

> Social Studies; Language Arts

Objectives

1. The students will listen to *Margaret and Margarita* by L. Reiser.
2. The students will use the context of the story to figure out the unknown words.
3. The students will discuss similarities between the girls in the book.
4. The students will discuss differences between the girls in the book.
5. The students will make a Venn Diagram.
6. The students will match corresponding Spanish and English words.
7. The students will start a Spanish/English word list.
8. The students will read books about different languages to construct a dictionary.
9. The students will read/listen to more stories about Hispanics' history, culture, and contributions.

Materials

- *Margaret and Margarita* by L. Reiser
- Copies of the corresponding Spanish and English words from the story
- Materials for making a Venn Diagram
- Materials for making word cards
- Chart paper
- Materials for making dictionaries
- Other suggested books about languages
- Other suggested books about Hispanic people

Introducing Selection

Activating Prior Knowledge

Ask English-speaking students if they know any Spanish words. Write them on the board. Do the same with Spanish-speaking children.

Setting Purpose for Reading Selection

Introduce the selection *Margaret and Margarita* by Lynn Reiser. Tell students the story is written in both Spanish and English. Ask them to look for words they can understand that are not written in their native tongue.

Reading and Responding

Read Selection

Have students read/listen to *Margaret and Margarita*.

Respond to Selection

Go over the meaning of the story as a class. Discuss the differences and similarities between the girls. Figure 3.2 shows a Venn Diagram; in cooperative groups, ask students to complete Venn Diagrams of the two girls in the story.

Extending the Literature

Activity 1

Hand out a card with a Spanish word from the story on it to each child in half of the room. Hand out a card with a corresponding English word from the story on it to each child in the other half of the room.

Place students who have a Spanish word on one side of the room and place students who have an English word on the other side of the room.

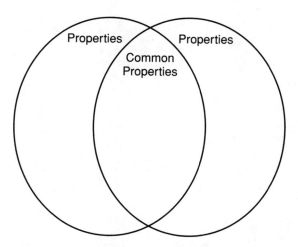

FIGURE 3.2   Venn Diagram

Have each student find the person who has the same word in the other language. Repeat this activity several times, giving all children a chance to look for both Spanish and English words. Have students write matching words on large chart paper. Display chart throughout the unit.

Activity 2

Break the class up into small groups of three to five to make picture dictionaries in languages other than English. Have each group research the numbers one through ten in the language they have been assigned. On each page they should write the word for each number and draw a picture to represent that number. Refer to books in Languages section of the Concept Book List to help the students with this assignment.

Activity 3

Have students read books from the Languages section of the Concept Book List.

CHAPTER

4

Focusing on Our Own and Others' History, Cultures, and Contributions

Lesson 4.1: Slavery Is Wrong!

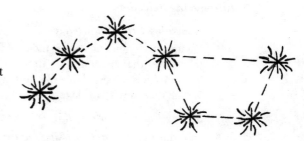

Books

Follow the Drinking Gourd
by J. Winter
Other suggested books about
slavery, the Underground
Railroad, and the Civil War

Purposes

- To introduce children to the concept of slavery and how it is wrong.
- To introduce children to the history of African Americans, especially in regard to slavery, the Underground Railroad, and the Civil War.

Appropriate Age Group

Primary

Thematic Unit Connections

African American History; Slavery; Understanding Self and Others

Curriculum Connections

Language Arts; Social Studies

Objectives

1. The students will read/listen to a story about the Underground Railroad.
2. The students will react to the story through a story line.
3. The students will do a readers' theater or an informal play about *Follow the Drinking Gourd*.
4. The students will research slavery, the times of slavery, the Underground Railroad, and the Civil War.
5. The students will make a time line depicting African American slavery from its onset to its abolishment.

Materials

- *Follow the Drinking Gourd* by J. Winter
- Materials for making a story line
- Materials to do a readers' theater or play
- Video camera
- Materials for writing a research report
- Materials for making a time line concerning slavery in the United States.
- Other suggested books about slavery, the times of slavery, the Underground Railroad, and the Civil War

Introducing Selection

Activating Prior Knowledge

Do an activity that takes the students' freedom away for no good reason; for example, take away the students' free time on playground or in classroom for several days. Then discuss what it feels like to have your privileges and/or freedom taken away. Relate this activity to slavery.

Setting Purpose for Reading Selection

1. Introduce *Follow the Drinking Gourd* by J. Winter.
2. Tell the students to listen to the story to find out the ways the slaves used the stars at night to help them escape to their freedom.

Reading and Responding

Read Selection

Read *Follow the Drinking Gourd* aloud to the students or provide enough copies so the students can read the book independently.

Respond to Selection

Ask the students to make or help you make a story line of *Follow the Drinking Gourd*. Major occurrences in the story could be paraphrased or drawn on the story line in the sequence in which they really happened. For example, the story line could begin and end as shown in Figure 4.1.

Extending the Literature

Activity 1

Have the students get into cooperative groups. Have each group do a readers' theater of *Follow the Drinking Gourd*. Or have the students informally act out the book. If they want to be more formal and elaborate, they can make costumes and so on. Videotape the different groups' versions of the play. The videotapes can be shared with other classes. A music specialist can be incorporated in order to integrate all the activities in this lesson.

Peg	Mollie,
Leg	James,
Joe	Isaiah,
taught	Hattie,
the	and
slave	George
families	crossed
the	the
song	shores
"Follow	of
the	Lake Erie
Drinking	to
Gourd"	freedom

FIGURE 4.1 **Students' Story Line for** *Following the Drinking Gourd*

Activity 2

Have the students learn the song at the end of the book. Tell the students that this was a real song the slaves learned in order to escape. It told them the way to navigate their way at night by following the Big Dipper. The students can include this song in their videotaped plays.

Activity 3

1. Tell children that they are going to be making a time line that depicts the history of slavery, the Underground Railroad, heroes and heroines of the Underground Railroad, Abraham Lincoln's connection to the freeing of the slaves, and the Civil War.

2. Have children get into cooperative groups, and have each group research information about

    a. People who helped the slaves escape on the Underground Railroad;

    b. The history of African American slavery—from its onset to its abolishment;

    c. What role Abraham Lincoln played in freeing the slaves; or

    d. What role the Civil War played in freeing the slaves.

3. Younger students may need help from buddies in the older grades.

4. In order to research their assigned topics, the students can use books from the list below.

    P   Adler, D. A. 1993. *A Picture Book of Frederick Douglass.* Holiday House. (African American history, civil rights, social activism)

    I   Armstrong, J. 1992. *Steal Away to Freedom.* Scholastic. (African American history, slavery)

    I   Beatty, P. 1991. *Jayhawker.* Morrow. (Civil War, slavery)

I   Beatty, P. 1992. *Who Comes with Cannons?* Morrow. (Underground Railroad)

I   Bentley, J. 1990. *Harriet Tubman.* Watts. (African American history)

I   Collier, J. L., & Collier, C. 1981. *Jump Ship to Freedom.* Delacorte. (Civil War, slavery)

I   Collier, J. L., & Collier, C. 1994. *With Every Drop of Blood: A Novel of the Civil War.* Delacorte. (Civil War, slavery)

I   Evitts, W. J. 1985. *Captive Bodies, Free Spirits: The Story of Southern Slavery.* Children's Book Press. (Slavery)

I   Fleishman, P. 1993. *Bull Run.* HarperCollins. (Civil War—different perspectives)

I   Fox, P. 1973. *The Slave Dancer.* Bradbury. (Slavery)

I   Freeman, F. B. 1971. *Two Tickets to Freedom: The True Story of Ellen and William Craft, Fugitive Slaves.* New York: Peter Bedrik. (Slavery)

I   Hamilton, V. 1993. *Many Thousand Gone: African Americans from Slavery to Freedom.* Knopf. (African American history, slavery)

I   Hansen, J. 1988. *Out from This Place.* Walker. (Civil War, slavery)

I   Haskins, J. 1993. *Get On Board: The Story of the Underground Railroad.* Scholastic. (Underground Railroad)

P, I   Johnson, D. 1993. *Now Let Me Fly: The Story of a Slave Family.* Macmillan. (Slavery, African American history)

P, I   Johnson, D. 1994. *Seminole Diary: Remembrance of a Slave.* Macmillan. (Slavery)

P, I   Levine, E. 1988. *If You Traveled on the Underground Railroad.* Scholastic. (Slavery, African American history)

I   McCurdy, M. 1994. *Escape from Slavery: The Boyhood of Frederick Douglass in His Own Words.* Knopf. (African American history, slavery, social activism)

I   McGovern, A. 1965. *Runaway Slave: The Story of Harriet Tubman.* Four Winds. (African American women in history, slavery, social activism)

I   McKissack, P., & McKissack, F. 1988. *A Long Hard Journey: The Story of the Pullman Porter.* Walker. (Civil rights movement)

I   Meltzer, M., ed. 1989. *Voices from the Civil War: A Documentary of the Great American Conflict.* HarperCollins. (Civil War, prejudice)

I   Mettger, Z. 1994. *The Victory Is Won: Black Soldiers in the Civil War.* Lodestar. (African American history, Civil War)

P   Monjo, F. N. 1970. *The Drinking Gourd.* Harper & Row. (African American history, slavery)

I   Moore, K. 1994. *If You Lived at the Time of the Civil War.* Scholastic. (African American history, Civil War)

I   Moore, Y. 1991. *Freedom Songs.* (African American history)

I   O'Dell, S. 1989. *My Name Is Not Angelica.* Houghton Mifflin. (Slavery, African American history)

I   Paulsen, G. 1993. *Night John.* Bantam Doubleday Dell. (African American history, slavery)

P, I   Polacco, P. 1994. *Pink and Say.* Philomel. (Civil War)

I   Rappaport, D. 1991. *Escape from Slavery: Five Journeys to Freedom.* Harper-Collins. (Slavery, African American history)

I   Ray, D. 1991. *Behind the Blue and Gray: The Soldier's Life in the Civil War.* Lodestar. (Civil War)

P   Ray, M. L. 1994. *Shaker Boy.* Browndeer. (Civil War, Shaker family)

I   Reit, S. 1988. *Behind Rebel Lines: The Incredible Story of Emma Edmonds, Civil War Spy.* Gulliver/Harcourt Brace Jovanovich. (Civil War)

P   Ringgold, F. 1992. *Aunt Harriet's Underground Railroad.* Crown. (Famous African American women)

I   Robinet, H. G. 1991. *Children of the Fire.* Atheneum. (Slavery, Underground Railroad, social activism)

I   Ruby, L. 1994. *Steal Away Home.* Macmillan/Simon & Schuster. (Underground Railroad)

I   Santrey, L. 1983. *Young Frederick Douglass: Fight for Freedom.* Troll. (African American history, slavery, social activism)

I   Smucker, B. 1977. *Runaway to Freedom.* Harper. (African American history)

I   Turner, A. 1987. *Nettie's Trip South.* Macmillan. (Civil War, prejudice)

P   Winter, J. 1992. *Follow the Drinking Gourd.* Knopf. (African American history, slavery, social activism)

Lesson 4.2: Why Do We Have to Leave Home?

Books

> *The Bracelet* by Y. Uchida and J. Yardley
>
> *Baseball Saved Us* by K. Mochizuki
>
> Other Books about Japanese/Japanese American history, culture, and contributions

Purposes

> ■ To introduce children to Japanese/Japanese American history, culture, and contributions.
>
> ■ To introduce children to the injustice of the internment camps.

Appropriate Age Group

> Second and third graders. Kindergarten and first grade teachers can also select individual activities that they feel are appropriate to the needs of their students.

Thematic Unit Connections

> Japanese American History; Family; Understanding Self and Others

Curriculum Connections

> Social Studies; Language Arts

Objectives

1. The students will read/listen to a story about a family that was sent to an internment camp.
2. The students will retell the story through a sequencing activity.
3. The students will make a collage.
4. The students will talk about something that is special to them.
5. The students will compare and contrast two stories about the same subject.
6. The students will read/listen to other stories relating to Japanese/Japanese American history, culture, and contributions.

Materials

- Chart paper
- *The Bracelet* by Y. Uchida and J. Yardley
- Materials for recording the sequence of the story
- Materials for making collages
- Reference materials about internment camps
- Something special from home
- *Baseball Saved Us* by K. Mochizuki
- Other books about Japanese/Japanese American history, culture, contributions

Introducing Selection

Activating Prior Knowledge

1. Have the students close their eyes and listen to you tell them a story. Tell the students that they have come home from school, and "You are at the table eating dinner with your family. There is a knock at the door. Your mom or dad gets up from the table to answer the door. You and the rest of your family follow. A man at the door tells you and your family that he is taking all of you away and that you can't bring anything with you. Your family gets in the back of a van and you are driven away."
2. Alternatively, read a selection that evokes the same feelings.
3. Have the class open their eyes. Have the students react to the story you told them. Ask them if they think it is fair to be taken from your house for no reason. You can write their feelings down on chart paper.

Setting Purpose for Reading Selection

1. Introduce *The Bracelet* by Y. Uchida and J. Yardley

2. Have the students study the front cover of the book and tell what they think the story could be about. After you hear their responses, tell them that the girl in this story and her family were taken from their home. Have the students listen to the story to find out about the kinds of feelings this family felt throughout the story. Also, have the students pay close attention to the sequence of events.

Reading and Responding

Read Selection

Have students read/listen to *The Bracelet* by Y. Uchida and J. Yardley.

Respond to Selection

1. Ask second and third grade students to share how Emi felt about being taken away from her home and her friend. Write down their responses on chart paper.

2. Have the children break up into groups of four or five. Give each student a piece of paper. Have each group discuss the order of events in the story. The group can decide on four or five of the most important events in the story. Then have each student in the group draw an event.

3. For kindergarteners and first graders, have the children help you decide on four or five of the most important events in the story. You can then draw pictures to represent the most important events the children decide on.

4. In front of the class, attach a string to two chairs or across the chalkboard to make a clothesline. Have each group bring their pictures and clip them in the order that the events occurred. Have the group retell the story by using the pictures on the clothesline.

Extending the Literature

Activity 1

1. Give each student a piece of construction paper. Provide the students with old magazines, glue, and scissors. Have the students make collages of things and memories that remind them of their home.

2. Ask students of all ages if they remember why Emi and her family were taken. If they forget, tell the children that during the war some people experienced unfounded fears about the Japanese Americans becoming involved with the war here in America, and so they moved Japanese Americans to internment camps.

3. Show only the older children pictures of internment camps from encyclopedias or other references. Have a discussion with the children about the cruelty of taking the Japanese Americans away from their homes.

Activity 2

Have the students bring in something special from home. Allow them to talk in front of class about what makes this object so special to them. Have them share the feelings and memories their special object would evoke if it were lost. Remind them that although Emi lost her bracelet, she was still able to hang on to her memories.

Activity 3

Read *Baseball Saved Us* by K. Mochizuki. Have students compare and contrast *Baseball Saved Us* with *The Bracelet*.

Activity 4

Have students read/listen to another book relating to Japanese/Japanese American history, culture, and contributions from the selection below. Ask them to look for the main ideas behind the story.

P, I   Coeer, E. 1993. *Sadako.* Putnam. (Hiroshima, Japanese history)

P   Coeer, E. 1977. *Sadako and the Thousand Cranes.* Putnam. (Hiroshima, Japanese history)

P, I   Hamanaka, S. 1994. *Peace Crane.* Morrow. (Japanese history, Hiroshima)

P, I   Maruki, T. 1980. *Hiroshima No Pika.* Lothrop. (Hiroshima, Japanese history)

P, I   Mochizuki, K. 1995. *Heroes.* New York: Lee & Low. (Stereotyping, Japanese American history)

P, I   Morimoto, J. 1987. *My Hiroshima.* Canada: Puffin Books. (Hiroshima, Japanese history)

P   Say, A. 1982. *The Bicycle Man.* Scholastic. (World War II, Japanese people, stereotyping)

P   Say, A. 1993. *Grandfather's Journey.* Houghton Mifflin. (Japanese family)

P   Uchida, Y. 1993. *The Magic Purse.* Margaret McElderry. (Japanese folktale)

P   Uchida, Y. 1994. *The Wise Old Women.* Margaret McElderry. (Japanese folktale)

Lesson 4.3: Jewish Celebrations

Books

Elijah's Angel by M. J. Rosen

A Family Hanukkah by B. Katz

Other suggested books about Jewish holidays; Jewish history, culture, and contributions; and holidays from different perspectives

Purposes

- To encourage children to understand that friendship is the same in any religion.
- To introduce children to Hanukkah.
- To introduce children to various Jewish holidays.

Appropriate Age Group

First, second, and third graders. Kindergarten teachers can select individual activities that they feel are appropriate to the needs of their students.

Thematic Unit Connections

Jewish American Holidays; Friendship; Understanding Self and Others

Curriculum Connections

Social Studies; Language Arts

Objectives

1. The students will read/listen to the story.
2. The students will make a KWL chart listing what they already know, want to know, and have learned about Hanukkah.
3. The students will record and discuss the main character's feelings.
4. The students will paint their favorite scene from the story.
5. The students will read/listen to books about other Jewish holidays.
6. The students will read/listen to books relating to holidays from different perspectives.

Materials

- *Elijah's Angel* by M. J. Rosen
- *A Family Hanukkah* by B. Katz
- KWL charts
- Journals
- Burlap or flax or canvas
- Tempera paints of various colors
- Other suggested books about Jewish holidays
- Other suggested books about holidays from different cultures

Introducing Selection

Activating Prior Knowledge

1. Children of all ages should listen to the story *A Family Hanukkah* by B. Katz in order to become familiar with Hanukkah.
2. Next, tell all students that they are going to read/listen to a story about two different people who celebrate two different holidays at the same time of the year. Ask the students to tell you what they already know about Hanukkah. Record the students' responses in the K ("Know") section of a KWL chart, as shown in Figure 4.2.
3. Ask students to tell you what else they want to know about Hanukkah. Record their responses in the W ("Want") section of the KWL chart.

What Do I Know	What Do I Want to Know?	What Did I Learn?

FIGURE 4.2   KWL Chart

Setting Purpose for Reading Selection

1. Ask students to read/listen to the story *Elijah's Angel* by M. J. Rosen to find out how Michael felt about the gift he received and why. Ask students to find out how this problem was resolved.

2. Tell students to be aware of the illustrations in the book. Explain how they are painted on scrap rag. Pass out examples of scrap rag (canvas or burlap). Have them note the apparent texture of the paintings in the book.

Reading and Responding

Read Selection

Read *Elijah's Angel* to the students, noting the illustrations.

Respond to Selection

1. Have younger students discuss how Michael felt about Elijah's gift. Discuss the importance of friendship across different religions.

2. Have older students use their journals to record how Michael felt about Elijah's gift. Have the students share their reactions in their literature groups. (Remember to place three to five students in each literature group.) Pull the entire class back together to discuss the importance of friendship and how it is universal across all religions.

Extending the Literature

Activity 1

1. Flip through the story again, paying special attention to the artwork.

2. Cover an area with newspaper and have each student use different paints to illustrate their favorite part of the story on burlap.

3. Have the students describe their illustration and then explain why they chose that particular scene.

Activity 2

Have students read a book from the list below to learn other facts about Hanukkah. Ask students to record one thing they learned. Place their responses in the L section of the KWL chart.

P, I   Adler, D. A. 1995. *One Yellow Daffodil: A Hanukkah Story.* Gulliver. (Jewish holiday)

P   Behrens, J. 1983. *Hanukkah.* Regensteiner. (Jewish holiday)

P   Kimmel, E. 1989. *Hershel and the Hanukkah Goblins.* Holiday House. (Jewish tale)

P   Kimmel, E. 1988. *The Chanukkah Guest.* Holiday House. (Jewish holiday)

P   Weiss, N. 1992. *The First Night of Hanukkah.* Putnam/Grosset & Dunlap. (Jewish holiday)

Activity 3

Ask students to listen to/read a story about another Jewish holiday from the books listed below. Ask the children to see if they can make connections between what is happening in the story and what is happening in their own lives.

P   Cohen, B. 1994. *Make a Wish, Molly.* Doubleday. (Jewish holiday)

P, I   Fluek, T., & Finkler, L. 1994. *Passover: As I Remember It.* Doubleday. (Jewish history, Jewish holiday)

P, I   Gordon, G. 1993. *My Two Worlds.* Clarion. (Holiday)

I   Jaffe, N. 1993. *The Uninvited Guest and Other Jewish Holiday Tales.* Scholastic. (Jewish holiday tales)

P   Koltach, A. 1992. *The Jewish Child's First Book of Why?* Jonathan David. (Jewish history, Jewish holidays)

P   Portnay, M. A. 1994. *Matzah Ball.* Kar-Ben Copies. (Jewish food, Jewish holiday)

P   Schotter, R. 1995. *Passover Magic.* Little, Brown. (Jewish holiday)

P, I   Schnur, S. 1995. *The Tie Man's Miracle: A Chanukah Tale.* Morrow. (Jewish tale, Jewish holiday)

P, I   Schwartz, L. S. 1994. *The Four Questions.* New York: Puffin. (Passover story)

Related Books

Refer to the Holidays section in the Concept Book List.

Lesson 4.4: But We Were Here First

Books

> *The People Shall Continue* by S. Ortiz
>
> *The Land of the Gray Wolf* by T. Locker
>
> Other suggested books about native American history, culture, and contributions

Purposes

- To introduce children to the feelings of the Native Americans when the settlers arrived.
- To introduce children to Native American history, culture, and contributions.

Appropriate Age Group

First, second, and third graders. Kindergarten teachers can select individual activities that they feel are appropriate to the needs of their students.

Thematic Unit Connections

Native American History; Environment; Understanding Self and Others

Curriculum Connections

Social Studies; Language Arts

Objectives

1. The students will listen to *The People Shall Continue* by S. Ortiz.
2. The students will make a list of adjectives that describe how they feel when someone makes them do something they don't want to do.
3. The students will discuss an incident when they were forced to do something they didn't want to.
4. The students will respond to the story through response journals and literature groups.
5. The students will draw a picture of how the North American land appeared before and after the settlers came.
6. The students will figure out how they feel—and why they feel that way—as they read/listen to stories and accounts of Native American history, culture, and contributions.

Materials

- *The People Shall Continue* by S. Ortiz
- *The Land of the Gray Wolf* by T. Locker
- Crayons and/or Magic Markers; 11-by-17-inch paper
- Literature logs/response journals
- Other suggested books about Native American history, culture, and contributions

Introducing Selection

Activating Prior Knowledge

1. Have the students discuss a time when they were forced to do something they didn't want to do.

2. Brainstorm all the adjectives the students can think of to describe the feelings they had when they were forced to do something they didn't want to do.

Setting Purpose for Reading Selection

Ask the students to listen to the story to find out about the feelings the Native Americans had when the settlers came to their land.

Reading and Responding

Read Selection

Have the students listen to/read *The People Shall Continue* by S. Ortiz.

Respond to Selection

Discuss how Native Americans felt when the settlers came to their land, when their land was taken away, and so on.

Extending the Literature

Activity 1

1. Have students answer the following open-ended questions in their literature logs or response journals:

   Did you have strong feelings as you read the story?

   What did the author do to make you feel this way?

2. Discuss the journal responses in small discussion groups.

3. In a total group, talk about some of the reactions that the students had to the story.

Activity 2

1. Read *The Land of the Gray Wolf* by T. Locker. Tell the children to notice the illustrations and think about how the world looked back then. After the story is read, flip through the pages again, paying special attention to the appearance of the land.

2. Pass out 11-by-17-inch paper. Have the students fold it in half. On one half of the paper, have the children illustrate what the land was like before the settlers came. On the other half, have them draw what it was like after the settlers came.

Activity 3

Have students read/listen to a story, tale, or other account about Native American history, culture, and contributions from the list provided below. Ask the students to be able to discuss how the account made them feel and why.

P   Adler, D. A. 1993. *A Picture Book of Sitting Bull.* Holiday House. (Native American history)

P   Aliki. 1976. *Corn Is Maize: The Gift of the Indians.* HarperCollins. (Native Americans)

P   Ata, T. 1989. *Baby Rattlesnake.* Children's Book Press. (Native American tale)

P, I   Baylor, B. 1986. *Hawk, I'm Your Brother.* Macmillan. (Native American tale)

P   Baylor, B. 1994. *The Table Where the Rich People Sit.* Scribner's. (Native Americans)

P   Bernhard, E. 1993. *Spotted Eagle and Black Crow: A Lakota Legend.* Holiday House. (Lakota legend)

P   Bierhorst, J. 1993. *The Woman Who Fell from the Sky: The Iroquois Story of Creation.* Morrow. (Iroquois story of creation)

P   Bruchac, J. 1993. *The First Strawberries.* Dial. (Native American tale)

P, I   Bruhac, J., & London, J. 1992. *Thirteen Moons on Turtle's Back: A Native American Year of Moons.* Philomel. (Native American tale)

P, I   Bruchas, J., & Ross, G. 1994. *The Girl Who Married the Moon: Tales from Native North America.* Bridgewater. (Native American tales)

P, I   Chief Dan George. 1989. *My Heart Soars.* Hancock House. (Native American poems)

P, I   Clark, A. N. 1941. *In My Mother's House.* New York: Viking. (Native American poems)

P   Cohlene, T. 1990. *Turquoise Boy: A Navajo Legend.* Rourke Corporation. (Navajo legend)

P   Crowder, J. 1986. *Tonibah and the Rainbow.* Upper Strata Ink. (Native American tale)

P, I   Dayrell, E. 1991. *Why the Sun and the Moon Live in the Sky.* Scholastic. (Native American tale)

P, I   DeArmond, D. 1987. *The Seal Oil Lamp.* Sierra Club/Little, Brown. (Eskimo tale)

P   dePaola, T. 1988. *The Legend of the Indian Paintbrush.* Putnams. (Native American tale)

P   dePaola, T. 1989. *The Legend of the Bluebonnet: An Old Tale of Texas.* Scholastic. (Native American tale)

P   Dixon, A. 1992. *How Raven Brought Light to People.* Margaret McElderry. (Tlingit Indian legend)

P, I   Drinking Hawk Sneve, V. 1988. *Dancing Teepees: Poems of American Indian Youth.* Holiday House. (Native American poems)

P, I   Eskoomiak, N. 1990. *Arctic Memories.* Holt. (Inuit family, Inuit history)

P, I   Gates, F. 1994. *Owl Eyes.* Lothrop. (Mohawk legend)

Lesson 4.5: Famous African American Women

Books

Dinner at Aunt Carrie's House
by F. Ringgold

Other suggested books about famous African
Americans, women in particular

Other suggested books about African/African
American history, culture, and contributions

Purposes

- To encourage children to learn about famous
  African American women.
- To introduce children to African American
  history, culture, and contributions.

Appropriate Age Group

Primary

Thematic Unit Connections

Famous African Americans; Famous Women; Understanding Self and Others

Curriculum Connections

Social Studies; Language Arts

Objectives

1. The students will read/listen to stories about famous African American women in *Dinner at Aunt Carrie's House* by Faith Ringgold.
2. The students will brainstorm and read for specific information.
3. The students will discuss their findings.
4. The students will read other books by Faith Ringgold and compare and contrast them to *Dinner at Aunt Carrie's House.*
5. The students will construct a "self-history" scrapbook.
6. The students will read/listen to a story, poem, or tale relating to African American history, culture, and contributions.
7. The students will tell what they learned about African American history, culture, and contributions from what they read.

Materials

- *Dinner at Aunt Carrie's House* by F. Ringgold
- Response journals

- Other books by Faith Ringgold
- Other books about the famous African American women in *Dinner at Aunt Carrie's House*
- Video camera
- Materials to make "self-history" scrapbook
- Other suggested books about African/African American history, culture, and contributions

Introducing Selection

Activating Prior Knowledge and Setting Purpose for Reading Selection

Get students into small groups of two to three students each. Give each group the name of one of the famous African American women from the book, including author Faith Ringgold. Each group needs to read/listen to a book from the list under "Extending the Literature" below to find out what contribution(s) one of the following women made:

1. Rosa Parks
2. Fannie Lou Hamer
3. Mary McLeod Bethune
4. Augusta Savage
5. Dorothy Dandridge
6. Zora Neale Hurston
7. Maria W. Steward

8. Bessie Smith
9. Harriet Tubman
10. Sojourner Truth
11. Marian Anderson
12. Madame C. J. Walker
13. Faith Ringgold

Reading and Responding

Read Selection

Have students read/listen to *Dinner at Aunt Carrie's House* by F. Ringgold.

Respond to Selection

After students read/listen to *Dinner at Aunt Carrie's House,* have them get into their groups to discuss and write down in their response journals the contributions their famous women made.

Extending the Literature

Activity 1

The same groups of students can read another book or an excerpt from another book about the women they were assigned from *Dinner at Aunt Carrie's House.* The books are listed below. After the students finish reading, videotape them as they role-play what the women did to make them famous.

P   Adler, D. A. 1993. *A Picture Book of Rosa Parks.* Holiday House.

P   Adler, D. A. 1994. *A Picture Book of Sojourner Truth.* Holiday House.

P, I Ashby, R., & Ohrn, D. G. 1995. *Herstory: Women Who Changed the World.* Viking. (Sojourner Truth, Bessie Smith, Zora Neale Hurston)

I Bentley, J. 1990. *Harriet Tubman.* Watts.

Bogart, M., ed. 1989. *African American Biographies.* Globe. (Zora Neale Hurston, Marian Anderson)

I Ferris, J. 1988. *Go Free or Die: A Story about Harriet Tubman.* Carolrhoda.

I Ferris, J. 1988. *Walking the Road to Freedom: A Story about Sojourner Truth.* Carolrhoda.

I Ferris, J. 1994. *What I Was Singing: The Story of Marian Anderson.* Carolrhoda.

P, I Greenfield, E. 1973. *Rosa Parks.* Crowell.

P, I Lee, G. L. 1989. *Interesting People: Black American History Makers.* Ballantine. (Harriet Tubman, Rosa Parks, Augusta Savage, Bessie Smith, Fannie Lou Hamer, Dorothy Dandridge)

P Livingston, M. C. 1994. *Keep on Singing: A Ballad of Marian Anderson.* Anderson.

I McGovern, A. 1965. *Runaway Slave: The Story of Harriet Tubman.* Four Winds.

P, I McKissack, P., & McKissack, F. 1991. *Mary McLeod: A Great Teacher.* Enslow.

P, I McKissack, P., & McKissack, F. 1993. *Madame C. J. Walker: Self-Made Millionaire.* Enslow.

I Meltzer, M. 1984. *The Black Americans: A History of Their Own Times.* HarperCollins. (Rosa Parks, Fannie Lou Hamer, Augusta Savage, Bessie Smith, Harriet Tubman).

P Miller, W. 1994. *Zora Hurston and the Chinaberry Tree.* Lee & Low.

I Parks, R., with J. Haskins. 1992. *Rosa Parks: My Story.* Dial.

I Porter, A. P. 1992. *Jump at de Sun: The Story of Zora Neale Hurston.* Carolrhoda.

I Potter, J. 1994. *African American Firsts: Famous, Little-Known, and Unsung Triumphs of Blacks in America.* Pinto. (Dorothy Dandridge, Sojourner Truth, Harriet Tubman)

P, I Rubel, D. 1990. *Fannie Lou Hamer: From Sharecropping to Politics.* Silver Burdett.

I Speigel, B. 1992. *The Year They Walked: Rosa Parks and the Montgomery Bus Boycott.* Simon & Schuster.

I Time-Life Books, Editors of. 1994. *Creative Fire: African American Voices of Triumph.* Time-Life. (Famous African Americans)

P, I Turner, G. 1989. *Take a Walk in Their Shoes.* Cobblestone. (Rosa Parks, Mary McLeod Bethune)

I Turner, R. M. 1992. *Faith Ringgold.* Little, Brown.

P, I Wolfe, R. E. 1992. *Mary McLeod Bethune.* Watts.

P, I Yannuzzi, D. A. 1996. *Zora Neale Hurston: Southern Storyteller.* Enslow.

Activity 2

1. Read other books written by the same author, Faith Ringgold: *Aunt Harriet's Underground Railroad* and *Tar Beach*.

2. Discuss what seems to make this particular author's work unique.

Activity 3

Have students bring in pictures of themselves. With these pictures they can construct a "self-history" scrapbook that they can share with the class or put on display.

Activity 4

Have students read/listen to a book from the list below. Ask them to be able to discuss what they learned about African American history, culture, and contributions from what they read.

P, I   Aardema, V. 1975. *Why Mosquitoes Buzz in People's Ears: A West African Tale.* Dial. (African American tale)

P, I   Aardema, V. 1981. *Bringing the Rain to Kapiti Plain.* Dial. (African American tale)

P   Adler, D. A. 1989. *A Picture Book of Martin Luther King, Jr.* Scholastic. (African American history, social activism)

P   Adler, D. A. 1993. *A Picture Book of Frederick Douglass.* Holiday House. (African American history, civil rights, social activism)

P   Adoff, A. 1973. *Black Is Brown Is Tan.* Harper. (African American poetry)

P   Ashe-Moutoussamy, J. 1993. *Daddy and Me: A Photo Story of Arthur Ashe and His Daughter, Camera.* Knopf. (Famous African American, family dealing with AIDS)

P, I   Bray, R. L. 1995. *Martin Luther King, Jr.* Greenwillow. (Famous African American, civil rights movement)

P, I   Bryan, A. 1974. *Walk Together Children: Black American Spirituals.* Atheneum. (African American songs)

P   Carlstom, N. W. 1987. *Wild Wild Sunflower Child Anna.* Macmillan. (African American family)

P   Chocolate, D. 1995. *On the Day I Was Born.* New York: Scholastic. (African American cultures)

P, I   Coles, R. 1995. *The Story of Ruby Bridges.* Scholastic. (African American women in history)

P   Cowen-Fletcher, J. 1994. *It Takes a Village.* Scholastic. (Extended African family)

P   Dupree, R. 1993. *The Wishing Chair.* Carolrhoda. (African American history, African American family)

P, I   Ets, M. H. 1971. *Soul Looks Back in Wonder.* Dial. (African American poems)

P, I   Everett, G. 1992. *Li'l Sis and Uncle Willie: A Story Based on the Life and Paintings of William H. Johnson.* Rizzoli. (Famous African Americans)

P   Greenfield, E. 1978. *Honey, I Love.* Dial. (African American poems)

P   Greenfield, E. 1988. *Nathaniel Talking.* Black Butterfly Books. (African American poems)

P, I   Greenfield, E. 1991. *Night on Neighborhood Street.* Black Butterfly Books. (African American poems)

P, I   Grifalconi, A. 1986. *The Village of Round and Square Houses.* Little, Brown. (African American tales)

P, I   Guthrie, D. W. 1993. *Nobiah's Well: A Modern African Folktale.* Ideals. (African American tale)

P, I   Hudson, W. 1993. *Pass It On: African American Poetry for Children.* Scholastic. (African American poetry)

P   Jackson, G. N. 1993. *Elijah McCoy, Inventor.* Modern Curriculum Press. (Famous African American)

P, I   Johnson, J. W. 1995. *Lift Ev'ry Voice and Sing.* Scholastic. (African American songs)

P   Jones, K. 1994. *Happy Birthday, Dr. King!* Simon & Schuster. (African American history, social activism)

P, I   Keats, E. J. 1965. *John Henry.* Pantheon. (African American tall tale)

P, I   Lawrence, J. 1993. *The Great Migration: An American Story.* HarperCollins. (African American history, migration)

P   Lester, H. 1994. *John Henry.* New York: Dial. (African American tall tale)

P, I   Lester, J. 1989. *How Many Spots Does a Leopard Have?: And Other Tales.* Scholastic. (African- and Jewish-based tales)

P   McDermott, G. M. 1972. *Anansi the Spider.* Scholastic. (African American tale)

P   Marzollo, J. 1993. *Happy Birthday, Martin Luther King, Jr.* Scholastic. (African American history)

P, I   Mattern, J. 1992. *Young Martin Luther King, Jr.: "I Have a Dream."* Troll. (African American history, social activism)

P   Mattox, C. W. 1989. *Shake It to the One That You Love the Best.* Jig. (African American songs)

P   Mederias, A. S. 1989. *Our People.* Atheneum. (African American history, elderly)

P   Mederias, A. S. 1991. *Dancing with the Indians.* Holiday House. (Family, African American history, Native American history)

P, I   Mitchell, M. K. 1993. *Uncle Jed's Barber Shop.* Simon & Schuster. (African American history)

P, I   Myers, W. D. 1993. *Brown Angels: An Album of Pictures and Verse.* HarperCollins. (African Americans)

P   Onyefulu, I. 1993. *A Is for Africa.* Cobblehill Books. (African history)

I   Parker, M. 1990. *What Is Martin Luther King Jr. Day?* Children's Press. (African American history)

P, I Phumla. 1972. *Nomi and the Magic Fish.* (Zulu version of *Cinderella*)

P, I Rucki, A. 1992. *Turkey's Gift to the People.* Northland. (Native American tale)

P   Polacco, P. 1992. *Mrs. Katz and Tush.* Dell. (Elderly, Jewish history, African American history)

P   Ringgold, F. 1992. *Aunt Harriet's Underground Railroad.* Crown. (Famous African American women)

P   Seeger, P. 1994. *Abiyoyo.* Aladdin. (Modern African American tale)

P, I Straight, S. 1990. *Aquaboogie.* Milkweed. (African American tale)

P, I Strickland, D., & Strickland, M. 1993. *Families: Poems Celebrating the African American Experience.* Albert Whitman. (Family, African American poems)

P, I Thomas, J. C. 1993. *Brown Honey in Broomwheat Tea.* HarperCollins. (African American poems)

P   Williams, S. A. 1992. *Working Cotton.* Harcourt Brace Jovanovich. (African American history)

Lesson 4.6: Tending the Land

Books

A Day's Work by E. Bunting

Amelia's Road by L. J. Altman and E. O. Sanquez

Lights on the River by M. Dooling

Other suggested books about migrant workers

Purposes

- To introduce children to the plight of migrant workers.

- To help children understand that not all migrant workers are Hispanic and that not all Hispanic people are migrant workers.

Appropriate Age Group

Second and third graders. Kindergarten and first grade teachers can select individual activities that they feel are appropriate to the needs of their students.

Thematic Unit Connections

Our Own and Others' History, Culture, and Contributions

Curriculum Connections

Social Studies, Language Arts

Objectives

1. The students will read/listen to and respond to stories about migrant workers.

2. The students will read/listen to other books in order to become more familiar with the plight of migrant workers.

3. The students will be able to tell you what they wondered about as they read/listened to the book.

Materials

- *A Day's Work* by E. Bunting
- *Amelia's Road* by L. J. Altman & E. O. Sanquez
- *Lights on the River* by J. R. Thomas
- Other suggested books about migrant workers

Introducing Selection

Activating Prior Knowledge

1. Read *A Day's Work* by E. Bunting.

2. Talk to students about migrant farmworkers and how they harvest the food that others eat. Discuss the plight of migrant workers, making sure to mention that

   a. The work is so hard that their muscles ache;

   b. They have to work all day, every day;

   c. The pay is minimal;

   d. The workers must always pay for rent and buy food;

   e. The children have to work;

   f. The families have to move from place to place to harvest crops; and

   g. The children do not get to attend school regularly.

Setting Purpose for Reading Selection

1. Tell students that they are going to be reading/listening to a story about migrant farmworkers—*Amelia's Road* by L. J. Altman and E. O. Sanquez.

2. Ask first, second, and third graders to be able to

   a. Name the main characters in this story;

   b. Discuss what the main characters did for a living in this story, including the children; and

   c. Discuss how being a migrant worker affected the lives of the characters in this story.

Reading and Responding

Read Selection

Have all students read/listen to *Amelia's Road* by L. J. Altman & E. O. Sanquez.

Respond to Selection

1. Older students should get into groups in order to name the main characters; younger students should help you name the main characters.

2. Ask younger students to help you discuss the following, and ask older students to stay in their groups to discuss the following:

   a. What the main characters, including the children, did for a living in this story;

   b. How being a migrant worker affected the lives of the characters in this story; and

   c. How the students would personally feel if they did not have a permanent place to come home to every night.

Extending the Literature

Activity 1

Ask all students to make a list of items they would bury in the ground if they had the chance. Explain that the items they choose should tell something about them as a person. Have students share their lists with the rest of the class.

Activity 2

Ask the students to read/listen to one of the books listed below in order to become more familiar with the plight of migrant workers. Ask them to be able to tell you what they wondered about as they read/listened to the book.

P, I   Atkin, B. A. 1993. *Voices from the Fields: Children of Migrant Farmworkers Tell Their Stories.* Joy Street. (Migrant workers)

P, I   Covault, R. 1994. *Pablo and Pimiento.* Northland. (Migrant workers, Hispanic people)

P   Dorros, A. 1993. *Radio Man.* HarperCollins. (Migrant workers, Hispanic people)

P   Williams, S. A. 1992. *Working Cotton.* Harcourt Brace Jovanovich. (Migrant workers)

Activity 3

1. Have students listen to/read *Lights on the River* by J. R. Thomas.

2. Make sure students listen to/read the Author's Note at the end of the book; students should understand that not all migrant workers are Hispanics and that not all Hispanics are migrant workers.

3. Have students read/listen to other books, chosen from the list below, that depict the roles of different Hispanics. Ask the children to think about how they feel as they listen to the story.

   P   Ancona, G. 1994. *The Pinata Maker: El Pinatero.* Harcourt Brace. (Mexican fiestas, Spanish–English language)

   P   Behrens, J. 1978. *Fiesta!* Regensteiner. (Hispanic holidays)

P Bernier-Grand, C. T. 1995. *Poets of Puerto Rico: Don Luis Munoz Marin.* Orchard. (Famous Puerto Rican)

P, I Bunting, E. 1994. *Smoky Nights.* Harcourt Brace. (Los Angeles riots)

P Cherry, L. 1995. *The Great Kapok Trees.* Dial. (Environment, Latinos)

P, I Codye, C. 1990. *Vilma Martinez.* Raintree/Steck-Vaughn. (Famous Hispanic women, social activism)

P Conrad, P. 1991. *Pedro's Journal.* Scholastic. (Columbus—different perspectives)

P Cowcher, H. 1988. *Rain Forest.* Starburst. (Environment)

P, I Czernecki, S., & Rhodes, T. 1992. *Pancho's Pinata.* Hyperion. (Hispanic family)

P, I Delacre, L. 1990. *Las Navidades: Popular Christmas Songs from Latin America.* Scholastic. (Latin American songs, Latin American holiday)

P Doherty, C. A., & Doherty, K. M. 1991. *Nine Days until Christmas: A Mexican Story.* Puffin. (Mexican holiday)

P Dorros, A. 1993. *Radio Man.* HarperCollins. (Migrant workers, Hispanic people)

P Gonzales, L. M. 1994. *The Bossy Gallito.* Scholastic. (Cuban folktale retold in Spanish and English)

P, I Gordon, G. 1993. *My Two Worlds.* Clarion. (Dominican Republic Christmas)

P Grossman, P. 1994. *Saturday Market.* Lothrop, Lee & Shepard. (Hispanic people)

P Haggerty, M. E. 1993. *A Crack in the Wall.* Lee & Low. (Family, holiday, Hispanic people)

P, I Hewett, F. P. 1990. *Hector Lives in the United States Now: The Story of a Mexican American Child.* Lippincott. (Immigration, Mexican American family)

P Hughes, M. 1996. *A Handful of Seeds.* Orchard. (Hispanic family, foods— different perspectives)

P Kuklin, S. 1992. *How My Family Lives in America.* Bradbury. (Immigrant families)

P, I Lattimore, D. N. 1988. *Why There Is No Arguing in Heaven: A Mayan Myth.* Harper. (Maya creation story)

P, I Lewis, R. 1991. *All of You Was Singing.* Atheneum. (Aztec myth)

P Mohr, N. 1993. *All for the Better: A Story of El Barrio.* Raintree/Steck-Vaughn. (Puerto Rican contributions, social activism)

P, I Mohr, N., & Martorell, A. 1995. *The Song of El Coqui and Other Tales of Puerto Rico.* Viking. (Puerto Rican culture)

P Mora, P. 1992. *A Birthday Basket for Tia.* Macmillan. (Hispanic family)

P Nieves, E. R. 1994. *Juan Bobo: Four Folktales from Puerto Rico.* HarperCollins. (Puerto Rican folktales)

P Pena, S. C. 1987. *Kikiriki Stories and Poems in English and Spanish for Children.* Arte Publico. (Puerto Rican poems, Spanish and English languages)

P Pico, F. 1994. *The Red Comb.* Bridgewater. (Puerto Rican slavery)

P   Ringgold, F. 1979. *Tar Beach.* Crown. (Puerto Rican history)

P   Sánchez, I. 1991. *Mis Primeros . . . Números.* Barron's. (Spanish language)

P   Schotter, R. 1993. *The Fruit and Vegetable Man.* Little, Brown. (Hispanic people)

P, I Spurr, E. 1995. *Lupe & Me.* Gulliver. (Mexican culture, immigration)

P   Stanek, M. 1990. *I Speak English for My Mom.* Albert Whitman. (Spanish language)

P   Van Laan, N. 1991. *The Legend of El Dorado: A Latin American Tale.* Knopf. (Latin American tale)

P, I Volkmer, J. A. *Song of Chrimia: A Guatemalan Folktale/La Musica de la Chrimia: Folktale Guatemalteco.* Carolrhoda. (Guatemalan folktale)

P   Winter, J. 1991. *Diego.* Knopf. (Latino history)

P, I Zak, M. 1994. *Save My Rainforest.* Volcano Press. (Environment, South America)

CHAPTER

5 Focusing on Deconstructing Stereotyping

Lesson 5.1: East Meets West

Books

> *Gila Monsters Meet You at the Airport*
> by M. W. Sharmat

> Other suggested books about deconstructing stereotyping

Purposes

- To encourage children to become more aware of Eastern and Western cultures.

- To encourage children to become more aware of others' cultures.

- To help children understand why it is not good to have preconceived notions about other people.

Appropriate Age Group

> First, second, and third graders. Kindergarten teachers can select individual activities that they feel meet the needs of their students.

Thematic Unit Connections

> Feelings; Deconstructing Stereotyping; Weather

Curriculum Connections

> Social Studies; Language Arts

Objectives

1. The students will read/listen to the story.
2. The students will list some common stereotypes about cities, countries, and peoples.
3. The students will compare and contrast the eastern United States and the western United States.
4. The students will research and report the weather in the eastern United States and the western United States.

5. The students will create their own version of the story using the same plot.

6. The students will create their own book cover.

Materials

- *Gila Monsters Meet You at the Airport* by M. W. Sharmat
- Chart paper and Magic Markers or chalkboard and chalk
- Materials to make Big Books
- Daily newspapers
- Costumes and scenery for conducting a weather report
- Video camera
- Other suggested books about deconstructing stereotyping

Introducing Selection

Activating Prior Knowledge

Brainstorm common preconceived notions or stereotypes about what children in countries such as China and Mexico eat, wear, do, and so forth.

Setting Purpose for Reading Selection

1. Introduce *Gila Monsters Meet You at the Airport* by M. W. Sharmat.

2. Ask the students to listen for the preconceived notions or stereotypes one boy in the story has about the western part of the United States and the other boy has about the western part of the United States.

Reading and Responding

Read Selection

Have students read/listen to *Gila Monsters Meet You at the Airport.*

Respond to Selection

1. Have a discussion about the preconceived notions or stereotypes the boys in the story had about the eastern and western parts of the United States. List older students' reponses on chart paper or on chalkboard.

2. Ask all students what the boy who was moving west learned about children who live in the West. Ask the older students what they think the boy who was moving east will learn about children who live in the East.

3. With older students, discuss the implications of children having preconceived notions about other children.

Extending the Literature

Activity 1

Have students use the daily newspaper to find out today's weather in the eastern and western parts of the country. Break students into small groups so they can take turns being TV weather forecasters. Videotape.

Activity 2

1. Have older students create their own versions of *Gila Monsters Meet You at the Airport*. Younger students can do a shared writing of their own version of the story. For example, students can write about a child from the United States moving to another country and a child from the other country moving to the United States. Be sure to have multiple copies of *Gila Monsters* so the students can use the same format as used in the story.

2. The student stories/class story can be published in the form of Big Books.

3. Share the younger students' version of the story with the class. Have older students share their Big Books with younger students.

4. Again discuss the implications of children having preconceived notions about children from other countries.

5. Make sure to place student-written book(s) in the classroom library.

Activity 3

Have the students create their own book cover.

Related Books

Find books about Stereotyping and Prejudice in the Concept Book List.

Lesson 5.2: Are There Really Big Bad Wolves?

Books

Any classic version of *Little Red Riding Hood*

Nonfiction books that depict wolves in a good light

The True Story of the Three Little Pigs by A. Wolf by J. Scieszka

Purposes

- To encourage children to recognize the meaning of stereotyping.
- To help children realize that stereotyping can be wrong.

Appropriate Age Group

Primary

Thematic Unit Connections

Fairy Tales; Wolves; Deconstructing Stereotyping

Curriculum Connections

Social Studies; Language Arts

Objectives

1. The students will list and categorize the good and bad characteristics of wolves.
2. The students will read/listen to a classic version of *Little Red Riding Hood* and nonfiction books about wolves.
3. The students will compare and contrast wolves in fiction and in nonfiction books.
4. The students will write a letter to a friend talking about what they have learned about the wolves in fairy tales versus in true stories.
5. The students will participate in a shared writing of the wolf's version of *Little Red Riding Hood.*
6. The students will perform in a readers' theater.

Materials

- Any classic version of *Little Red Riding Hood*
- Any factual book about wolves, such as *The Eyes of the Gray Wolf* by J. London; *Eyewitness Juniors: Amazing Wolves, Dogs, & Foxes* by M. Ling; or *Gray Wolf, Red Wolf* by D. H. Patent
- Semantic map
- Friendly letter form
- *The True Story of the 3 Little Pigs by A. Wolf* by J. Scieszka
- Materials for writing play
- Materials for performing readers' theater
- Materials for making posters

Introducing Selection

Activating Prior Knowledge

1. Younger children should first have fairy tales about wolves read to them.
2. For all students:
   a. Place the word *Wolves* in an oval on a semantic map, as shown in Figure 5.1.
   b. Tell the students to brainstorm all the words they can think of to describe wolves or that relate to wolves.
   c. Use the different shapes on the semantic map (e.g., ovals, rectangles, and circles) to categorize the different types of information the students provide.

Setting Purpose for Reading Selection

Tell students that they are going to be reading/listening to true stories about wolves. Have them be ready to tell you the similarities and differences between wolves in fairy tales and wolves in true stories.

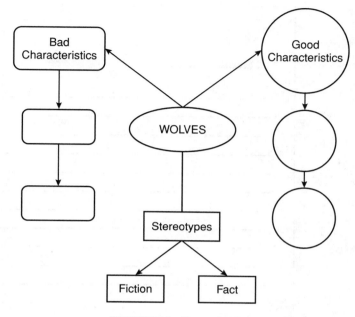

FIGURE 5.1   Semantic Map

Reading and Responding to Selections

Read Selections

Read or let the students read factual books about wolves.

Respond to Selections

1. Discuss with the children the similarities and differences they find between the wolf in *Little Red Riding Hood* and wolves in the factual books.

2. Have a discussion about

    a. How the students feel wolves have been portrayed in folk and fairy tales;

    b. Why the students feel wolves have been stereotyped as bad animals; and

    c. Whether the students feel wolves really are bad animals.

3. Then ask the students how they think they could change people's prejudices toward wolves.

Extending the Literature

Activity 1

Have students write a letter to their friend discussing what they have learned about the way wolves have been portrayed in folk and fairy tales and whether wolves are really bad animals. For younger students, refer to the format for writing a friendly letter in Figure 5.2. If your classroom or school does not already have a mail system for students,

FIGURE 5.2   Informal Letter Format

make sure to set up mailboxes in your classroom and/or school so students can send and receive letters such as the one they just wrote.

Activity 2

Retell the classic version of *The Three Little Pigs* and J. Scieszka's version—*The True Story of the 3 Little Pigs by A. Wolf.* Discuss how A. Wolf is telling his own version of what really happened in the story of the three little pigs. Do a shared writing of the wolf's version of *Little Red Riding Hood* in a play format. Have the class break into small groups of three to five students each. Let the small groups use the readers' theater format to act out the different parts in their own versions of *Little Red Riding Hood.*

Activity 3

Have students make posters inviting other classes to sign up to see their own version of *Little Red Riding Hood.* Each troupe could then perform in other classrooms.

Related Books

Refer to the section on Wolves in the Concept Book List to find comparable tales about wolves, foxes, and coyotes as well as more true stories about wolves.

Lesson 5.3: Alone in a New Country

Books

Angel Child, Dragon Child by M. M. Surat

Other suggested books about Vietnamese/
Vietnamese American history, culture,
and contributions

Purposes

- To encourage children to learn the pitfalls
  of stereotyping.
- To encourage children to be aware of our
  cultural differences and similarities.
- To encourage children to examine others' likes and dislikes.
- To introduce students to Vietnamese/Vietnamese American history, culture, and
  contributions.

Appropriate Age Group

Primary

Thematic Unit Connections

Self-Concept; Cultures; Understanding Similarities and Differences; Deconstructing
Stereotyping

Curriculum Connections

Social Studies; Language Arts

Objectives

1. The students will read or listen to the story *Angel Child, Dragon Child* by Michele
   Maria Surat.
2. The students will respond to the issues of cultural similarities/differences and stereotyping raised in the story.
3. The students will write their reason(s) for liking the story and will draw a picture to
   illustrate what the story was about.
4. The students will interview partners regarding their likes and dislikes.
5. The students will compare their partners' likes and dislikes with their own.
6. The students will share information about their partners with the rest of the class.
7. The students will make a necklace.
8. The students will read/listen to a book about Vietnamese history, culture, and contributions and will think about whether the author provided any clues in the book to help
   them anticipate the outcome.

Materials

- *Angel Child, Dragon Child* by Michele Maria Surat
- World map
- I Liked My Book Because . . . form
- Materials for writing/illustrating
- Materials for interviewing
- Materials for making rice noodle necklaces
- Other suggested books about Vietnamese/Vietnamese American history, culture, and contributions

Introducing Selection

Activating Prior Knowledge

Ask the students if they have ever moved and gone to a new school.

Discuss the students' experiences.

Setting Purpose for Reading Selection

1. Tell the students the following legend: Vietnamese people believe that Vietnam's first king was the son of an angelic fairy and that he married the daughter of a noble dragon king. Therefore, it is said that all people from Vietnam are descendants of angels and dragons.
2. Find Vietnam on a map and ask students to find the mouth and tail of the dragon.
3. Go over some of the meanings of the names of the children in the story.
4. Ask students to listen to/read the story to find out how *(a)* Ut was different from the other children in the story; *(b)* Ut was the same as the other children in the story; *(c)* Ut was stereotyped by the little boy in the story.

Reading and Responding

Read Selection

Have students read/listen to the story *Angel Child, Dragon Child* by Michele Maria Surat.

Respond to Selection

Lead students in discussion of how *(a)* Ut was different from the rest of the children; *(b)* Ut was the same as the other children; *(c)* Ut was being stereotyped by the little boy; and *(d)* this problem was resolved.

Extending the Literature

Activity 1

Ask students to fill out a paper (Figure 5.3) discussing why they liked the story *Angel Child, Dragon Child* and illustrating a scene from the book.

Name _____

Date _____

Title of Book _____

Author of Book _____

I Liked My Book because _____

_____

_____

_____

Here Is a Picture about My Book

FIGURE 5.3   Story Response Sheet

Activity 2

1. Tell students they are going to do an activity in which they are going to compare their own likes and dislikes with those of another student in the classroom.

2. Place students in pairs. Have one student in each pair ask the other student about his or her likes and dislikes regarding food, clothes, music, games, sports, videos, and so on. One student should be taking notes while the other is talking.

3. Then have students switch places.

4. Have students write about each other's likes and dislikes.

5. Have students share their partners' likes and dislikes with the class and/or make a bulletin board with their papers.

Activity 3

For an art activity, string rice noodles to make chains or necklaces, as Ut's brother did in the book.

Activity 4

Have students read/listen to a book about Vietnamese history, culture, and contributions from the list below. Ask the children if the author provided any clues in the book to help them anticipate the outcome.

P, I   Bunting, E. 1990. *The Wall.* Clarion. (Vietnamese history)

I   Coburn, J. R. 1976. *Beyond the East Wind: Legends and Folktales As Told by Duomg Van Quyen.* Burn Hart. (Vietnamese legends and tales)

P   Garland, S. 1994. *The Lotus Seed.* Harcourt Brace Jovanovich. (Vietnamese people)

P, I   Hoyt-Goldsmith, D. 1992. *Hoang Anh: A Vietnamese–American Boy.* Holiday House. (Vietnamese, immigration)

P   Keller, H. 1994. *Grandfather's Dream.* Greenwillow. (Elderly, Vietnamese history)

P, I   Kid, D. 1991. *Onion Tears.* Orchard. (Vietnamese people, immigrants)

P, I   Nhuong, H. Q. 1982. *The Land I Lost: Adventures of a Boy in Vietnam.* Harper. (Vietnamese people)

I   Paterson, K. 1989. *Park's Quest.* Puffin. (Vietnamese people)

P   Tran, K. 1987. *The Little Weaver of Thai-Shen Village.* Children's Book Press. (Vietnamese American tale)

I   Vuong, L. D. 1993. *The Golden Carp and Other Tales of Vietnam.* Lothrop. (Vietnamese tales)

I   Vuong, L. D. 1993. *Sky Legends from Vietnam.* HarperCollins. (Vietnamese stories, poems, song)

Lesson 5.4: Anybody Can Do Anything!

Books

Amazing Grace by M. Hoffman and C. Binch

Other suggested books about self-concept

Purposes

- To encourage children to believe in themselves.
- To encourage children to realize they can be anything they want to be.
- To help children realize they can overcome being stereotyped.

Appropriate Age Group
> Primary

Thematic Unit Connections
> Self-Concept; Feelings; Deconstructing Stereotyping; Growing Up

Curriculum Connections
> Social Studies; Language Arts

Objectives

1. The students will make predictions about the story through a story map.
2. The students will read/listen to the story.
3. The students will take part in a class discussion to find out whether or not their predictions were verified when they read/listened to the story.
4. The students will design a mobile to illustrate what they want to be now or when they grow up.
5. The students will role-play different characters in stories.
6. The students will listen to a panel of speakers who have chosen occupations that go against the traditional male/female job stereotypes.

Materials

- *Amazing Grace* by M. Hoffman and C. Binch
- Story map
- Materials for making mobiles: coat hangers and art supplies
- Materials for role playing
- Panel of speakers
- Other suggested books about self-concept

Introducing Selection

Activating Prior Knowledge

Ask students to brainstorm things they want to do now or when they grow up.

Setting Purpose for Reading Selection

1. Introduce the book selection *Amazing Grace* by M. Hoffman and C. Binch.
2. Hold the book up in front of the class. Introduce the name of the title, author, and illustrator. Flip through the book, giving the students a chance to see what they think will happen. Show the children a story map prediction strategy chart (see Figure 5.4). Review with the children definitions of story setting, characters, and problem. Ask children to predict the setting, characters, and story problem. Record group predictions on story map.

SETTING	TIME	PLACE

CHARACTERS

PROBLEM

ACTION

OUTCOME

FIGURE 5.4   Story Map

Reading and Responding

Read Selection

Have students read/listen to *Amazing Grace* by M. Hoffman and C. Binch.

Respond to Selection

1. Have a discussion with the students to find out whether or not their predictions were verified when they read/listened to the story.

2. Ask students who Grace wanted to be in the school play.

3. Have a discussion about how Grace's classmates felt at first about her being Peter Pan. Explain how this is called stereotyping, and how Grace was stereotyped because she was African American and a girl. Then talk about how Grace was an amazing Peter Pan because she kept in mind that she could be anything she wanted to be.

4. Ask students if they ever wanted to do something that was not acceptable to people around them. Ask them how they handled the situation. You may have to refer to Grace's decision to be Peter Pan.

5. Tell students that they are capable of accomplishing their dreams and goals no matter what others say if they put their minds and hearts into it. Explain to the class that it is important to believe in and be proud of themselves so that when others say they can't become something because of their race and/or gender they can do it anyway.

Extending the Literature

Activity 1

Have the students think of three things that they want to be now or when they grow up (e.g., join a sports team or be a musician). Help students assemble objects that symbolize the things they want to be now or when they grow up. Attach string to each and tie them to a coat hanger. Have the students present their mobiles to the class.

Activity 2

Have students role-play different characters in books they have read. Remind them that they can role-play any part, regardless of the character's gender, age, or race.

Activity 3

Set up a panel of speakers who have chosen occupations that go against the traditional male/female job stereotypes; for example, a female conductor, a male nurse, and so on. This will help children avoid gender stereotyping.

Activity 4

Have each child or group of children read/listen to another story about self-concept from the list below. The children can share how the character's problem was resolved by the end of the story.

P   Ashley, B. 1991. *Cleversticks.* Crown. (Self-concept, Asian Americans)

P   Baehr, P. 1989. *School Isn't Fair.* Simon & Schuster. (Self-concept)

P   Carle, E. 1984. *The Mixed-Up Chameleon.* Harper. (Self-concept)

P   Carlson, N. 1990. *I Like Me.* Penguin. (Self-concept)

P   Cogancherry, H. 1990. *All I Am.* Bradbury. (Self-concept)

P   Greenfield, E. 1977. *African Dream.* Harper. (Self-concept, African Americans)

P   Hudson, C. W., & Ford, G. F. *Bright Eyes, Brown Skin.* Sundance. (Self-concept, African Americans)

P   Kirk, D. 1994. *Miss Spider's Tea Party.* Scholastic. (Self-concept)

P   Lester, H. 1988. *Tacky the Penguin.* Houghton Mifflin. (Self-concept)

P   McKee, D. 1989. *Elmer.* Lothrop, Lee & Shepard. (Self-concept)

P   Mitchell, R. P. 1993. *Hue Boy.* Dial. (Family, self-concept, African people)

P   Payne, L. M. 1993. *Just Because I Am.* Free Spirit. (Self-concept)

P   Pfister, M. 1992. *Rainbow Fish.* North–South. (Self-concept)

P, I   Seuss, Dr. 1990. *Oh, the Places You'll Go.* Random House. (Self-concept)

I   Stevens, J. R. 1993. *Carlos and the Cornfield.* Northland. (Hispanic people, self-concept)

P   Waber, B. 1966. *You Look Ridiculous: Said the Rhinoceros to the Hippopotamus.* Houghton Mifflin. (Self-concept)

P   Tsaitui, Y. 1988. *Anna in Charge.* Viking. (Self-concept)

P   Yarbrough, C. 1979. *Cornrows.* Coward-McCann. (Self-concept, African Americans)

P   Young, E. 1987. *I Wish I Were a Butterfly.* Harcourt Brace. (Self-concept)

P   Zolotow, C. 1972. *William's Doll.* Harper & Row. (Self-concept, gender equity)

Lesson 5.5: "I'm Not the Bad Guy"

Books
- *Heroes* by K. Mochizuki
- Other suggested books about deconstructing stereotypes

Purposes
- To encourage children to think about other cultures.
- To encourage children to see people for who they are and not for what race they are.

Appropriate Age Group
Primary

Thematic Unit Connections
Languages; Heroes; Deconstructing Stereotyping

Curriculum Connections
Social Studies; Language Arts

Objectives
1. The students will read/listen to a story about an Asian boy in America.
2. The students will respond to the story.
3. The students will investigate the meanings of words.
4. The students will research, write, and make presentations about American heroes from various ethnic backgrounds.
5. The students will make a mask/costume of their hero.

Materials

- *Heroes* by Ken Mochizuki
- Large butcher paper
- Who, What, Where, When worksheet
- Crayons, markers, and/or colored pencils
- Materials to make a word bank
- Books to research heroes
- Materials for doing a report
- Old clothes for dressing up
- Other suggested books about deconstructing stereotypes

Introducing Selection

Activating Prior Knowledge

1. Have a discussion about how children are stereotyped; for example, because they are good students or skinny or athletic, or because they come from different countries.
2. Ask the students if they have ever been teased for something. Ask if that is like being stereotyped.
3. Discuss with the students what a hero is.

Setting Purpose for Reading Selection

1. Introduce students to the book *Heroes* by Ken Mochizuki. Ask the students to predict what it will be about. Record their predictions on butcher paper.
2. Have students listen to/read the story to find out how the boy in the story is being stereotyped.
3. Ask students to find out what happens in the story that helps the boy overcome his problem.

Reading and Responding

Read Selection

Have students read/listen to *Heroes* by Ken Mochizuki.

Respond to Selection

1. Ask students if their predictions were correct.
2. Ask students why they think Donnie was always the "bad guy" in the children's games.
3. Ask students why they think the children in the story always played war games.
4. Discuss what Donnie's uncle and dad did to help solve Donnie's problem.
5. Separate the students into cooperative groups. Ask each group to respond to the story by filling in a Who, What, Where, When worksheet (Figure 5.5).

Who, What, Where, When?

Name: _____   Date: _____

Title: _____

Author: _____

Who was in this book? _____

_____

What did they do? _____

_____

Where did they do it? _____

_____

When did they do it? _____

_____

How did you like this book? _____

_____

FIGURE 5.5   Who, What, Where, When Worksheet

Extending the Literature

Activity 1

Have the class create or add to a word bank. The purpose is to collect the meanings of important words the students come across while reading. Pair off the students. Assign each pair of students a word that is vitally important to the meaning of the story and that you believe is not explicitly defined in the text. Let the students use the context of the story, structural analysis, and/or the dictionary to define their word. Students can share the meanings of their words with the entire class. Then the words can be placed in individual word banks or a class word bank.

Activity 2

1. Have students research American heroes from various ethnic backgrounds.

   Have younger children work in cooperative groups to choose a hero they want to learn more about. Students from older grades can help the younger students research and write about their heroes. Have the small groups take turns in reporting about their heroes. (The younger students can draw a mask of their hero and wear it as they make their presentation; see Activity 3 below.)

Give older students time to individually plan, research, and write a report about their hero. (The older students can be dressed up like their hero as they make their presentation; see Activity 3 below.)

2. Students could submit their finished reports to a writing contest or place their finished reports on a special writing display in the hall.

Activity 3

Have the students make a mask of the hero they researched. Older students can also make a costume to go with the mask. These outfits can be worn during the presentations outlined in Activity 2 above.

Related Books

Find additional books on Stereotyping in the Concept Book List.

6 Focusing on Different Perspectives

Lesson 6.1: Many Versions of *The Three Little Pigs*

Books

An original version of *The Three Little Pigs*

The Three Javelinas by S. Lowell

The True Story of the 3 Little Pigs by A. Wolf by J. Scieszka

Other classic tales from different perspectives

Purposes

■ To help children to see the same story from different perspectives.

■ To help children view the same concept from many different perspectives.

Appropriate Age Group

Primary

Thematic Unit Connections

Fairy Tales; Different Perspectives

Curriculum Connections

Social Studies; Language Arts

Objectives

1. The students will listen to/read *The Three Little Pigs* and *The Three Javelinas*.
2. The students will compare and contrast *The Three Little Pigs* and *The Three Javelinas*.
3. The students will retell the story with a flannel board.
4. The students will write the wolf's perspective in his diary.
5. The students will record their favorite part of another version of *The Three Little Pigs*.

Materials

- An original version of *The Three Little Pigs*
- *The Three Javelinas* by S. Lowell
- Venn Diagram
- Flannel board/flannel-board pieces
- *The True Story of the 3 Little Pigs by A. Wolf* by J. Scieszka
- Materials to make wolf's diary
- Other versions of *The Three Little Pigs*
- Tape recorder
- Audiotapes
- Other classic tales from different perspectives

Introducing Selection

Activating Prior Knowledge

For younger students, read *The Three Little Pigs* aloud.

Older students can help you retell the story of *The Three Little Pigs*.

Setting Purpose for Reading Selection

Tell the students that they will be comparing another version of *The Three Little Pigs* with the original version of *The Three Little Pigs*. Introduce *The Three Javelinas* by S. Lowell. Ask students to listen for the similarities and differences between the original version of *The Three Little Pigs* and *The Three Javelinas*. Have students pay special attention to the characters, setting, and plot (problem and resolution).

Reading and Responding

Read Selection

Have students read/listen to *The Three Javelinas* by S. Lowell.

Respond to Selection

Make a Venn Diagram (Figure 6.1) on the chalkboard or overhead projector, or draw on chart paper. Ask the students to discuss the similarities and differences between the *Three Little Pigs* and *The Three Javelinas,* especially between the characters, setting, and plot of the two stories. Fill in the Venn Diagram with their responses.

Extending the Literature

Activity 1

Make flannel-board pieces to correspond to the setting and characters from *The Three Javelinas*. Provide a time and place for small groups of students to retell the story with a flannel board.

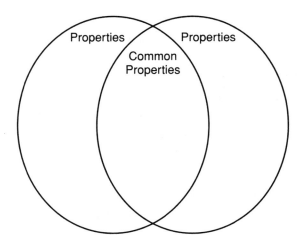

FIGURE 6.1   Venn Diagram

Activity 2

Have the students read/listen to *The True Story of the 3 Little Pigs by A. Wolf* by J. Scieszka. Students can pretend to be the wolf in this story and write an entry for the wolf's diary telling one reason why people should believe that his story is really the true story of *The Three Little Pigs.*

Activity 3

Place students in cooperative groups. Have each group read one of the other versions of *The Three Little Pigs* that can be found in the Classic Tales from Different Per-spectives section of the Concept Book List. Have each group record their favorite part of the story on a cassette tape. The tapes can be played back to the entire class in order to entice everyone into reading all the versions of *The Three Little Pigs.*

Related Books

Refer to the Classic Tales from Different Perspectives section of the Concept Book List.

Lesson 6.2: Ways Children Get to School

Books

> *This Is the Way We Go to School:*
> *A Book about Children around*
> *the World* by E. Baer

Other suggested books about
differences and likenesses

Purposes

- To help children learn that children around the world go to school in different ways.
- To help children view the same concept from many different perspectives.

Appropriate Age Group

Primary.

Thematic Unit Connections

Transportation; Geography; Different Perspectives

Curriculum Connections

Social Studies; Language Arts

Objectives

1. The students will read/listen to the story.
2. The students will respond to the story through a graphic organizer.
3. The students will use map skills.
4. The students will research climates in different regions of the world.
5. The students will create a picture flip book.
6. The students will create a mode of transportation out of clay.

Materials

- *This Is the Way We Go to School* by E. Baer
- Graphic organizer
- World map
- Newspapers
- Materials to make a flip book
- Clay
- Other suggested books about differences and likenesses

Introducing Selection

Activating Prior Knowledge

Take a class poll of how students get to school.

Setting Purpose for Reading Selection

Have students listen to the story to find out if children from other places in the United States and around the world get to school in the same way they do.

Reading and Responding

Read Selection

Have students read/listen to *This Is the Way We Go to School* by E. Baer.

Respond to Selection

1. Ask students what they feel the story is mainly about (the many ways children around the world go to school). Come to a class consensus. Tell the students that this is also called a main idea. Record in the first main idea portion of a graphic organizer, as shown in Figure 6.2.

2. Ask students to list the various ways the children go to school in the book. Record their responses on the "Support" lines of the graphic organizer. Explain that these are supporting ideas because they all support the main idea.

Extending the Literature

Activity 1

Have students place push pins in a world map to represent where the different characters in the book live. Use newspapers to find out what the climate is like in those regions of the world. Ask if the climate affects the mode of transportation the children use to go to school.

IDEA ONE

Support

1 _____

2 _____

3 _____

IDEA TWO

Support

1 _____

2 _____

3 _____

IDEA THREE

Support

1 _____

2 _____

3 _____

FIGURE 6.2 Graphic Organizer

Activity 2

Have the class create a picture flip book to show the different ways the students come to school.

Activity 3

Have the students make clay models of the modes of transportation they use to go to school.

Related Books

Additional books about Differences and Likenesses can be found in the Concept Book List.

Lesson 6.3: Houses, Homes, and the Homeless

Books

This Is My House by A. Dorros

Fly Away Home by E. Bunting

Other suggested books about houses, homes, and the homeless

Purposes

- To encourage children to learn about many different kinds of houses/homes.
- To help children view the same concept from many different perspectives.
- To introduce children to the concept of homelessness.

Appropriate Age Group

Primary

Thematic Unit Connections

Houses, Homes, and the Homeless; Different Perspectives

Curriculum Connections

Language Arts; Social Studies

Objectives

1. The students will read a story about different types of houses.
2. The students will make dioramas.
3. The students will respond to the story through a KWL chart.
4. The students will create a bookmark.

5. The students will listen to others talk about homelessness.

6. The students will become active in social issues.

Materials

- *This Is My House* by A. Dorros
- KWL chart
- Materials to make dioramas
- World map
- Materials to make bookmark
- *Fly Away Home* by E. Bunting
- Other suggested books about houses, homes, and the homeless

Introducing Selection

Activating Prior Knowledge

1. Tell the students that they are going to read a book about all different kinds of houses/homes. Ask them to tell you what they already know about houses/homes. Write responses in the K ("Know") column of KWL chart, as shown in Figure 6.3.

2. Ask students what they want to learn about homes. Write their responses in the W ("Want to Know") column of the KWL chart.

3. Ask students if a car or an airport can be a home for some people.

Setting Purpose for Reading Selection

1. Introduce the selection—*This Is My House* by A. Dorros.

What Do I Know	What Do I Want to Know?	What Did I Learn?

FIGURE 6.3   KWL Chart

2. Ask students to read/listen to the story to find out some of the answers to what they wanted to know about houses/homes. Also, have the students pay attention to the many different kinds of homes that people in different parts of the world live in.

Reading and Responding

Read Selection

Have students read/listen to *This Is My House* by A. Dorros.

Respond to Selection

1. Discuss the following:

    a. Did we find out the answers to our questions by reading/listening to the story? What was the most interesting or surprising thing you learned? What have you learned by reading this that you didn't know before? Write the students' descriptions in the L ("Learned") section of the KWL chart.

    b. What questions do we still need to find out more about? Add the students' responses to the W column of the KWL chart.

2. Ask students if a car or an airport can be a home to some people. Explain that a house can be anything that protects us; it is the people who live in the house that make it a home.

Extending the Literature

Activity 1

Have the students work with a partner. Assign each group a home mentioned in the story. Supply the children with materials to construct a diorama of the type of house/home. Have students:

1. Share their diorama with the class; and

2. Point out on the world map the area where their type of house/home is located, according to the information given in the book.

Activity 2

Have the students draw, color, or paint a picture of their own home on a bookmark.

Activity 3

This is a good time to talk to the children about the homeless. Show the class a photo of people living in a car. Explain to the students that some people do not have a home. You could read *Fly Away Home* by Eve Bunting to illustrate the concept of homelessness. Have the class collect cans of food for a nearby homeless shelter and/or have a guest speaker from a shelter come and talk to the class about being homeless.

Related Books

Other books about Houses, Homes, and the Homeless can be found in the Concept Book List.

Lesson 6.4: Pilgrimages/Immigration

Books

Across the Wide Dark Sea:
The Mayflower Journey
by J. Van Leeuwen

How Many Days to America?:
A Thanksgiving Story by E. Bunting

Molly's Pilgrim by B. Cohen

Other suggested books about viewing
Pilgrims from different perspectives

Other suggested books about different
kinds of pilgrimages, immigration,
and migration

Purposes

- To introduce children to the concepts of pilgrimages and immigration/immigrants.
- To help children view the same concept from many different perspectives.

Appropriate Age Group

Second and third graders. Kindergarten and first grade teachers can select individual
activities that are appropriate for their students.

Thematic Unit Connections

Pilgrimages; Immigration; Examining Our Own Heritage; Different Perspectives

Curriculum Connections

Social Studies; Language Arts

Objectives

1. The students will identify reasons why the United States celebrates Thanksgiving.
2. The students will read/listen to stories about different kinds of pilgrimages.
3. The students will compare and contrast two different pilgrimages.
4. The students will create a pilgrim that reflects their own heritage.
5. The students will use their library skills to find books about specific subjects.
6. The students will read stories telling about daily life during the times of the Pilgrims
   from several different perspectives.

Materials

- *Across the Wide Dark Sea: The Mayflower Journey* by J. Van Leeuwen
- *How Many Days to America?: A Thanksgiving Story* by E. Bunting

- Response journals
- Venn Diagram on chart paper
- *Molly's Pilgrim* by B. Cohen
- Clothespins, markers, yarn, fabrics, and other materials for making "pilgrims"
- K. Waters's books portraying the times of the Pilgrims from several different perspectives
- Other suggested books about different kinds of pilgrimages, immigration, and migration

Introducing Selection

Activating Prior Knowledge

1. Read *Across the Wide Dark Sea: The Mayflower Journey* by J. Van Leeuwen.
2. Discuss why people like the Pilgrims came to America.

Setting Purpose for Reading Selection

Introduce the book *How Many Days to America?* by E. Bunting. Show the cover and flip through the pages. Have the students make predictions about what the story might be about. Tell the students to listen for the similarities and differences between the pilgrimages described in *Across the Wide Dark Sea* and in *How Many Days to America?*

Reading and Responding

Read Selection

Have students read/listen to *How Many Days to America?* by E. Bunting.

Respond to Selection

1. In their journals, have the students record the similarities and differences they noted between *Across the Wide Dark Sea* and *How Many Days to America?*
2. As a class, make a Venn Diagram (refer to Figure 6.1, page 92) on a large chart to note all of the student's responses.

Extending the Literature

Activity 1

Read *Molly's Pilgrim* by B. Cohen. Have the children make pilgrims out of clothespins that will reflect their own heritage. Encourage them to be creative in making outfits, accessories, hairdos, and so on. Be sure to get parents and relatives involved so that these pilgrims' costumes authentically reflect the children's various heritages.

Activity 2

1. Have older students break into groups. Each group can go to the library and find other books about pilgrimages/immigrations (refer to Related Books below). These books reflect the different kinds of nationalities of the people who immigrated to this country.

2. Have each student in each group take turns reading the book the group has chosen or have all the students in each group read in unison.

3. Give the students time to discuss how their book relates to the concept of different kinds of pilgrimages and how their book relates to the different kinds pilgrimages discussed previously in this lesson.

4. Then the students can share their findings with the total group while you record their findings on a chart or chalkboard. The class can later compare and contrast their findings.

Activity 3

Have the students read/listen to books from the following list about the experiences of different people during the Pilgrim times.

I   Sewall, M. 1995. *Thunder from a Clear Sky*. Atheneum. (Pilgrims—different perspectives)

P, I   Waters, K. 1989. *Sarah Morton's Day: A Day in the Life of a Pilgrim Girl*. Scholastic. (Pilgrims—different perspectives)

P, I   Waters, K. 1989. *Samuel Easton: A Day in the Life of a Pilgrim Boy*. Scholastic. (Pilgrims—different perspectives)

P, I   Waters, K. 1996. *Tamenum's Day: A Wampanoag Indian Boy in Pilgrim Times*. Scholastic. (Pilgrims—different perspectives)

P, I   Waters, K. 1996. *On the Mayflower: Voyage of the Ship's Apprentice & a Passenger Girl*. Scholastic. (Pilgrims—different perspectives)

Related Books

Additional books about different kinds of Pilgrimages, Immigration, and Migration can be found in the Concept Book List.

Lesson 6.5: Quilt Stories

Books

The Quilt Story by T. Johnston

The Canada Geese Quilt
by N. Kinsley-Warcock

Any combination of or all of the
following books:

The Keeping Quilt by P. Polacco

The Rag Coat by L. Mills

Patchwork Quilt by V. Flournoy

Sweet Clara and the Freedom Quilt
by D. Hopkinson

Purposes
- To encourage children to think about how different people can share similar customs.
- To help children view the same concept from many different perspectives.

Appropriate Age Group
   Primary

Thematic Unit Connections
   Quilts; History; Different Perspectives

Curriculum Connections
   Social Studies; Language Arts; Art

Objectives
1. The students will read/listen to stories about quilts.
2. The students will examine what quilts mean to different story characters.
3. The students will create a class quilt.
4. The students will conduct an analysis of a character in a book.

Materials
- *The Quilt Story* by T. Johnston
- Any combination of or all of the following books:
   The Keeping Quilt by P. Polacco
   The Rag Coat by L. Mills
   Patchwork Quilt by V. Flournoy
   Sweet Clara and the Freedom Quilt by D. Hopkinson

- Response journals
- Colored construction paper; glue
- *The Canada Geese Quilt* by N. Kinsley-Warcock
- Character Analysis Chart

Introducing Selection

   Activating Prior Knowledge
1. Ask the students what a quilt is. Ask the students if they ever had a quilt or blanket that was special to them.
2. Introduce students to *The Quilt Story* and any combination of or all of the other books —*Sweet Clara and the Freedom Quilt, The Keeping Quilt, The Rag Coat,* and *Patchwork Quilt.* Tell the children that they will be reading some or all of the books you have

chosen in the next few days. Ask them to look at the books and their titles and to tell you what they think they are about. Discuss their predictions.

Setting Purpose for Reading Selection

Introduce students to *The Quilt Story* by T. Johnston. Ask students to read/listen to the story to find out what

a. the little girl from long ago and the little girl of today shared; and

b. the importance of and/or the relationship of the quilt was to the two little girls.

Reading and Responding

Read Selection

Have students read/listen to *The Quilt Story* by T. Johnston.

Respond to Selection

Ask students what the two little girls in the story shared. Discuss what the importance and/or relationship of the quilt was to the two little girls in this story.

Extending the Literature

Activity 1

Ask the students to get into cooperative groups. Have each group read one of the following books: *Sweet Clara and the Freedom Quilt, The Keeping Quilt, The Rag Coat,* or *Patchwork Quilt.* Ask each group to find out what the importance of and/or the relationship of the quilt was to the character(s) in their book. Have each student record his or her own findings in a response journal. Let students discuss their findings within their own groups. Then have each group quickly retell their quilt story and share their findings with the class as a whole.

Activity 2

Have the students make a class quilt. You can ask them to do this with squares of construction paper. Ask the students to make a quilt square that reflects who they are. Then put all the students' quilt pieces together to make a class quilt.

Activity 3

Each day, read a chapter from the book *The Canada Geese Quilt* by N. Kinsley-Warcock.

1. After the first chapter, ask the students to pretend to be Ariel. Then ask: What kind of a person are you? How do you feel? What does the author do to tell you what kind of a person you are and to make you feel this way?

2. After each chapter thereafter, ask what kind of a person Ariel is in this chapter. How does Ariel feel in this chapter? What does the author do to tell you what kind of a person Ariel is and how Ariel is feeling in this chapter?

3. Have the students help you complete a character analysis chart of Ariel at the conclusion of the story (see Figure 6.4). Ask students to describe the traits of Ariel, and ask for story evidence to support each description.

Character Analysis Chart for _____

Character Trait	How Trait Is Revealed in Story

FIGURE 6.4   Character Analysis Chart

Related Books

Additional Quilt Stories from different perspectives can be found in the Concept Book List.

Lesson 6.6: Another Look at Jack and the Beanstalk

Books

A traditional version of *Jack and the Beanstalk*

Jim and the Beanstalk by R. Briggs

Other suggested classic tales from different perspectives

Purposes

- To encourage children to examine different versions of the same fairy tale.
- To help children view the same concept from many different perspectives.

Appropriate Age Group

Primary

Thematic Unit Connections

Fairy Tales; Elderly; Different Perspectives

Curriculum Connections

Social Studies; Language Arts

Objectives

1. The students will construct a web for the traditional story of Jack and the beanstalk.
2. The students will collectively read *Jim and the Beanstalk.*
3. The students will predict and confirm different aspects of the story.
4. The students will compare and contrast *Jack and the Beanstalk* and *Jim and the Beanstalk.*
5. The students will retell *Jim and the Beanstalk* by using transparencies.
6. The students will rate the story.
7. The students will write questions to ask the giant.

Materials

- Web
- A traditional version of *Jack and the Beanstalk*
- Double-entry journal
- *Jim and the Beanstalk* by R. Briggs
- Venn Diagram
- Transparencies/overhead projector
- Materials to make graph

Introducing Selection

Activating Prior Knowledge

Ask students if they know the fairy tale *Jack and the Beanstalk.* Construct a web on the board as the students tell you the different components of the story (refer to Figure 6.5). If enough young children don't know the story, read it aloud to them.

Setting Purpose for Reading Selection

1. Before and during the reading of *Jim and the Beanstalk* by Raymond Briggs, have the children make predictions about and respond to the story using a double-entry journal. Figure 6.6 shows an example of a double-entry journal format. On the left side of the journal page, the students write/illustrate predictions for different parts of the story before they read/listen to the book. On the right side of the journal page, the students write/illustrate responses to the different parts of the book after they read/listen to it.
2. Begin this activity by telling the students the title and author of *Jim and the Beanstalk* by Raymond Briggs. Show the cover of the book and ask the students to draw/ illustrate what they think the story is going to be about in the first prediction box.
3. In the second prediction box, ask the students to write/illustrate predictions about the giant in this story. Then read up to the part of the book that describes the giant and ask the children to write/illustrate their responses in the corresponding response box.
4. Continue to have the students make predictions about the story before and respond to the story after you read a few pages at a time. At the very end of the story, let the students write their personal reactions to the story in the first response box.

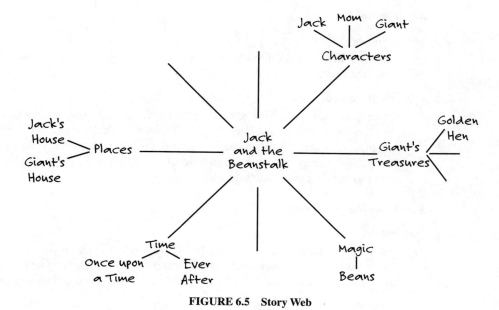

FIGURE 6.5   Story Web

PREDICTIONS	RESPONSES

FIGURE 6.6   Double-Entry Journal

Reading and Responding

Read Selection

Separate the students into cooperative groups and ask them to reread *Jim and the Beanstalk* together.

Respond to Selection

After the groups have finished reading the story, ask each group to do a Venn Diagram to compare and contrast *Jim and the Beanstalk* with *Jack and the Beanstalk*. An example of a Venn Diagram can be seen in Figure 6.1, page **000**. As a class, discuss the different properties that the individual groups came up with. Students can add other groups' ideas to their own diagrams.

Extending the Literature

Activity 1

Make a transparency of the giant. Break the students into small groups. Let them make transparencies of the different objects that Jim brought the giant in *Jim and the Beanstalk*. Let each group retell the story by using the props (transparencies).

Activity 2

Conduct a poll of the students' reactions to the book; for example, "terrific," "good," "OK," "so-so," and "awful." Graph the students' reactions on a display board.

Activity 3

Have students write out some questions they would like to ask the giant. Pair up the students so one child can ask questions while the other answers as if he or she were the giant.

Related Books

Refer to the Classic Tales from Different Perspectives section of the Concept Book List.

CHAPTER

7 Focusing on Social Action

Lesson 7.1: Helping the Elderly

Books

Not So Fast Songololo by N. Daly

How Can You Help?: Creative Volunteer Projects for Kids Who Care by L. Schwartz

Other suggested books about the elderly

Purposes

- To encourage children not to stereotype the elderly.
- To encourage children to help elderly people.

Appropriate Age Group

Primary

Thematic Unit Connections

Social Action/Helping Others; Elderly

Curriculum Connections

Language Arts; Social Studies

Objectives

1. The students will list things they do with older people.
2. The students will read/listen to *Not So Fast Songololo* by N. Daly.
3. The students will contribute to a discussion about the story.
4. The students will perform a puppet show.
5. The students will identify ways in which they can help older people.
6. The students will help older people in various ways.

Materials

- *Not So Fast Songololo* by N. Daly
- Materials needed for a sequencing activity
- Materials needed to create and put on a puppet show
- World map
- Materials needed to do activities with an adopted grandparent
- *How Can You Help?: Creative Volunteer Projects for Kids Who Care* by L. Schwartz
- Other suggested books about the elderly

Introducing Selection

Activating Prior Knowledge

Ask students to list things they do with or for older people. Accept any answers they provide. You can write up the list on a chalkboard, chart paper, or overhead projector.

Setting Purpose for Reading Selection

Tell the students to read or listen to *Not So Fast Songololo* by N. Daly to find out about who the little boy in the story helps and what he does to help this person.

Reading and Responding

Read Selection

Have students read/listen to *Not So Fast Songololo* by N. Daly.

Respond to Selection

Have the students fold a piece of paper into three sections. Ask the students to illustrate the three ways in which Sheperd helped his Granny in sequential order. On the back of the paper, the students can illustrate what Granny did for Sheperd.

Extending the Literature

Activity 1

Ask students to get into cooperative groups. Have each group put together a puppet show based on *Not So Fast Songololo*. Each group can create puppets to depict the characters in the book. They can also paint the scenery for their puppet show. The different groups of students can perform their puppet shows in different classrooms around the school.

Activity 2

Ask the students to talk about where their grandparents live. These locations can be marked on a map. Whose grandparents live the farthest away? Whose grandparents live in certain states? How many students' grandparents live in the same city they live in?

Activity 3

1. Discuss the following:

   a. Some children don't have grandparents living nearby;

   b. Some older people don't have grandchildren living nearby;

   c. Some children don't have any grandparents at all; and

   d. Some older people don't have any grandchildren at all.

2. Tell the students that these are good reasons for "adopting" a grandparent. There are agencies in every area that will match children up with elderly people.

3. Ask the students to brainstorm activities they could do with an adopted grandparent. *How Can You Help?: Creative Volunteer Projects for Kids Who Care* by L. Schwartz provides ideas for projects such as

   a. Eating lunch together;

   b. Being pen pals;

   c. Reading a book together;

   d. Playing a game together; or

   e. Creating a story together.

4. Pick some activities and do them with students' adopted grandparents.

Related Books

Refer to books about the Elderly and/or Death in the Concept Book List.

Lesson 7.2: Environmental Awareness

Books

Brother Eagle, Sister Sky by S. Jeffers

The Earth and I by F. Asch

Every Kid's Guide to Saving the Earth by J. Berry

Other suggested books about the environment

Purposes

- To encourage children to appreciate the earth.
- To encourage children to become actively involved in their community.

Appropriate Age Group

Primary

Thematic Unit Connections

Social Action; Helping Our Environment

Curriculum Connections

Social Studies; Language Arts

Objectives

1. The students will read/listen to stories about the environment.
2. The students will write/illustrate a response to *Brother Eagle, Sister Sky.*
3. The students will make a list of the things they can do to help conserve and preserve the environment.
4. The students will keep a record of things they have done to help conserve and preserve the environment.
5. The students will share their record of things they have done to help conserve and preserve the environment.
6. The students will write a letter to the editor of a local newspaper.

Materials

- *The Earth and I* by F. Asch
- Response journals
- *Brother Eagle, Sister Sky* by S. Jeffers
- *Every Kid's Guide to Saving the Earth* by J. Berry
- Materials for keeping a list of the things the students can do to help conserve and preserve the environment
- Format for writing business letter
- Other suggested books about the environment

Introducing Selection

Activating Prior Knowledge

The students will read/listen to *The Earth and I* by F. Asch. Discuss how the boy feels about the earth. Ask the students how they feel about the earth.

Setting Purpose for Reading Selection

Explain that a famous Native American chief, Chief Seattle, gave a speech about our earth and that the book *Brother Eagle, Sister Sky* by S. Jeffers is his speech. Ask the students to read/listen to the book to find out who the chief says our relatives are and why he feels it is important for us to protect the earth.

Reading and Responding

Read Selection

Have students read/listen to *Brother Eagle, Sister Sky* by Susan Jeffers.

Respond to Selection

1. Discuss who Chief Seattle says our relatives are and why it is important for us to protect the earth.

2. Ask students to write a reaction to the story. They need to include in their reaction *(a)* the title; *(b)* the author; and *(c)* their response. Two examples of ways in which students can respond include:

    a. Writing about how the book made them feel and why.

    b. Drawing a picture to show how the story made them feel and writing one or two sentences about the picture.

3. Ask students to share their reactions in literature groups or with the entire class.

Extending the Literature

Activity 1

Have the students look through *Every Kid's Guide to Saving the Earth* by Joy Berry and make a list of things they can do to help conserve and preserve the environment.

Activity 2

Have students take a day to keep records of all the things they do to help conserve and preserve the environment. Make sure you let others at your school know what your students are doing to help the environment. Ideas for accomplishing this goal include:

1. Reading students' lists at daily announcement time over the PA system.

2. Sharing students' lists with other adults, then writing a note to each student describing adults' responses.

Activity 3

Have students write a letter to the editor of your local newspaper stating what we need to do to conserve and preserve our earth. Figure 7.1 shows the format for writing a business letter.

Related Books

Refer to books in the Environment section of the Concept Book List.

(blank business letter template with ruled lines)

FIGURE 7.1 **Business Letter Format**

Lesson 7.3: Saving Our Earth

Books

> *The Lorax* by Dr. Seuss
>
> *How Can You Help?: Creative Volunteer Projects for Kids Who Care* by L. Schwartz
>
> *Every Kid's Guide to Saving the Earth* by J. Berry
>
> Other suggested books about the environment and social action

Purpose

- To help children get actively involved in social action.

Appropriate Age Group
> Primary

Thematic Unit Connections
> Social Action; Helping Our Environment; Conservation

Curriculum Connections
> Social Studies; Language Arts

Objectives
1. The students will brainstorm the benefits of trees.
2. The students will read/listen to *The Lorax* by Dr. Seuss.
3. The students will create a simple story frame.
4. The students will write an epilogue to the story.
5. The students will plant and care for a tree or flowers.

Materials
- Chart paper
- *The Lorax* by Dr. Seuss
- Simple story frame
- Materials for writing an epilogue to the story
- Materials for planting a tree or flowers
- *How Can You Help?: Creative Volunteer Projects for Kids Who Care* by L. Schwartz
- *Every Kid's Guide to Saving the Earth* by J. Berry
- Other suggested books about the environment

Introducing Selection

Activating Prior Knowledge

Ask the students to brainstorm the benefits of trees. You can list their responses on the chalkboard or on chart paper. One possible title for the assignment would be "The Benefits of Trees." The students' responses should include shade, food, home and shelter, beauty, wood, oxygen, and so forth.

Setting Purpose for Reading Selection

1. Ask students to read/listen to the story to find out:
   a. What did the Truffula trees provide?
   b. What happened to the trees?
   c. How might the Truffula trees be saved?

2. Ask students to pay special attention to the characters, setting, problem, and solution of the story while reading/listening to *The Lorax.*

Reading and Responding

Read Selection

Have students read/listen to *The Lorax* by Dr. Seuss.

Respond to Selection

1. Have a discussion about what the Truffula trees provided, what happened to the trees, and how the Truffula trees were possibly going to be saved.
2. Ask students to help you fill in a simple story frame (Figure 7.2) noting the characters, setting, problem, and solution for *The Lorax.*

NAME OF STORY

CHARACTERS

SETTING

PROBLEM

SOLUTION

FIGURE 7.2   Simple Story Frame

Extending the Literature

Activity 1

Have younger children collectively dictate an epilogue to the story. Older children can individually write their own epilogues to the story, then share the epilogues with the entire class.

Activity 2

Use moneys collected from selling the Class Cookbook (Lesson 3.4 of this book) to buy saplings or plant flowers from a local nursery. The nursery might even donate the tree and/or flowers to you when they find out that your class is planting them for a good cause. Plant and care for trees/flowers at your school or in a nearby town park. Have students look in books such as *How Can You Help?: Creative Volunteer Projects for Kids Who Care* by L. Schwartz and *Every Kid's Guide to Saving the Earth* by J. Berry to find step-by-step directions for planting and caring for trees/flowers.

Activity 3:

Refer to the Social Action section in the Concept Book List to find more books the students can read/listen to relating to people who have become involved in social causes. For example, a ten-year-old boy's actions become the impetus for efforts to save the Mexican rain forest in the true story *Save My Rainforest* by M. Zak (Volcano Press).

Related Literature

Find books related to both the Environment and Social Action in the Concept Book List.

PART THREE

Multicultural Book Lists

CONCEPT BOOK LIST

The following list organizes books alphabetically according to concept headings. The designations "P" and "I" indicate books suitable for children at the primary and/or intermediate levels. For a list of all the concept headings, see this book's table of contents.

African American History, Slavery, Civil War

P   Adler, D. A. 1995. *A Picture Book of Abraham Lincoln.* New York: Holiday House. (African American history)

P   Adler, D. A. 1993. *A Picture Book of Frederick Douglass.* New York: Holiday House. (African American history, civil rights, social activism)

P   Adler, D. A. 1989. *A Picture Book of Martin Luther King, Jr.* New York: Scholastic. (African American history, social activism)

P   Adler, D. A. 1993. *A Picture Book of Rosa Parks.* New York: Holiday House. (African American history, civil rights, social activism)

P   Adler, D. A. 1994. *A Picture Book of Sojourner Truth.* New York: Holiday House. (African American women in history)

I   Armstrong, J. 1992. *Steal Away to Freedom.* New York: Scholastic. (African American history, slavery)

P, I   Ashby, R., & Ohrn, D. G. 1995. *Herstory: Women Who Changed the World.* New York: Viking. (Famous women)

P   Ashe-Moutoussamy, J. 1993. *Daddy and Me: A Photo Story of Arthur Ashe and His Daughter, Camera.* New York: Knopf. (Famous African American, family dealing with AIDS)

I   Beatty, P. 1991. *Jayhawker.* New York: Morrow. (Civil War, slavery)

I   Beatty, P. 1992. *Who Comes with Cannons?* New York: Morrow. (Underground Railroad)

I   Bentley, J. 1990. *Harriet Tubman.* New York: Watts. (African American history)

I   Bial, R. 1995. *The Underground Railroad.* Boston: Houghton Mifflin. (African American history, Underground Railroad)

P, I   Bogart, M., ed. 1989. *African American Biographies.* Englewood Cliffs, NJ: Globe. (Famous African American women)

I   Brashler, W. 1994. *The Story of Negro League Baseball.* New York: Ticknor & Fields. (Famous African Americans)

P, I   Bray, R. L. 1995. *Martin Luther King, Jr.* New York: Greenwillow. (Famous African American, civil rights movement)

I   Bullock, S. 1993. *Free at Last: A History of the Civil Rights Movement and Those Who Died in the Struggle.* New York: Oxford University Press. (African American history, civil rights)

I   Burns, K., & Miles, W. 1995. *Black Stars in Orbit: NASA's African American Astronauts.* New York: Gulliver. (Famous black Americans)

P   Chocolate, D. 1995. *On the Day I Was Born.* New York: Scholastic. (African American cultures)

P, I   Coles, R. 1995. *The Story of Ruby Bridges.* New York: Scholastic. (African American women in history)

I   Collier, J. L., & Collier, C. 1981. *Jump Ship to Freedom.* New York: Delacorte. (Civil War, slavery)

I   Collier, J. L., & Collier, C. 1994. *With Every Drop of Blood: A Novel of the Civil War.* San Diego: Delacorte. (Civil War, slavery)

I   Cooper, M. 1995. *Bound for the Promised Land: The Great Black Migration.* New York: Lodestar. (African American history, migration)

I   Cox, C. 1993. *The Forgotten Heroes: The Story of the Buffalo Soldiers.* New York: Scholastic. (African American history)

I   Curtis, C. P. 1995. *The Watsons Go to Birmingham: 1963.* San Diego: Delacorte. (Civil rights movement)

I   Doctor, B. A. 1992. *Malcolm X for Beginners.* New York: Writers and Readers. (Famous African American, civil rights)

P   Dupree, R. 1993. *The Wishing Chair.* Minneapolis: Carolrhoda. (African American history, African American family)

P, I   Everett, G. 1992. *Li'l Sis and Uncle Willie: A Story Based on the Life and Paintings of William H. Johnson.* New York: Rizzoli. (Famous African Americans)

I   Evitts, W. J. 1985. *Captive Bodies, Free Spirits: The Story of Southern Slavery.* San Francisco: Children's Book Press. (Slavery)

P, I   Feelings, M. 1995. *The Middle Passage: White Ships/Black Cargo.* New York: Dial. (African American history, slavery)

I   Ferris, J. 1988. *Go Free or Die: A Story about Harriet Tubman.* Minneapolis: Carolrhoda. (African American history, social activism)

I   Ferris, J. 1988. *Walking the Road to Freedom: A Story about Sojourner Truth.* Minneapolis: Carolrhoda. (African American women in history)

I   Ferris, J. 1994. *What I Was Singing: The Story of Marian Anderson.* Minneapolis: Carolrhoda. (Famous African American women)

I   Fleishman, P. 1993. *Bull Run.* New York: HarperCollins. (Civil War—different perspectives)

I   Fox, P. 1973. *The Slave Dancer.* New York: Bradbury. (Slavery)

I   Freeman, F. B. 1971. *Two Tickets to Freedom: The True Story of Ellen and William Craft, Fugitive Slaves.* New York: Peter Bedrik. (Slavery)

I   Greenberg, K. E. 1992. *Magic Johnson: Champion with a Cause.* Minneapolis: Lerner. (Famous African American)

P, I   Greenfield, E. 1973. *Rosa Parks.* New York: Crowell. (African American women in history, social activism)

I   Hamilton, V. 1993. *Many Thousand Gone: African Americans from Slavery to Freedom.* New York: Knopf. (African American history, slavery)

I   Hansen, J. 1988. *Out from This Place.* New York: Walker. (Civil War, slavery)

I   Haskins, J. 1992. *Against All Opposition: Black Explorers in America.* New York: Walker. (African American history; Columbus—different perspectives)

I   Haskins, J. 1996. *Black Eagles: African Americans in Aviation.* New York: Scholastic. (Famous African Americans)

I   Haskins, J. 1993. *Get On Board: The Story of the Underground Railroad.* New York: Scholastic. (Underground Railroad)

I   Haskins, J. 1992. *I Have a Dream: The Life and Words of Martin Luther King, Jr.* Brookfield, CT: Millbrook. (African American history, social activism)

I   Haskins, J. 1991. *Outward Dreams: Black Inventors and Their Inventions.* New York: Walker. (Famous African Americans)

I   Hooks, W. H. 1990. *The Ballad of Belle Dorcas.* New York: Knopf. (African American history, slavery)

P, I   Hoyt-Goldsmith, D. 1994. *Celebrating Kwanza.* New York: Holiday House. (African American history)

I   Hudson, K. E. 1994. *The Will and the Way: Paul R. Williams, Architect.* New York: Rizzoli. (Famous African American)

P   Jackson, G. N. 1993. *Elijah McCoy, Inventor.* Cleveland: Modern Curriculum Press. (Famous African American)

P, I   Johnson, D. 1993. *Now Let Me Fly: The Story of a Slave Family.* New York: Macmillan. (Slavery, African Americans)

P, I   Johnson, D. 1994. *Seminole Diary: Remembrance of a Slave.* New York: Macmillan. (Slavery)

P   Jones, K. 1994. *Happy Birthday, Dr. King!* New York: Simon & Schuster. (African American history, social activism)

I   Katz, W. L. 1995. *Black Women of the Old West.* New York: Atheneum. (African American history)

I   Katz, W. L., & Franklin, P. A. 1993. *Proudly Red and Black: Stories of African and Native Americans.* New York: Atheneum. (African American history, Native American history)

P, I   Lawrence, J. 1993. *The Great Migration: An American Story.* New York: HarperCollins. (African American history, migration)

P, I   Lee, G. L. 1989. *Interesting People: Black American History Makers.* New York: Ballantine. (Famous African American women)

P, I   Levine, E. 1988. *If You Traveled on the Underground Railroad.* New York: Scholastic. (Slavery, African American history)

P, I   Lincoln, A. 1995. *The Gettysburg Address.* Boston: Houghton Mifflin. (Abraham Lincoln)

P   Livingston, M. C. 1994. *Keep on Singing: A Ballad of Marian Anderson.* London: Anderson. (African American Women in history)

I   Lyons, M. E. 1993. *Stitching Stars: The Story Quilts of Harriet Powers.* New York: Scribner's. (African American history, quilt story)

P   Marzollo, J. 1993. *Happy Birthday, Martin Luther King, Jr.* New York: Scholastic. (African American history)

P, I   Mattern, J. 1992. *Young Martin Luther King, Jr.: "I Have a Dream."* Mahwah, NJ: Troll. (African American history, social activism)

I   McCurdy, M. 1994. *Escape from Slavery: The Boyhood of Frederick Douglass in His Own Words.* New York: Knopf. (African American history, slavery, social activism)

P, I   McKenna, N. D. 1986. *A Zulu Family.* Minneapolis: Lerner. (African American culture)

I McKissack, P. 1989. *Jesse Jackson: A Biography.* New York: Scholastic. (African American history, social activism)

I McKissack, P., & McKissack, F. 1984. *African-American Inventors.* Brookfield, CT: Millbrook. (Famous African Americans)

I McKissack, P., & McKissack, F. 1994. *Black Diamond: The Story of the Negro Baseball Leagues.* New York: Scholastic. (African American history)

I McKissack, P., & McKissack, F. 1994. *Christmas in the Big House, Christmas in the Quarters.* New York: Scholastic. (African American history, Civil War, holidays)

I McKissack, P., & McKissack, F. 1988. *A Long Hard Journey: The Story of the Pullman Porter.* New York: Walker. (Civil rights movement)

P, I McKissack, P., & McKissack, F. 1993. *Madame C. J. Walker: Self-Made Millionaire.* Springfield, NJ: Enslow. (Famous African American women)

P, I McKissack, P., & McKissack, F. 1991. *Mary McLeod: A Great Teacher.* Springfield, NJ: Enslow. (Famous African American women)

I McKissack, P., & McKissack, F. 1996. *Red-Tails Angels: The Story of the Tuskegee Airmen of World War II.* New York: Walker. (African American history, famous African Americans)

I Mederias, A. S. 1993. *Come This Far to Freedom: A History of African Americans.* New York: Atheneum. (African American history)

P Mederias, A. S. 1991. *Dancing with the Indians.* New York: Holiday House. (Family, African American history, Native American history)

P Mederias, A. S. 1989. *Our People.* New York: Atheneum. (African American history, elderly)

I Meltzer, M. 1984. *The Black Americans: A History of Their Own Times.* New York: HarperCollins. (African American history)

I Meltzer, M., ed. 1989. *Voices from the Civil War: A Documentary of the Great American Conflict.* New York: HarperCollins. (Civil War, prejudice)

I Mettger, Z. 1994. *The Victory Is Won: Black Soldiers in the Civil War.* New York: Lodestar. (African American history, Civil War)

I Miller, R. 1992. *Reflections of a Black Cowboy.* Morristown, NJ: Silver Burdett. (African American history)

P Miller, W. 1994. *Zora Hurston and the Chinaberry Tree.* New York: Lee & Low. (Famous African American women)

P, I Mitchell, M. K. 1993. *Uncle Jed's Barber Shop.* New York: Simon & Schuster. (African American history)

P Monjo, F. N. 1970. *The Drinking Gourd.* New York: Harper & Row. (African American history, slavery)

I Moore, K. 1994. *If You Lived at the Time of the Civil War.* New York: Scholastic. (African American history, Civil War)

I Moore, Y. 1991. *Freedom Songs.* New York: Orchard. (African American history)

Myers, W. D. 1993. *The Great Migration: An American Story.* New York: HarperCollins. (African American history, migration)

I   Myers, W. D. 1995. *One More River to Cross: An African American Photograph Album.* San Diego: Harcourt Brace. (African American history)

I   O'Dell, S. 1989. *My Name Is Not Angelica.* Boston: Houghton Mifflin. (Slavery, African American history)

P   Onyefulu, I. 1993. *A Is for Africa.* New York: Cobblehill Books. (African history)

I   Parker, M. 1990. *What Is Martin Luther King Jr. Day?* Chicago: Children's Press. (African American history)

I   Parks, R., with J. Haskins. 1992. *Rosa Parks: My Story.* New York: Dial. (Famous African American women)

I   Paulsen, G. 1993. *Night John.* New York: Bantam Doubleday Dell. (African American history, slavery)

P   Polacco, P. 1992. *Mrs. Katz and Tush.* New York: Dell. (Elderly, Jewish history, African American history)

P, I   Polacco, P. 1994. *Pink and Say.* New York: Philomel. (Civil War)

I   Porter, A. P. 1992. *Jump at de Sun: The Story of Zora Neale Hurston.* Minneapolis: Carolrhoda. (Famous African American women)

I   Potter, J. 1994. *African American Firsts: Famous, Little-Known, and Unsung Triumphs of Blacks in America.* New York: Pinto. (African American history)

I   Rappaport, D. 1991. *Escape from Slavery: Five Journeys to Freedom.* New York: HarperCollins. (Slavery, African American history)

I   Ray, D. 1991. *Behind the Blue and Gray: The Soldier's Life in the Civil War.* New York: Lodestar. (Civil War)

P   Ray, M. L. 1994. *Shaker Boy.* San Diego: Harcourt. (Civil War, Shaker family)

I   Reit, S. 1988. *Behind Rebel Lines: The Incredible Story of Emma Edmonds, Civil War Spy.* New York: Gulliver/San Diego: Harcourt Brace Jovanovich. (Civil War)

P   Ringgold, F. 1992. *Aunt Harriet's Underground Railroad.* New York: Crown. (Famous African American women)

P, I   Ringgold, F. 1993. *Dinner at Aunt Carrie's House.* New York: Hyperion. (African American women in history)

I   Robinet, H. G. 1991. *Children of the Fire.* New York: Atheneum. (Slavery, Underground Railroad, social activism)

P, I   Rubel, D. 1990. *Fannie Lou Hamer: From Sharecropping to Politics.* Englewood Cliffs, NJ: Silver Burdett. (Famous African American women)

I   Ruby, L. 1994. *Steal Away Home.* New York: Macmillan/Simon & Schuster. (Underground Railroad)

I   Santrey, L. 1983. *Young Frederick Douglass: Fight for Freedom.* Mahwah, NJ: Troll. (African American history, slavery, social activism)

I   Schlissel, L. 1995. *Black Frontiers: A History of African American Heroes in the Old West.* New York: Simon & Schuster. (African American history)

P, I   Shorto, R. 1991. *Abraham Lincoln and the End of Slavery.* Brookfield, CT: Millbrook. (African American history)

I   Smucker, B. 1977. *Runaway to Freedom.* New York: Harper. (African American history)

I   Speigel, B. 1992. *The Year They Walked: Rosa Parks and the Montgomery Bus Boycott.* New York: Simon & Schuster. (African American history, social activism)

I   Taylor, E. E. 1990. *Thank You, Dr. Martin Luther King, Jr.!* New York: Watts. (African American family, African American history)

I   Taylor, M. D. 1995. *The Well: David's Story.* New York: Dial. (African American history)

I   Time-Life Books, Editors of. 1994. *Creative Fire: African American Voices of Triumph.* New York: Time-Life. (Famous African Americans)

I   Turner, A. 1987. *Nettie's Trip South.* New York: Macmillan. (Civil War, prejudice)

P, I   Turner, G. 1989. *Take a Walk in Their Shoes.* New York: Cobblestone. (African American history, social activism)

I   Turner, R. M. 1992. *Faith Ringgold.* Boston: Little, Brown. (Famous African American women)

P   Williams, S. A. 1992. *Working Cotton.* San Diego: Harcourt Brace Jovanovich. (African American history)

P   Winter, J. 1992. *Follow the Drinking Gourd.* New York: Knopf. (African American history, slavery, social activism)

P, I   Wolfe, R. E. 1992. *Mary McLeod Bethune.* New York: Watts. (Famous African American woman)

P, I   Yannuzzi, D. A. 1996. *Zora Neale Hurston: Southern Storyteller.* Springfield, NJ: Enslow. (Famous African American woman)

Asian/Asian American History, Culture, and Contributions

I   Atkins, J. 1995. *Aani & the Tree Huggers.* New York: Lee & Low. (India, environment)

P   Ashley, B. 1991. *Cleversticks.* New York: Crown. (Self-concept, Asian Americans)

I   Baile, A. *Little Brother.* New York: Viking. (Cambodian family)

I   Balgassi, H. 1996. *Peacebound Trains.* New York: Clarion. (Korean War)

P   Bannerman, H. 1996. *The Story of Little Babaji.* New York: HarperCollins. (Indian history, culture, contributions)

P, I Bash, B. 1996. *In the Heart of the Village: The World of the Indian Banyan Tree.* Boston: Little Brown. (Tale from India)

P, I Bond, R. 1995. *Binja's Blue Umbrella.* Honesdale, PA: Boyds Mills Press. (Indian history, culture, contributions)

P Bond, R. 1996. *Cherry Tree.* Honesdale, PA: Boyds Mills Press. (Indian history, culture, contributions)

I Bosse, M. *Tusk and Stone.* Honesdale, PA: Front Street Press. (Indian history, culture, contributions; slavery)

P Chin, K. 1995. *Sam and the Lucky Money.* New York: Lee & Low. (Chinese New Year)

I Chui, C. 1996. *Lives of Notable Asian Americans: Literature and Education.* New York: Chelsea House. (Famous Asian Americans, Asian American culture)

P, I Coeer, E. 1993. *Sadako.* New York: Putnam. (Hiroshima, Japanese history)

P Coeer, E. 1977. *Sadako and the Thousand Cranes.* New York: Putnam. (Hiroshima, Japanese history)

I Das, P. 1996. *I Is for India.* Englewood Cliffs, NJ: Silver Burdett. (Indian history, culture, contributions)

P Demi. 1997. *One Grain of Rice: A Mathematical Folktale.* New York: Scholastic. (Tale from India)

P, I Ginsburg, M. 1988. *The Chinese Mirror.* San Diego: Harcourt Brace Jovanovich. (Chinese tales)

P Godden, R. 1997. *Premlata and the Festival of Lights.* New York: Greenwillow. (Indian holiday)

I Hamanaka, S. 1990. *The Journey: Japanese Americans, Racism, and Renewal.* New York: Orchard. (Japanese American history, World War II, racism)

P, I Hamanaka, S. 1994. *Peace Crane.* New York: Morrow. (Japanese history, Hiroshima)

I Haskins, J. 1989. *India under Indira and Ravij Gandi.* Springfield, NJ: Enslow. (Indian history, culture, contributions)

I Hoobler, D., & Hoobler, T. 1994. *The Chinese American Family Album.* New York: Oxford University Press. (Chinese American culture)

I Hoobler, D., & Hoobler, T. 1995. *The Japanese American Family Album.* New York: Oxford University Press. (Japanese American culture)

I Howard, D. E. 1996. *India.* Chicago: Children's Press. (Indian history, culture, contributions)

I Howard, E. 1987. *Her Own Song.* New York: Atheneum. (Adopted family—one Chinese and one American)

P, I Jacobs, J., ed. 1994. *Indian Fairy.* New York: Dover. (Tales from India)

P Jaffrey, M. 1997. *Robi Dobi: The Marvelous Adventures of an Indian Elephant.* New York: Dial. (Indian history, culture, contributions)

I   Japanese American Curriculum Project. 1985. *The Japanese American Journey.* San Mateo, CA: AACP. (Japanese American culture)

P   Kalman, M. 1995. *Swami on Rye: Max in India.* New York: Viking. (Indian history, culture, contributions)

I   Katz, E. 1996. *India in Pictures.* Minneapolis: Lerner. (Indian history, culture, contributions)

P, I   Kipling, R. 1987. *The Jungle Book.* New York: Puffin. (Tales from India)

P, I   Kipling, R. 1865–1936. *The Jungle Book.* New York: Arcade. (Tales from India)

I   Kipling, R. 1987. *The Jungle Book: The Mowgli Stories.* New York: Morrow. (Tales from India)

P   Kipling, R. 1997. *Rikki-Tikki-Tavi.* New York: Morrow. (Tales from India)

P, I   Kipling, R.; Ashachik, D.; & Hannon, H. 1992. *The Jungle Book.* Mahwah, NJ: Troll. (Tales from India)

I   Kodama, T. 1995. *Shin's Tricycle.* New York: Walker. (Hiroshima, Japanese history)

I   Laure, J. 1992. *Bangladesh.* Chicago: Children's Press. (Indian history, culture, contributions)

I   Leathers, N. L. 1991. *The Japanese in America.* Minneapolis: Lerner. (Japanese American history)

P   Lee, H. V. 1994. *At the Beach.* New York: Holt. (Mandarin Chinese language)

I   Levine, E. 1995. *A Fence away from Freedom: Japanese Americans and World War II.* New York: Putnam. (Japanese American history, internment camps)

P   Lewis, T. 1995. *Sacred River.* New York: Clarion. (Indian history, culture, contributions)

P, I   Livingston, M. C. 1996. *Festivals.* New York: Holiday House. (Holidays in India)

P   Mahy, M. 1990. *The Seven Chinese Brothers.* New York: Scholastic. (Chinese history)

P   Margolies, B. A. 1992. *Kanu of Kathmandu: A Journey in Nepal.* New York: Simon & Schuster. (Indian history, culture, contributions)

P   Martin, R. 1997. *The Monkey Bridge.* New York: Knopf. (Tale from India)

P   Martin, R., & Anderson, B. 1998. *The Brave Little Parrot.* New York: Putnam. (Tale from India)

P, I   Maruki, T. 1980. *Hiroshima No Pika.* New York: Lothrop. (Hiroshima, Japanese history)

I   Meltzer, M. 1980. *The Chinese Americans.* New York: HarperCollins. (Chinese American history)

P, I   Mochizuki, K. 1993. *Baseball Saved Us.* New York: Lee & Low. (Japanese American history, internment camps)

P, I   Mochizuki, K. 1995. *Heroes.* New York: Lee & Low. (Stereotyping, Japanese American history)

Morimoto, J. 1987. *My Hiroshima.* New York: Viking. (Hiroshima, Japanese history)

P   Nunes, S. M. 1995. *The Last Dragon.* New York: Clarion. (Chinese American culture)

I   Prior, K. 1997. *The History of Emigration from the Indian Subcontinent.* New York: Watts. (Indian history, immigration)

P   Rajpust, M. 1997. *The Peacock's Pride.* New York: Disney Press. (Tale from India)

P   Reddix, V. 1991. *Dragon Kite of Autumn Moon.* New York: Lothrop, Lee & Shepard. (Elderly, Chinese holiday)

P   Say, A. 1982. *The Bicycle Man.* New York: Scholastic. (World War II, stereotyping)

I   Schmidt, J. 1994. *In the Village of the Elephants.* New York: Walker. (Indian history, culture, contributions)

P   Shepard, A. 1995. *The Gifts of Wali Dad: A Tale of India & Pakistan.* New York: Atheneum. (Tale from India)

P   Shepard, A. 1992. *Savitri: A Tale of Ancient India.* New York: Philomel. (Tale from India)

P   Souhami, J. 1997. *Rama and the Demon King: An Ancient Tale from India.* New York: DK. (Tale from India)

I   Stanley, J. 1994. *I Am an American: A True Story of Japanese Internment.* New York: Crown. (Japanese American history, internment camps)

I   Stern, J. 1990. *The Filipino Americans.* New York: Chelsea House. (Filipino American history)

I   Takaki, R. 1994. *In the Heart of Filipino America: Immigrants from the Pacific Isles.* New York: Chelsea House. (Filipino American history, Filipino immigrants)

I   Uchida, Y. 1983. *The Best of a Bad Thing.* New York: Macmillan. (Japanese American culture)

I   Uchida, Y. 1985. *Journey to Topaz: Story of the Japanese–American Evacuation.* New York: Scribner's. (Japanese American history)

I   Uchida, Y. 1987. *Picture Bride.* Flagstaff, AZ: Northland. (Japanese Americans)

I   Uchida, Y. 1985. *Samurai of Gold Hill.* San Francisco: Creative Arts Books. (Japanese American culture)

P   Uchida, Y., & Yardley, J. 1993. *The Bracelet.* New York: Philomel. (Japanese American history, internment camps)

P   Waters, K., & Slvenz-Low, M. 1990. *Lion Dancer: Ernie Wan's Chinese New Year.* New York: Scholastic. (Chinese holiday)

P   Wolf, G. 1996. *The Very Hungry Lion: A Folktale.* Toronto: Annick Press. (Tale from India)

I   Yep, L. 1988. *Child of the Owl.* New York: Harper & Row. (Chinese American family, elderly, Chinese American culture)

I   Yep, L. 1995. *Hiroshima: A Novella.* New York: Scholastic. (Japanese history, Hiroshima)

P   Young, E. 1992. *Seven Blind Mice.* Morton Grove, IL: Albert Whitman. (Tale from India)

The Challenged

P   Adler, D. 1990. *A Picture Book of Helen Keller.* New York: Holiday House. (Challenged—blind and deaf)

I   Alexander, S. H. 1990. *Mom Can't See Me.* New York: Macmillan. (Challenged—blind; family)

P, I Bahr, M. 1992. *The Memory Box.* Morton Grove, IL: Albert Whitman. (Challenged—Alzheimers; family)

P   Barrett, M. B. 1994. *Sing to the Stars.* Boston: Little, Brown. (Challenged—blind)

P   Cairo, S.; Cairo, J.; & Cairo, T. 1985. *Our Brother Has Down's Syndrome.* Toronto: Annick Press. (Family; challenged—Down syndrome)

P   Condra, E. 1994. *See the Ocean.* Nashville: Ideals. (Family, challenged)

I   Davis, D. 1994. *My Brother Has AIDS.* New York: Atheneum. (Family; challenged—AIDS)

P, I DenBoer, H. 1994. *Please Don't Cry, Mom.* Minneapolis: Carolrhoda. (Family; challenged—depression)

I   Drimmer, F. 1988. *Born Different: Amazing Stories of Very Special People.* New York: Atheneum. (Family, challenged)

P   Fleming, V. 1993. *Be Good to Eddie Lee.* New York: Philomel. (Stereotyping; challenged—mentally retarded)

P   Greenfield, E. 1980. *Alesia.* New York: Philomel. Darlene Methuen. (Challenged—wheelchair)

I   Haldane, S. 1991. *Helping Hands: How Monkeys Assist People Who Are Disabled.* New York: Dutton. (Challenged)

I   Hall, L. 1990. *Halsey's Pride.* New York: Scribner's. (Challenged)

P, I Harshman, M. 1995. *The Storm.* New York: Cobblehill. (Challenged—wheelchair)

I   Hesse, K. 1993. *Lester's Dog.* New York: Crown. (Challenged—hearing impaired).

I   Hill, D. 1994. *See Ya, Simon.* New York: Dutton. (Challenged—muscular dystrophy)

I   Hooks, W. H. 1988. *A Flight of Dazzle Angels.* New York: Macmillan. (Family; challenged—clubfooted)

P   Kroll, V. 1994. *Pink Paper Swans.* Grand Rapids, MI: Eerdman's. (Challenged—arthritis; Asian Americans)

I   Kudlinski, K. V. 1990. *Helen Keller: A Light for the Blind.* New York: Viking. (Challenged—blind and deaf)

P   Lears, L. 1998. *Ian's Walk: A Story about Autism.* Morton Grove, IL: Albert Whitman. (Challenged—autism)

I   Martin, A. M. 1990. *Kristy and the Secret of Susan.* New York: Scholastic. (Challenged—autism)

I   Padden, C., & Humphries, T. 1988. *Deaf in America: Voices from a Culture.* New York: Orchard. (Challenged—deaf)

P   Pirner, C. W. 1991. *Even Little Kids Get Diabetes.* Morton Grove, IL: Albert Whitman. (Challenged—diabetes)

P   Quinlan, P. 1994. *Tiger Flowers.* New York: Dial. (Challenged—AIDS)

P   Rogers, A. 1987. *Luke Has Asthma, Too.* Burlington, VT: Waterfont. (Challenged—asthma)

P   Schick, E. 1993. *I Have Another Language: The Language Is Dance.* Louisville, KY: American Printing House for the Blind. (Challenged, languages)

I   Smith, D. B. 1994. *Remember the Red-Shouldered Hawk.* New York: Putnam. (Family; challenged—Alzheimer's; elderly)

I   Springer, M. 1991. *Colt.* New York: Dial. (Challenged—spina bifida)

P   Thompson, M. 1996. *Andy and His Yellow Frisbee.* Warwick, RI: Woodbine House. (Challenged—autism)

P   Watson, E. 1996. *Talking to Angels.* San Diego: Hartcourt Brace. (Challenged—autism)

I   Werlin, M. 1996. *Are You Alone on Purpose?* Boston: Houghton Mifflin. (Challenged—autism)

I   Whelan, G. 1991. *Hannah.* New York: Knopf. (Challenged—blind)

P   Wild, M. 1993. *All the Better to See You With.* Morton Grove, IL: Albert Whitman. (Challenged—handicap)

I   Wood, J. R. 1992. *The Man Who Loved Clowns.* Morton Grove, IL: Albert Whitman. (Challenged—Down syndrome)

I   Wood, J. R. 1995. *When Pigs Fly.* New York: Putnam. (Challenged—Down syndrome)

Classic Tales from Different Perspectives

P, I   Andersen, H. C. 1984. *The Emperor's New Clothes.* Boston: Little, Brown. (Classic tale)

I   Belting, N. M. 1992. *Moon Was Tired of Walking on Air.* Boston: Houghton Mifflin. (South American Indian myths)

P, I   Berenzy, A. 1989. *A Frog Prince.* New York: Holt. (Classic fairy tale)

P, I   Black, S. 1994. *Upside Down Tales: Hansel and Gretel and The Witch's Tale.* New York: Carol Publishing Group. (Classic and witch's versions of *Hansel and Gretel*)

P, I   Briggs, R. 1970. *Jim and the Beanstalk.* New York: Coward-McCann. (Elderly version of *Jack and the Beanstalk*)

P, I   Bruhac, J., & London, J. 1992. *Thirteen Moons on Turtle's Back: A Native American Year of Moons.* New York: Philomel. (Native American tale)

P, I   Calmenson, S. 1989. *The Principal's New Clothes.* New York: Scholastic. (Modern version of *The Emperor's New Clothes*)

P, I   Climo, S. 1989. *The Egyptian Cinderella.* New York: HarperCollins. (Egyptian version of *Cinderella*)

I   Climo, S. 1993. *The Korean Cinderella.* New York: HarperCollins. (Korean version of *Cinderella*)

P, I   Cole, B. 1992. *Prince Cinders.* New York: Putnam. (Gender-equity version of *Cinderella*)

P, I   Crawford, E. D. 1983. *The Little Red Cap.* New York: Morrow. (Version of *Little Red Riding Hood*)

P, I   Dove, M. 1990. *Coyote Stories.* Lincoln: University of Nebraska Press. (Native American tales)

P   Eisen, A. 1992. *Treasury of Children's Literature.* Boston: Houghton Mifflin. (Anthology of tales)

P, I   Emberly, M. 1990. *Ruby.* Boston: Little, Brown. (Version of *Little Red Riding Hood*)

P, I   French, F. 1992. *Snow White in New York.* New York: Oxford University Press. (Modern version of *Snow White*)

P, I   Granowsky. A. 1993. *Point of View Stories: Cinderella and That Awful Cinderella.* Austin: Steck-Vaughn. (Classic and stepsisters' versions of *Cinderella*)

P, I   Granowsky. A. 1993. *Point of View Stories: Peter Pan: The Classic Tale and Grow Up, Peter Pan!* Austin: Steck-Vaughn. (Classic and So-and-So's versions of *Peter Pan*)

P, I   Granowsky. A. 1993. *Point of View Stories: Snow White: The Classic Tale and The Unfairest of Them All.* Austin: Steck-Vaughn. (Classic and stepmother's versions of *Snow White*)

I   Hamilton, V. 1988. *In the Beginning: Creation Stories from around the World.* San Diego: Harcourt Brace Jovanovich. (Tales—different perspectives)

P   Heins, P. 1974. *Snow White.* Boston: Little, Brown. (Classic fairy tale)

P   Hooks, W. H. 1989. *The Three Little Pigs and the Fox.* New York: Macmillan. (Appalachian version of *The Three Little Pigs*)

P, I   Jacobs, J. 1989. *Tattercoats.* New York: Putnam. (Translation of *Cinderella*)

P   Kroll, S. 1993. *Queen of the May.* New York: Holiday House. (Variation of Cinderella story)

P   Lewis, J. P. 1994. *The Frog Princess.* New York: Dial. (Fairy tale)

P, I   Louie, A. L. 1982. *Yeh-Shen: A Cinderella Story from China.* New York: Sandcastle. (Chinese version of *Cinderella*)

P, I   Lowell, S. 1992. *The Three Little Javelinas*. New York: Scholastic. (Southwestern version of *The Three Little Pigs*)

P, I   Lum, D. 1994. *The Golden Slipper: A Vietnamese Legend*. Mahwah, NJ: Troll. (Vietnamese version of *Cinderella*)

P   Marshall, J. 1988. *Goldilocks and the Three Bears*. New York: Scholastic. (Classic version of fairy tale)

P, I   Martin, R. 1992. *The Rough-Faced Girl*. New York: Putnam. (Native American version of *Cinderella*)

P   Mathers, P. 1991. *Borreguita and the Coyote*. New York: Knopf. (Mexican tale)

P   Mayo, G. W. 1993. *Meet Tricky Coyote*. New York: Walker. (Native American tales)

P   McKissack, P. 1986. *Flossie and the Fox*. New York: Dial. (African American version of *The Three Little Pigs*)

I   Minard, R. 1975. *Womenfolk and Fairy Tales*. Boston: Houghton Mifflin. (Tales, gender equity)

P, I   Minters, F. 1994. *Cinder-elly*. New York: Viking/Penguin. (Modern version of *Cinderella*)

P   Montresor, B. 1991. *Little Red Riding Hood*. New York: Doubleday. (Classic fairy tale)

I   Osborne, M. P. 1993. *Mermaid Tales from around the World*. New York: Scholastic. (Tales—different perspectives)

   Paxton, T. 1990. *Belling the Cat and Other Aesop's Fables*. New York: Morrow. (American tall tales)

P, I   San Souci, R. D. 1993. *Cut from the Same Cloth: American Women of Myth, Legend, and Tall Tales*. New York: Philomel. (Tales, gender equity)

P, I   San Souci, R. D. 1994. *Sootface: An Ojibwa Cinderella Story*. New York: Doubleday. (Ojibwa version of *Cinderella*)

P, I   Scieszka, J. 1991. *The Frog Prince: Continued*. New York: Viking. (Modern version of *The Frog Prince*)

P, I   Scieszka, J. 1989. *The True Story of the 3 Little Pigs by A. Wolf*. New York: Viking. (The wolf's version of *The Three Little Pigs*)

P, I   Scieszka, J., and Smith, L. 1992. *The Stinky Cheese Man and Other Fairly Stupid Tales*. New York: Viking. (Humorous folktales and fairy tales)

P, I   Shorto, R. 1994. *The Untold Story of Cinderella: Upside Down Tales*. New York: Carol Publishing Group. (Classic and stepmother's versions of *Cinderella*)

P, I   Steptoe, J. 1987. *Mufaro's Beautiful Daughters: An African Tale*. New York: Lothrop, Lee & Shepard. (African American version of *Cinderella*)

P, I   Trivias, E., & Oxenbury, H. 1993. *The Three Little Wolves and the Big Bad Pig*. New York: Margaret McElderry. (Humorous version of *The Three Little Pigs*)

P, I   Yolen, J. 1986. *Favorite Folktales from Around the World*. New York: Pantheon. (Multicultural tales)

P   Young, E. 1989. *Lon Po Po*. New York: Philomel. (Chinese *Little Red Riding Hood*)

Columbus—Different Perspectives

P   Adler, D. A. 1991. *A Picture Book of Christopher Columbus.* New York: Holiday House. (Columbus—different perspectives)

I   Brenner, B. 1991. *If You Were There in 1492.* New York: Bradbury. (Columbus—different perspectives)

P   Conrad, P. 1991. *Pedro's Journal.* New York: Scholastic. (Columbus—different perspectives)

I   Dyson, J. 1991. *Westward with Columbus: Set Sail on the Voyage That Changed the World.* New York: Scholastic. (Columbus—different perspectives)

I   Haskins, J. 1992. *Against All Opposition: Black Explorers in America.* New York: Walker. (African American history; Columbus—different perspectives)

P, I   Jacobs, F. 1992. *The Tainos: The People Who Welcomed Columbus.* New York: Putnam. (Columbus—different perspectives)

I   Levison, N. S. 1990. *Christopher Columbus: Voyager to the Unknown.* New York: Lodestar. (Columbus—different perspectives)

P, I   Littlechild, G. 1993. *This Land Is My Land.* Emeryville, CA: Children's Book Press. (Native Americans; Columbus—different perspectives)

I   Maestro, B., & Maestro, G. 1991. *The Discovery of the Americas.* New York: Lothrop. (Columbus—different perspectives)

I   Meltzer, M. 1990. *Columbus and the World around Him.* New York: Watts. (Columbus—different perspectives)

I   Pelta, K. 1991. *Discovering Christopher Columbus: How History Is Invented.* Minneapolis: Lerner. (Columbus—different perspectives)

I   Roop, P., & Roop, C., eds. 1990. *I, Columbus: My Journal—1492–3.* New York: Walker. (Columbus—different perspectives)

P   Sis, P. 1991. *Follow the Dream: The Story of Christopher Columbus.* New York: Knopf. (Columbus—different perspectives)

P, I   Yolen, J. 1992. *Encounter.* San Diego: Harcourt Brace Jovanovich. (Columbus—different perspectives)

Differences and Likenesses

P   Baer, E. 1990. *This Is the Way We Go to School: A Book about Children around the World.* New York: Scholastic. (Differences and likenesses)

P   Cannon, J. 1993. *Stellaluna.* San Diego: Harcourt Brace. (Differences and likenesses)

P, I   Copsey, S. E., with Kindersley, A. *Children Just Like Me.* New York: DK. (Differences and likenesses)

P   Dooley, N. 1991. *Everybody Cooks Rice.* Minneapolis: Carolrhoda. (Differences and likenesses)

P   Hamanaka, S. 1994. *All the Colors of the Earth.* New York: Morrow. (Differences and likenesses)

P   Lacapa, K., & Lacapa, M. 1994. *Less Than Half, More Than Whole.* Flagstaff, AZ: Northland. (Differences and likenesses)

P, I   Lankford, M. D. 1992. *Hopscotch around the World.* New York: Morrow. (Differences and likenesses)

I   Lowes, J. 1995. *Looking at Photographs.* San Francisco: Chronicle. (Differences and likenesses)

P   Lyon, G. E. 1992. *Who Came Down That Road?* New York: Orchard. (Native American history; differences and likenesses)

P   McKee, D. 1989. *Elmer.* New York: Lothrop, Lee & Shepard (Self-concept; differences and likenesses)

P   Morris, A. 1989. *Bread, Bread, Bread.* New York: Lothrop, Lee & Shepard. (Differences and likenesses)

P   Morris, A. 1989. *Hats, Hats, Hats.* New York: Lothrop, Lee & Shepard. (Differences and likenesses)

P   Morris, A. 1990. *Houses and Homes.* New York: Lothrop, Lee & Shepard. (Differences and likenesses)

P   Morris, A. 1990. *Loving.* New York: Lothrop, Lee & Shepard. (Differences and likenesses)

P   Nikola-Lisa, W. 1995. *Being with You This Way.* New York: Lee & Low. (Differences and likenesses)

P   Raffi. 1994. *Like Me and You.* New York: Crown. (Differences and likenesses)

P   Robinson, M. 1993. *Cock-a-Doodle Doo!: What Does It Sound Like to You?* New York: Stewart, Tabori, & Chang. (Differences and likenesses, languages)

P   Simon, N. 1975. *All Kinds of Families.* Chicago: Albert Whitman. (Family; differences and likenesses)

I   Simon, N. 1976. *Why Am I Different?* Chicago: Albert Whitman. (African Americans)

P, I   Spier, P. 1980. *People.* New York: Doubleday. (Differences and likenesses)

Elderly and/or Death

P   Alexandra, M. 1992. *Where Does the Sky End, Grandpa?* San Diego: Harcourt Brace Jovanovich. (Family, elderly)

P   Andrews, J. 1991. *The Auction.* New York: Macmillan. (Elderly)

P, I   Bahr, M. 1992. *The Memory Box.* Morton Grove, IL: Albert Whitman. (Elderly— Alzheimers; family)

P   Buckley, H. E. 1994. *Grandfather and I.* New York: Lothrop, Lee & Shepard. (Family, elderly)

P   Castaneda, O. S. 1993. *Abuela's Weave.* New York: Lee & Low. (Family, elderly)

P   Choi, S. N. 1993. *Halmouni and the Picnic.* Boston: Houghton Mifflin. (Korean family, elderly)

P   Clifton, L. 1983. *Everett Anderson's Goodbye.* New York: Holt. (Elderly, death)

P   Daly, N. 1985. *Not So Fast Songololo.* New York: Puffin. (Family, elderly)

P   dePaola, T. 1978. *Nana Upstairs & Nana Downstairs.* New York: Puffin. (Elderly, death)

P   Dorros, A. 1991. *Abuela.* New York: Dutton. (Elderly; Hispanic people)

P   Franklin, K. L. 1992. *The Old, Old Man and the Very Little Boy.* New York: Atheneum. (African family, elderly)

I   Godden, R. 1993. *Great Grandmother's House.* New York: Greenwillow. (Japanese family, elderly)

P   Gray, N. 1988. *A Balloon for Grandad.* New York: Orchard. (Elderly)

P   Greenfield, E. 1988. *Grandpa's Face.* New York: Philomel. (Family, elderly)

P   Greenfield, E. 1993. *William and the Good Old Days.* New York: HarperCollins. (Elderly, death, African American family)

P   Hazen, B. 1985. *Why Are People Different?* Racine, WI: Western. (African American, elderly)

P   Hesse, K. 1993. *Poppy's Chair.* New York: Macmillan. (Family, elderly, death)

P   Hest, A. 1989. *The Midnight Eaters.* New York: Simon & Schuster. (Family, elderly)

P   Johnson, A. 1990. *When I Am Old with You.* New York: Orchard. (African American family, elderly).

P   Johnston, T. 1991. *Grandpa's Song.* New York: Dial. (Family, elderly)

P   Keller, H. 1989. *The Best Present.* New York: Greenwillow. (Family, elderly)

P   Keller, H. 1994. *Grandfather's Dream.* New York: Greenwillow. (Vietnamese family, elderly, Vietnamese history)

P   Kroll, V. 1995. *Fireflies, Peach Pies, and Lullabies.* New York: Simon & Schuster. (Elderly)

P   Lindbergh, R. 1993. *Grandfather's Lovesong.* New York: Viking. (Family, elderly)

P   Martin, B., & Archambault, B. 1989. *Knots on a Counting Rope.* New York: Holt. (Elderly, African American)

P, I   Mathis, S. B. 1975. *The Hundred Penny Book.* New York: Viking. (Family, elderly)

P, I Mederias, A. S. 1989. *Our People.* New York: Atheneum. (African American history, elderly)

P Miles, M. 1971. *Annie and the Old One.* Boston: Little, Brown. (Family, elderly, Native American)

P Moss, M. 1994. *In America.* New York: Dutton. (Elderly)

P Nelson, M. N. 1988. *Always Gramma.* New York: Putnam. (Elderly—nursing home)

I Nez, R. T., as told to K. Wilder. 1995. *Forbidden Talent.* Flagstaff, AZ: Northland. (Navajo family, elderly)

I Nodar, C. S. 1992. *Abuelita's Paradise.* Morton Grove, IL: Albert Whitman. (Puerto Rican family, elderly)

P Nye, N. S. 1993. *Siti's Secrets.* New York: Simon & Schuster. (Elderly; Palestinian/Arab American family)

I Perkins, M. 1993. *The Sunita Experiment.* Boston: Little, Brown. (Indian family, elderly)

P Polacco, P. 1990. *Babushka's Doll.* New York: Simon & Schuster. (Russian family, elderly)

P Polacco, P. 1992. *Mrs. Katz and Tush.* New York: Dell. (Elderly, Jewish history, African American history)

P Raczek, L. T. 1995. *The Night the Grandfathers Died.* Flagstaff, AZ: Northland. (Ute culture, elderly)

P Reddix, V. 1991. *Dragon Kite of Autumn Moon.* New York: Lothrop, Lee & Shepard. (Chinese family, elderly)

P Say, A. 1993. *Grandfather's Journey.* Boston: Houghton Mifflin. (Japanese family)

P Schwartz, L. 1994. *How Can You Help?: Creative Volunteer Projects for Kids Who Care.* New Hyde Park, NJ: Learning Works. (Social activism, helping the elderly)

P Stoltz, M. 1991. *Storm in the Night.* New York: Harper. (Elderly; African American family)

I Tobias, T. 1993. *Pot Luck.* New York: Lothrop. (Family, elderly)

P Waddell, M. 1990. *My Great-Grandpa.* New York: Putnam. (Family, elderly)

P, I Walker, A. 1967. *To Hell with Dying.* San Diego: Harcourt Brace Jovanovich. (Elderly)

P Wallace, I. 1984. *Chin Chiang and the Dragon's Dance.* New York: Atheneum/Macmillan. (Elderly, Chinese)

P Wild, M. 1994. *Our Granny.* Boston: Houghton Mifflin. (Elderly)

P, I Weisman, J. 1993. *The Storyteller.* New York: Rizzoli. (Native American family, elderly)

Environment

P, I Allen, J. 1992. *Tiger.* Cambridge, MA: Candlewick. (Environment, South China)

I Ancona, G. 1990. *Riverkeeper.* New York: Macmillan. (Environment, social activism)

P, I Anholt, L. 1992. *The Forgotten Forest.* San Francisco: Sierra Club. (Environment)

P, I Appelbaum, D. 1993. *Giants in the Land.* Boston: Houghton Mifflin. (Environment)

P Asch, F. 1993. *The Earth and I.* San Diego: Harcourt Brace. (Environment)

P, I Baker, J. 1991. *Window.* New York: Greenwillow. (Environment)

P, I Berry, J. 1993. *Every Kid's Guide to Saving the Earth.* Nashville: Ideals. (Environment)

P Bowen, B. 1991. *Antler, Bear, Canoe: A Northlands Alphabet Book.* Boston: Little, Brown. (Environment)

P Cherry, L. 1995. *The Great Kapok Trees.* New York: Dial. (Environment)

P, I Chief Jake Swamp. 1995. *Giving Thanks: A Native American Good Morning Message.* New York: Lee & Low. (Iroquois morning address, environment)

I Cone, M. 1992. *Come Back Salmon: How a Group of Dedicated Kids Adopted Pigeon Creek and Brought It Back to Life.* San Francisco: Sierra Club. (Environment, social activism)

P Cowcher, H. 1988. *Rain Forest.* New York: Farrar, Straus, & Giroux. (Environment)

I Davis, D. 1988. *The Secret of the Seal.* New York: Crown. (Environment, Inuit family)

P, I Durell, A.; Patterson, K.; George, J. C., eds. 1992. *The Big Book for Our Planet.* New York: Dutton. (Environment)

P, I Earth Works Group. 1994. *50 Simple Things Kids Can Do to Recycle.* Berkeley: Earth Works Press. (Ecology, social action)

I Elkington, J; Hailes, J.; Hill, D.; & Makower, J. 1990. *Going Green: A Kid's Handbook to Saving the Planet.* New York: Puffin. (Environment)

P, I Fife, D. H. 1991. *The Empty Lot.* San Francisco: Sierra Club. (Environment, social activism)

I Foster, J. 1991. *Cartons, Cans, and Orange Peels: Where Does Your Garbage Go?* New York: Clarion. (Environment)

P, I Frasier, D. 1991. *On the Day That You Were Born.* San Diego: Harcourt Brace Jovanovich. (Environment)

P, I Gibbons, G. 1992. *Recycle!: A Handbook for Kids.* Boston: Little, Brown. (Environment, social activism)

P Hallinan, P. K. 1992. *For the Love of Earth.* Nashville: Ideals. (Environment)

P, I Havill, J. 1993. *Sato and the Elephants.* New York: Lothrop. (Environment)

I   Huff, B. A. 1990. *Greening the City Streets: The Story of Community Gardens.* New York: Clarion. (Environment, social activism)

P   Iverson, D. 1993. *I Celebrate Nature.* Nevada City, CA: Dawn. (Environment)

P, I   Jeffers, S. 1991. *Brother Eagle, Sister Sky.* New York: Scholastic. (Native American, environment)

P   Koch, M. 1993. *World Water Watch.* New York: Greenwillow. (Environment)

P, I   Locker, T. 1991. *The Land of the Gray Wolf.* New York: Dial. (Native American history, environment)

P   MacGill-Callahan, S. 1991. *And Still the Turtle Watched.* New York: Dial. (Environment)

I   National Geographic Staff. 1988. *Adventures in Your National Parks.* Washington, DC: National Geographic Society. (Environment)

I   Presilla, M. E., & Soto, G. 1996. *Life around the Lake: Embroideries by the Women of Lake Patzcuaro.* New York: Holt. (Hispanic culture, environment)

P, I   Rand, G. 1992. *Prince William.* New York: Holt. (Environment, social activism)

I   Savan, B. 1991. *Earthwatch: Earthcycles and Ecosystems.* Boston: Addison Wesley. (Environment)

P   Siebert, D. 1991. *Sierra.* New York: HarperCollins. (Environment)

P, I   Schlein, M. 1995. *The Year of the Panda.* New York: Crowell. (Environment)

P   Schmid, E. 1992. *The Air around Us.* New York: North–South. (Environment)

P, I   Seuss, Dr. 1971. *The Lorax.* New York: Random House. (Environment)

I   Stile, D. 1990. *Water Pollution.* Chicago: Children's Press. (Environment)

I   Temple, L., ed. 1993. *Dear World: How Children around the World Feel about Our Environment.* New York: Random House. (Environment)

P, I   Thompson, C. 1992. *The Paper Bag Prince.* New York: Knopf. (Environment)

P, I   Tokuda, W., & Hall, R. 1986. *Humphrey the Lost Whale.* Union City, CA: Herian International. (Environment)

P, I   Turner, A. 1988. *Heron Street.* New York: Harper. (Environment)

P, I   Van Allsburg. 1990. *Just a Dream.* Boston: Houghton Mifflin. (Environment, social activism)

P, I   Weir, B., & Weir, W. 1991. *Panther Dream: A Story of the African Rainforest.* New York: Hyperion. (Environment)

I   Whitfield, P. 1989. *Can the Whales Be Saved?: Questions about the Natural World and the Threats to Its Survival Answered by the Natural History Museum.* New York: Viking. (Environment)

P   Yolen, J. 1987. *Owl Moon.* New York: Philomel. (Family, environment)

P, I   Zak, M. 1994. *Save My Rainforest.* Volcano, CA: Volcano Press. (Environment, South America)

P   Zolotow, C. 1992. *The Seashore Book.* New York: Harper. (Environment)

Family—Different Perspectives

P   Ackerson, K. 1993. *By the Dawn's Early Light*. New York: Atheneum. (African American family)

P   Adoff, A. 1982. *All Colors of the Race*. New York: Lothrop. (Biracial family)

I   Alexander, S. H. 1990. *Mom Can't See Me*. New York: Macmillan. (Challenged—blind; family)

I   Armstrong, W. H. 1969. *Sounder*. New York: Harper. (African American family)

P   Ashe-Moutoussamy, J. 1993. *Daddy and Me: A Photo Story of Arthur Ashe and His Daughter, Camera*. New York: Knopf. (Famous African American; family dealing with AIDS)

P, I   Bahr, M. 1992. *The Memory Box*. Morton Grove, IL: Albert Whitman. (Challenged—Alzheimers; family)

I   Baile, A. *Little Brother*. New York: Viking. (Cambodian family)

I   Banish, R. 1992. *A Forever Family: A Child's Story about Adoption*. New York: Harper. (Family—adoption)

P   Barrett, M. B. 1994. *Sing to the Stars*. Boston: Little, Brown. (Family)

I   Bell, C. 1990. *Perez Family*. New York: Norton. (Cuban American family)

P   Belton, S. 1994. *May'naise Sandwiches & Sunshine Tea*. New York: Simon & Schuster. (Importance of family)

I   Bial, R. 1993. *Amish Home*. Boston: Houghton Mifflin. (Amish family)

I   Brimner, L. D. 1992. *A Migrant Family*. Minneapolis: Lerner. (Mexican American migrant family)

P   Bunting, E. 1994. *A Day's Work*. New York: Clarion. (Migrant workers, Mexican American family)

P   Cairo, S.; Cairo, J.; & Cairo, T. 1985. *Our Brother Has Down's Syndrome*. Toronto: Annick Press. (Family; challenged—Down syndrome)

I   Cameron, A. 1988. *The Most Beautiful Place in the World*. New York: Random House. (Extended family)

P   Carlstom, N. W. 1987. *Wild Wild Sunflower Child Anna*. New York: Macmillan. (African American family)

I   Castaneda, O. S. 1993. *Among the Volcanoes*. New York: Lodestar. (Mayan family)

I   Childress, A. 1981. *Rainbow Jordon*. New York: Avon. (Family—foster homes; neglect)

I   Christiansen, C. B. 1994. *I See the Moon*. New York: Atheneum. (Family—adoption)

I   Christiansen, C. B. 1989. *My Mother's House, My Father's House*. New York: Atheneum. (Family—divorce)

P, I   Coer, E., & Young, E. 1986. *The Josefina Story Quilt*. New York: Harper & Row. (Quilt stories—Western movement version)

P   Cole, J. 1995. *How I Was Adopted.* New York: Morrow. (Families—adoption)

P   Condra, E. 1994. *See the Ocean.* Nashville: Ideals. (Family; challenged—blind)

P, I   Cooney, B. 1990. *Hattie and the Wild Waves: A Story from Brooklyn.* New York: Viking. (Family, immigration)

P   Cooper, M. 1993. *I Got a Family.* New York: Holt. (Extended family)

P   Cowen-Fletcher, J. 1994. *It Takes a Village.* New York: Scholastic. (Extended African family)

P   Cowen-Fletcher, J. 1993. *Mama Zooms.* New York: Scholastic. (Family; challenged —wheelchair)

P, I   Czernecki, S., & Rhodes, T. 1992. *Pancho's Pinata.* New York: Hyperion. (Hispanic family)

P, I   Daly, N. 1995. *My Dad.* New York: Margaret McElderry. (Family—alcoholism)

I   Davis, D. 1994. *My Brother Has AIDS.* New York: Atheneum. (Family; challenged —AIDS)

I   Davis, D. 1988. *The Secret of the Seal.* New York: Crown. (Inuit family)

P, I   DenBoer, H. 1994. *Please Don't Cry, Mom.* Minneapolis: Carolrhoda. (Family; challenged—depression)

P   Dionetti, M. 1991. *Coal Mine Peaches.* New York: Orchard. (Italian family)

P, I   Di Salvo-Ryan, F. D. 1992. *Uncle Willie and the Soup Kitchen.* New York: Morrow. (Family, hunger)

I   Dorris, M. 1992. *Morning Girl.* New York: Hyperion. (Taino Indian family)

P   Dorros, A. 1991. *Abuela.* New York: Dutton. (Elderly; Hispanic people)

I   Drimmer, F. 1988. *Born Different: Amazing Stories of Very Special People.* New York: Atheneum. (Family, challenged)

P   Dupree, R. 1993. *The Wishing Chair.* Minneapolis: Carolrhoda. (African American history, African American family)

P   Eisenberg, P. R. 1992. *You're My Nikki.* New York: Dial. (African American family)

P, I   Eskoomiak, N. 1990. *Arctic Memories.* New York: Holt. (Inuit family, Inuit history)

P, I   Fabers, D. 1991. *The Amish.* New York: Doubleday. (Amish family)

P   Freeman, D. 1968. *Corduroy.* New York: Viking. (African American family)

P   Freeman, D. 1983. *A Pocket for Corduroy.* New York: Penguin. (African American family)

P, I   Freidman, F. B. 1984. *How My Parents Learned to Eat.* Boston: Houghton Mifflin. (Biracial family)

I   Gay, K. 1988. *Changing Families: Meeting Today's Challenges.* Springfield, NJ: Enslow. (Families—different perspectives)

I   Graff, N. P. 1993. *Where the River Runs: A Portrait of a Refugee Family.* Boston: Little, Brown. (Refugee family)

P   Greenfield, E. 1993. *First Pink Light.* New York: Crowell. (African American family)

P   Greenfield, E. 1974. *She Come Bringing Me That Baby Girl.* Philadelphia: Lippincott. (African American family)

P   Haggerty, M. E. 1993. *A Crack in the Wall.* New York: Lee & Low. (Family, holiday, Hispanic people)

P, I   Harvey, B. 1988. *Cassie's Journey: Going West in the 1860's.* New York: Holiday House. (1860 family, migration)

P   Havill, J. 1986. *Jamaica's Find.* Boston: Houghton Mifflin. (African American family)

P   Havill, J. 1986. *Jamaica Tag Along.* Boston: Houghton Mifflin. (African American family)

P   Hazen, B. 1985. *Why Are People Different?* Racine, WI: Western. (African Americans, elderly)

P, I   Hest, A. 1990. *The Ring and the Window Seat.* New York: Scholastic. (Jewish family, Holocaust)

I   Hewett, F. P. 1990. *Hector Lives in the United States Now: The Story of a Mexican American Child.* Philadelphia: Lippincott. (Immigration, Mexican American family)

P   Hines, A. G. 1986. *Daddy Makes the Best Spaghetti.* New York: Clarion. (Family, gender equity)

I   Hirschfielder, A. B., & Singer, B. R., eds. 1991. *Rising Voices: Writings of Young Native Americans.* New York: Scribner's. (Native American family, Native American history)

P   Hoffman, M., & Binch, C. 1995. *Boundless Grace.* New York: Dial. (African American family)

I   Hook, W. H. 1988. *A Flight of Dazzle Angels.* New York: Macmillan. (Family, challenged)

I   Howard, E. 1987. *Her Own Song.* New York: Atheneum. (Adopted family—one Chinese and one American)

P   Howard, E. F. 1991. *Aunt Flossie Hats and Crab Cakes Later.* New York: Dutton. (African American family)

I   Hoyt-Goldsmith, D. 1992. *Arctic Hunter.* New York: Holiday House. (Inupiat family)

P   Hoyt-Goldsmith, D. 1993. *Cherokee Summer.* New York: Holiday House. (Native American family)

I   Hoyt-Goldsmith, D. 1996. *Migrant Worker: A Boy from the Rio Grande Valley.* New York: Holiday House. (Migrant workers, Hispanic family, social activism)

I   Hoyt-Goldsmith, D. 1991. *Pueblo Storyteller.* New York: Holiday House. (Native American family)

I   Hudson, J. 1989. *Sweetgrass.* New York: Philomel. (Blackfoot Indian history, Blackfoot Indian family)

P, I   Hudson, W. 1991. *Jamal's Busy Day.* Orange, NJ: Just Us Books. (African American family)

P   Hughes, M. 1996. *A Handful of Seeds.* New York: Orchard. (Hispanic family; foods—different perspectives)

P   Hurwitz, J. 1993. *New Shoes for Sylvia.* New York: Morrow. (Hispanic family)

I   James, B. 1994. *The Mud Family.* New York: Putnam. (Anasazi Indian family)

I   Jenness, A. 1988. *Families: A Celebration of Diversity, Commitment, and Love.* Boston: Houghton Mifflin. (Family—differences and likenesses)

I   Jenness, A., & Rivers, A. 1988. *In Two Worlds: A Yup'ik Eskimo Family.* Boston: Houghton Mifflin. (Eskimo family)

P   Johnson, A. 1993. *Do Like Kyla.* New York: Orchard. (African American family)

P   Johnson, A. 1990. *When I Am Old with You.* New York: Orchard. (African American family, elderly)

P, I   Johnson, D. 1993. *Now Let Me Fly: The Story of a Slave Family.* New York: Macmillan. (Slavery, African American family)

P   Johnson, D. 1990. *What Will Mommy Do When I'm at School?* London: Collier Macmillan. (African American family)

I   Jones, R. C. 1988. *The Believers.* New York: Arcade. (Family—adopted)

P   Joose, B. M. 1991. *Mama, Do You Love Me?* New York: Scholastic. (Native American/Eskimo/Inuit family)

P   Keats, E. J. 1967. *Peter's Chair.* New York: HarperCollins. (African American family)

I   King, S. 1993. *Shannon: An Ojibway Dancer.* Minneapolis: Lerner. (Ojibway family)

I   Kinsley-Warcock, N. 1989. *The Canada Geese Quilt.* New York: Cobblehill Books. (Quilt—Canadian; family)

P   Koeler, P. 1990. *The Day We Met You.* New York: Bradbury. (Family—adoption)

P   Kuklin, S. 1992. *How My Family Lives in America.* New York: Bradbury. (Immigrant families)

I   Lasky, K. 1994. *Days of the Dead.* New York: Hyperion. (Mexican family, holiday)

P   Lindbergh, R. 1993. *Grandfather's Lovesong.* New York: Viking. (Family, elderly)

P   Lindsay, J. W. 1994. *Do I Have a Daddy?: Story about a Single-Parent Child.* Buena Vista, CA: Morning Glory Press. (Family—single parent)

P   Loh, M. 1987. *Tucking Mommy In.* New York: Orchard. (Asian American family)

P   Long, D. J. 1995. *I Wish I Were the Baby.* Nashville: Ideal. (Family)

P, I   Lowrey, L. 1995. *Somebody Somewhere Knows My Name.* Minneapolis: Carolrhoda. (Abandoned children, homeless)

P, I   Luenn, N. 1990. *Nessa's Fish.* New York: Atheneum. (Family, elderly)

I   MacLachlin, P. 1985. *Sarah, Plain and Tall.* New York: Harper & Row. (Family)

P   Mederias, A. S. 1991. *Dancing with the Indians.* New York: Holiday House. (Family, African American history, Native American history)

P, I   Mederias, A. S. 1989. *Our People.* New York: Atheneum. (African American history, elderly)

P   Merriam, E. 1989. *Mommies at Work.* New York: Little Simon. (Gender equity, family)

P   Mitchell, B. 1993. *Down Buttermilk Lane.* New York: Lothrop. (Amish family)

P   Mitchell, R. P. 1993. *Hue Boy.* New York: Dial. (African family, self-concept)

P   Mora, P. 1992. *A Birthday Basket for Tia.* New York: Macmillan. (Hispanic family)

P   Mora, P. 1994. *Pablo's Tree.* New York: Macmillan. (Hispanic family)

I   Myers, W. D. 1988. *Won't Know Till I Get There.* New York: Puffin. (Family)

I   Namioka, L. 1995. *Yang the Third and Her Impossible Family.* Boston: Little, Brown. (Chinese American family)

I   Namioka, L. 1992. *Yang the Youngest and His Terrible Ear.* Boston: Little, Brown. (Chinese family, Anglo family)

P   Nelson, M. N. 1988. *Always Gramma.* New York: Putnam. (Elderly—nursing home)

P, I   Newman, L. 1995. *Gloria Goes to Gay Pride.* (Family, gay)

I   Nez, R. T., as told to K. Wilder. 1995. *Forbidden Talent.* Flagstaff, AZ: Northland. (Navajo family, elderly)

I   Nolan, D. 1988. *Wolf Child.* New York: Macmillan. (Family—different perspectives)

P   Nye, N. S. 1993. *Siti's Secrets.* New York: Simon & Schuster. (Elderly; Palestinian/Arab American family)

P   Otey, M. 1990. *Daddy Has a Pair of Striped Shorts.* New York: Farrar, Straus, & Giroux. (Family, stereotyping)

I   Perkins, M. 1993. *The Sunita Experiment.* Boston: Little, Brown. (Indian family, elderly)

P   Peterson, J. 1994. *My Mamma Sings.* New York: HarperCollins. (African American family)

P   Polacco, P. 1990. *Babushka's Doll.* New York: Simon & Schuster. (Russian family, elderly)

P   Polacco, P. 1992. *Chicken Sunday.* New York: Philomel. (Russian family, holiday)

P   Polacco, P. 1990. *Just Plain Fancy.* New York: Dell. (Amish family)

P   Polacco, P. 1988. *The Keeping Quilt.* New York: Simon & Schuster. (Family—quilt)

P   Polacco, P. 1988. *Rechenka's Eggs.* New York: Philomel. (Russian family, holiday)

P   Politi, L. 1994. *Three Stalks of Corn.* New York: Aladdin. (Hispanic family)

P   Pomerantz, C. 1989. *The Chalk Doll.* Philadelphia: Lippincott. (Jamaican family)

P, I   Powell, E. S. 1991. *Daisy.* Minneapolis: Carolrhoda/First Avenue. (Family—child abuse)

P   Quinlan, P. 1994. *Tiger Flowers.* New York: Dial. (Family—AIDS)

P   Ray, M. L. 1994. *Shaker Boy.* San Diego: Harcourt. (Civil War, Shaker family)

P, I   Rosen, M. J. 1992. *Elijah's Angel.* San Diego: Harcourt Brace. (Jewish family, Christians)

P   Ryland, C. 1982. *When I Was Young in the Mountains.* New York: Puffin. (Appalachian family)

I   Samuels, G. 1991. *Yours, Bret.* New York: Lodestar. (Family—foster care)

I   Sanders, D. 1990. *Clover: A Novel.* Boston: Hall. (Interracial family)

P   Say, A. 1993. *Grandfather's Journey.* Boston: Houghton Mifflin. (Japanese family)

P   Say, A. 1991. *Tree of Cranes.* Boston: Houghton Mifflin. (Family—adoption)

P   Scott, A. H. 1992. *On Mother's Lap.* New York: Clarion. (Asian American family)

P   Simon, N. 1975. *All Kinds of Families.* Chicago: Albert Whitman. (Family; differences and likenesses)

P, I   Singer, M. 1994. *Family Reunion.* New York: Macmillan/Simon & Schuster. (Extended family)

P   Skutch, R. 1995. *Who's in a Family?* Berkeley: Tricycle Press. (Family; differences and likenesses)

P   Smalls, I. 1992. *Jonathan and His Mommy.* Boston: Little, Brown. (African American family)

I   Smith, D. B. 1994. *Remember the Red-Shouldered Hawk.* New York: Putnam. (Family; challenged—Alzheimer's; elderly)

P   Sonneborn, R. 1970. *Friday Night Is Papa Night.* New York: Puffin. (Hispanic family)

P   Sorensen, V. 1983. *Plain Girl.* San Diego: Harcourt Brace. (Amish family)

P   Soto, G. 1993. *Too Many Tamales.* New York: Putnam. (Food—Hispanic)

P   Steptoe, J. 1980. *Daddy Is a Monster . . . Sometimes.* New York: Harper. (Single-parent family)

P   Stevens, J. R. 1993. *Carlos and the Squash Plant.* Flagstaff, AZ: Northland. (Hispanic family)

P   Stoltz, M. 1991. *Go Fish.* New York: HarperCollins. (African American family)

P   Sun, C. F. 1994. *Mama Bear.* Boston: Houghton Mifflin. (Asian American family)

P   Surat, M. M. 1983. *Angel Child, Dragon Child.* New York: Scholastic. (Vietnamese American family, stereotyping)

I   Taylor, E. E. 1990. *Thank You, Dr. Martin Luther King, Jr.!* New York: Watts. (African American family, African American history)

I   Taylor, M. D. 1976. *Roll of Thunder, Hear My Cry.* New York: Dial. (African American family, prejudice)

P, I   Thomas, J. R. 1994. *Lights on the River.* New York: Hyperion. (Migrant workers, Mexican family)

P   Tompert, A. 1994. *Will You Come Back for Me?* Morton Grove, IL: Albert Whitman. (Asian American family)

P   Tsaitui, Y. 1988. *Anna in Charge.* New York: Viking. (Self-concept, Japanese family)

P   Turner, A. 1990. *Through Moon and Stars and Night Skies.* New York: HarperCollins. (Family—adoption)

P   Udry, J. M. 1966. *What Mary Jo Shared.* New York: Scholastic. (African American family)

P, I   Vigna, J. 1995. *My Two Uncles.* New York: Whitman. (Gay uncle)

P, I   Wallner, A. 1992. *Since 1920.* New York: Doubleday. (Native American family; houses and homes)

P   Walter, M. P. 1983. *My Mama Needs Me.* New York: Macmillan. (African American family)

P, I   Weisman, J. 1993. *The Storyteller.* New York: Rizzoli. (Native American family, elderly)

P   Willhoite, M. 1990. *Daddy's Roommate.* Boston: Alyson Wonderland. (Family—gay)

P   Williams, V. B. 1982. *A Chair for My Mother.* New York: Scholastic. (Hispanic family)

P   Williams, V. B. 1982. *Music, Music for Everyone.* New York: Greenwillow. (Hispanic family)

P   Williams, V. B. 1982. *Something Special for Me.* New York: Greenwillow. (Hispanic family)

I   Willis, P. 1991. *A Place to Call Home.* New York: Clarion. (Family—orphan)

P   Wilson, B. P. 1990. *Jenny.* New York: Macmillan. (African American family)

I   Woodson, J. 1991. *The Dear One.* San Diego: Delacorte. (African American family)

I   Yep, L. 1988. *Child of the Owl.* New York: Harper & Row. (Chinese American family, elderly, Chinese American culture)

I   Yep, L. 1975. *Dragonwings.* New York: Harper. (Chinese American family)

I   Yep, L. 1995. *Later, Gator.* New York: Hyperion. (Chinese American family)

P   Yolan, J. 1987. *Owl Moon.* New York: Philomel. (Family, environment)

Foods—Different Perspectives/Hunger

P   Aliki. 1976. *Corn Is Maize: The Gift of the Indians.* New York: HarperCollins. (Food—different perspectives; Native Americans)

P, I   Blackmore, V. 1984. *Why Corn Is Golden: Stories about Plants.* Boston: Little, Brown. (Food—different perspectives; Mexican tales)

P   Brady, A. A. 1995. *Kwanzaa Karamu: Cooking and Crafts for a Kwanzaa Feast.* Minneapolis: Carolrhoda. (African American holiday, food)

P, I   Di Salvo-Ryan, F. D. 1992. *Uncle Willie and the Soup Kitchen.* New York: Morrow. (Family, hunger)

Dooley, N. 1991. *Everybody Cooks Rice.* Minneapolis: Carolrhoda. (Food—different perspectives)

P   Gershator, D., & Gershator, P. 1995. *Bread Is for Eating.* New York: Holt. (Food—different perspectives)

P   Hughes, M. 1996. *A Handful of Seeds.* New York: Orchard. (Hispanic family; foods—different perspectives)

P   Paulsen, G. 1995. *The Tortilla Factory.* San Diego: Harcourt Brace. (Food—different perspectives)

I   Penner, L. R. 1994. *The Native American Feast.* New York: Macmillan/Simon & Schuster. (Native American cooking)

I   Peters, R. M. 1992. *Clambake: A Wampanoag Tradition.* Minneapolis: Lerner. (Wampanoag culture)

P   Polacco, P. 1992. *Chicken Sunday.* New York: Philomel. (Russian family, holiday)

P   Politi, L. 1994. *Three Stalks of Corn.* New York: Aladdin. (Food—Hispanic)

P   Portnay, M. A. 1994. *Matzah Ball.* Rockville, MD: Kar-Ben Copies. (Food—Jewish; Jewish holiday)

P, I   Rattigan, J. K. 1993. *Dumpling Soup.* Boston: Little, Brown. (Holiday, Hawaiian new year)

P, I   Regguinti, G. 1991. *The Sacred Harvest: Ojibway Wild Rice Gathering.* Minneapolis: Lerner. (Ojibway wild rice gathering)

P, I   Rosen, M. J., ed. 1994. *The Greatest Table: A Banquet to Fight against Hunger.* San Diego: Harcourt Brace. (Hunger)

P   Soto, G. 1993. *Too Many Tamales.* New York: Putnam. (Food—Hispanic)

Gender Equity

P, I   Ashby, R., & Ohrn, D. G. 1995. *Herstory: Women Who Changed the World.* New York: Viking. (Famous women)

P, I   Blumberg, R. 1993. *Bloomers.* New York: Bradbury. (Women of the women's rights movement, social activism)

P, I   Bruchas, J., & Ross, G. 1994. *The Girl Who Married the Moon: Tales from Native North America.* Mahwah, NJ: Bridgewater. (Native American tales, gender equity)

P, I   Cole, B. 1992. *Prince Cinders.* New York: Putnam. (Fairy tale—gender-equity version of *Cinderella*)

I   Dorris, M. 1987. *Yellow Raft in Blue Water.* New York: Warner. (Native American women)

I   Fritz, J. 1995. *You Want Women to Vote, Lizzie Stanton.* New York: Putnam. (Suffrage campaign)

P, I   Hamilton, V. 1995. *Her Stories: African American Folktales, Fairy Tales, and True Tales.* New York: Blue Sky. (Tales from different cultures, gender equity)

P   Hines, A. G. 1986. *Daddy Makes the Best Spaghetti.* New York: Clarion. (Family, gender equity)

P   Hoffman, M. 1991. *Amazing Grace.* New York: Dial. (Self-concept, gender equity, African Americans)

P   Merriam, E. 1989. *Mommies at Work.* Boston: Little Simon. (Gender equity, family)

P, I   Munsch, R. 1980. *The Paper Bag Princess.* Toronto: Annick Press. (Fairy tale—gender equity)

Phelps, E. J. 1981. *The Maid of the North: Feminist Folk Tales from around the World.* New York: Holt. (Tales—gender equity)

P, I   San Souci, R. D. 1993. *Cut from the Same Cloth: American Women of Myth, Legend, and Tall Tales.* New York: Philomel. (Tales—gender equity)

I   Weatherford, D. 1995. *Foreign and Female: Immigrant Women in America 1840–1930.* New York: Facts on File. (Immigration, gender equity)

I   Wrede, P. 1990. *Dealing with Dragons.* New York: Harcourt Brace. (Gender equity)

P   Zolotow, C. 1972. *William's Doll.* New York: Harper & Row. (Self-concept, gender equity)

Hispanic History, Culture, and Contributions

P, I   Altman, L. J. 1993. *Amelia's Road.* New York: Lee & Low. (Migrant workers, Hispanic people)

P   Ancona, G. 1994. *The Pinata Maker: El Pinatero.* San Diego: Harcourt Brace. (Mexican fiestas; Spanish–English language)

I   Ashabranner, B. 1985. *Dark Harvest: Migrant Workers in America.* New York: Putnam. (Migrant workers, Hispanic people)

P, I   Ashby, R., & Ohrn, D. G. 1995. *Herstory: Women Who Changed the World.* New York: Viking. (Famous women)

I   Atkin, B. A. 1993. *Voices from the Fields: Children of Migrant Farmworkers Tell Their Stories.* Boston: Little, Brown. (Migrant workers)

P   Behrens, J. 1978. *Fiesta! Cinco de Mayo.* Chicago: Children's Press. (Hispanic holiday)

I   Belting, N. M. 1992. *Moon Was Tired of Walking on Air.* Boston: Houghton Mifflin. (South American Indian myths)

P   Bernier-Grand, C. T. 1995. *Poets of Puerto Rico: Don Luis Munoz Marin.* New York: Orchard. (Famous Puerto Rican)

I   Borton de Tevino, E. 1988. *El Guero: An Adventure Story.* New York: Farrar, Straus, & Giroux. (Mexican history)

I   Brimner, L. D. 1992. *A Migrant Family.* Minneapolis: Lerner. (Mexican American migrant family)

P   Bunting, E. 1994. *A Day's Work.* New York: Clarion. (Migrant workers, Latino American family, Latino American history)

P, I   Bunting, E. 1994. *Smoky Nights.* San Diego: Harcourt Brace. (Los Angeles riots)

P   Cherry, L. 1995. *The Great Kapok Trees.* New York: Dial. (Environment, Latinos)

P, I   Codye, C. 1990. *Vilma Martinez.* Chatham, NJ: Raintree/Steck-Vaughn. (Famous Hispanic women, social activism)

P   Conrad, P. 1991. *Pedro's Journal.* New York: Scholastic. (Columbus—different perspectives)

P   Cowcher, H. 1988. *Rain Forest.* Lancaster, PA: Starburst. (Environment)

I   Cumpian, C. 1994. *Poems about Latino Americans.* Chicago: Children's Press. (Poems, famous Latino Americans)

P, I   DeRuiz, D. C. 1993. *The Causa: The Migrant Farm Workers' Story.* Chatham, NJ: Raintree/Austin: Steck-Vaughn. (Famous Hispanic people—Cesar Chavez and Delores Huerta; social activism; migrant workers)

I   De Varona, F. 1993. *Miguel Hidalgo y Costilla: Father of Mexican Independence.* Brookfield, CT: Millbrook. (Hispanic heritage)

P   Doherty, C. A., & Doherty, K. M. 1991. *Nine Days until Christmas: A Mexican Story.* New York: Puffin. (Mexican holiday)

P   Dorros, A. 1993. *Radio Man.* New York: HarperCollins. (Migrant worker, Hispanic people, Spanish and English languages)

I   Fradin, D. B., & Fradin, J. B. 1995. *Puerto Rico.* Danbury, CT: Children's Press. (Puerto Rican history, Puerto Rican culture)

I   Garcia, G. 1995. *Spirit of the Maya: A Boy Explores His People's Mysterious Past.* New York: Simon & Schuster. (Maya culture)

P, I   Garcia, M. 1987. *The Adventures of Connie and Diego.* San Francisco: Children's Book Press. (Hispanic and biracial people)

I   Gernard, R. 1988. *The Cuban Americans.* New York: Chelsea House. (Cuban American history)

I   Gleiter, J. 1989. *Diego Rivera.* Milwaukee: Raintree. (Hispanic people)

P, I   Gordon, G. 1993. *My Two Worlds.* New York: Clarion. (Dominican Republic Christmas)

P   Grossman, P. 1994. *Saturday Market.* New York: Lothrop, Lee & Shepard. (Hispanic people)

I   Haskins, J. 1989. *Count Your Way through Mexico.* Minneapolis: Carolrhoda. (Mexican language)

I   Haskins, J. 1982. *The New Americans: Cuban Boat People.* New York: Chelsea House. (Cuban American history, Cuban immigration)

I   Hewett, F. P. 1990. *Hector Lives in the United States Now: The Story of a Mexican American Child.* Philadelphia: Lippincott. (Immigration, Mexican American family)

I   Hijuelos, O. 1989. *Mambo Kings Play Songs of Love: A Novel.* New York: Farrar, Straus, & Giroux. (Cuban Americans)

I   Hoobler, D. T. 1994. *The Mexican American Family Album.* New York: Oxford University Press. (Mexican American history, Mexican American immigration)

I   Hoobler, D. T., & Hoobler, T. 1995. *The Cuban American Family Album.* New York: Oxford University Press. (Cuban American history, Cuban American immigration)

I   Johnson, J. 1995. *Puerto Rico.* Minneapolis: Lerner. (Puerto Rican history, Puerto Rican culture)

I   Krull, K. 1994. *The Other Side: How Kids Live in a California Latino Neighborhood.* New York: Lodestar. (Latino American culture)

I   Krumgold, J. 1953. *And Now Miguel.* New York: Crowell. (Hispanic people)

I   Lasky, K. 1994. *Days of the Dead.* New York: Hyperion. (Mexican family, holiday)

P, I   Lattimore, D. N. 1988. *Why There Is No Arguing in Heaven: A Mayan Myth.* New York: Harper. (Maya creation story)

P, I   Lewis, R. 1991. *All of You Was Singing.* New York: Atheneum. (Aztec myth)

I   Machado, A. M. 1995. *Exploration into Latin America.* Parsippany, NY: New Discovery. (Latino American culture)

P, I   Markin, P. M. 1993. *The Little Painter of Sabana Grande.* New York: Bradbury. (Houses and homes)

P, I   McLeish, K., & McLeish, L. 1991. *Famous People.* Mahwah, NJ: Troll. (Famous people)

I   Meltzer, M. 1982. *The Hispanic Americans.* New York: HarperCollins. (Latino history)

I   Mendez, A. 1994. *Cubans in America.* Minneapolis: Lerner. (Cuban American history)

P   Mohr, N. 1993. *All for the Better: A Story of El Barrio.* Austin, TX: Raintree/Steck-Vaughn. (Puerto Rican contributions, social activism)

P, I   Mohr, N., & Martorell, A.1995. *The Song of El Coqui and Other Tales of Puerto Rico.* New York: Viking. (Puerto Rican culture)

P, I   Mora, F. 1994. *Pablo and Pimiento.* Flagstaff, AZ: Northland. (Migrant workers, Hispanic people, Spanish and English languages)

I   Morey, J., & Dunn, W. 1989. *Famous Mexican Americans.* New York: Cobblehill Books. (Mexican American history)

I   Nye, N. S. 1995. *The Tree Is Older Than You Are: A Bilingual Gathering of Poems and Stories from Mexico with Paintings by Mexican Artists.* New York: Simon & Schuster. (Bilingual literature, Mexican poems, Mexican culture)

I   Pelta, K. 1991. *Discovering Christopher Columbus: How History Is Invented.* Minneapolis: Lerner. (Columbus—different perspectives)

I   *Peoples of North America.* New York: Chelsea House. (Series of fifty-one books about immigration, etc.)

P   Pico, F. 1994. *The Red Comb.* Mahwah, NJ: Bridgewater. (Puerto Rican slavery)

I   Powers, T. J., & Galvin, J. L. 1989. *Champions of Change: Biographies of Famous Hispanic Americans.* Austin: Steck-Vaughn. (Hispanic history)

I   Presilla, M. E. 1994. *Feliz Nochebueño, Feliz Navidad: Christmas Feasts of the Hispanic Carribean.* New York: Holt. (Caribbean Christmas)

I   Presilla, M. E., & Soto, G. 1996. *Life around the Lake: Embroideries by the Women of Lake Patzcuaro.* New York: Holt. (Hispanic culture, environment)

I   Press, P. 1995. *Puerto Rican Americans.* New York: Benchmark. (Puerto Rican American culture)

I   Rappoport, K. 1993. *Bobby Bonnilla.* New York: Walker. (Famous Puerto Rican American)

P   Reisner, L. 1993. *Margaret and Margarita.* New York: Greenwillow. (Spanish and English languages)

P   Ringgold, F. 1979. *Tar Beach.* New York: Crown. (Puerto Rican history)

I   Sabin, L. 1992. *Roberto Clemente: Young Baseball Hero.* Mahwah, NJ: Troll. (Latino American history)

P   Sánchez, I. 1991. *Mis Primeros . . . Números.* New York: Barron's. (Spanish language)

P   Schotter, R. 1993. *The Fruit and Vegetable Man.* Boston: Little, Brown. (Hispanic people)

P, I   Spurr, E. 1995. *Lupe & Me.* New York: Gulliver. (Mexican culture; immigration; Spanish and English languages)

P   Stanek, M. 1990. *I Speak English for My Mom.* Niles, IL: Albert Whitman. (Spanish language)

P   Thomas, J. R. 1994. *Lights on the River.* New York: Hyperion. (Migrant workers; Spanish and English languages)

P   Van Laan, N. 1991. *The Legend of El Dorado: A Latin American Tale.* New York: Knopf. (Latin American tale)

I   Vazauez, A. M., & Casas, R. E. 1987. *Cuba: Enchantment of the World.* Chicago: Children's Press. (Cuban history, Cuban culture)

I   Westridge Young Writer's Workshop. 1992. *Kids Explore America's Hispanic Heritage.* Santa Fe, NM: John Muir. (Mexican American culture)

I   White, F. M. 1973. *Cesar Chavez: Man of Courage.* Champaign, IL: Garrard. (Hispanic history)

P   Winter, J. 1991. *Diego.* New York: Knopf. (Latino history)

P, I   Zak, M. 1994. *Save My Rainforest.* Volcano, CA: Volcano Press. (Environment, Mexicans, social activism)

I   Zapater, B. M. 1992. *Fiesta!* Cleveland, OH: Modern Curriculum Press. (Latin American history, Latin American holidays)

Holidays

P, I   Adler, D. A. 1995. *One Yellow Daffodil: A Hanukkah Story.* New York: Gulliver. (Jewish holiday)

P   Ancona, G. 1994. *The Pinata Maker: El Pinatero.* San Diego: Harcourt Brace. (Mexican fiestas; Spanish–English language)

P   Behrens, J. 1978. *Fiesta! Cinco de Mayo.* Chicago: Children's Press. (Hispanic holiday)

P   Behrens, J. 1982. *Gung Hay Fat Choy!* Chicago: Children's Press. (Asian American holiday)

P   Behrens, J. 1983. *Hanukkah.* Chicago: Children's Press. (Jewish holiday)

P   Brady, A. A. 1995. *Kwanzaa Karamu: Cooking and Crafts for a Kwanzaa Feast.* Minneapolis: Carolrhoda. (African American holiday, food)

P   Chin, K. 1995. *Sam and the Lucky Money.* New York: Lee & Low. (Chinese New Year)

P   Cohen, B. 1994. *Make a Wish, Molly.* New York: Doubleday. (Jewish holiday)

I   Cohn, J. 1995. *The Christmas Menorahs: How a Town Fought Hatred.* New York: Whitman. (Jewish and Christian holidays, prejudice)

P, I   Czernecki, S., & Rhodes, T. 1992. *Pancho's Pinata.* New York: Hyperion. (Holiday, Hispanic family)

P, I   Delacre, L. 1990. *Las Navidades: Popular Christmas Songs from Latin America.* New York: Scholastic. (Latin American songs, Latin American holiday)

P   Delacre, L. 1993. *Vejigante/Masquerader.* New York: Scholastic. (Latin American holiday)

P   Doherty, C. A., & Doherty, K. M. 1991. *Nine Days until Christmas: A Mexican Story.* New York: Puffin. (Mexican holiday)

P, I   Fluek, T., & Finkler, L. 1994. *Passover: As I Remember It.* New York: Doubleday. (Jewish history, Jewish holiday)

P   Godden, R. 1997. *Premlata and the Festival of Lights.* New York: Greenwillow. (Indian holiday)

P, I   Gordon, G. 1993. *My Two Worlds.* New York: Clarion. (Dominican Republic Christmas)

P   Haggerty, M. E. 1993. *A Crack in the Wall.* New York: Lee & Low. (Family, holiday, Hispanic people)

P   Harness, C. 1995. *Papa's Christmas Gift: Around the World the Night before Christmas.* New York: Simon & Schuster. (Christmas around the world)

I   Hoyt-Goldsmith, D. 1994. *Days of the Dead: A Mexican–American Celebration.* New York: Holiday House. (Mexican American holiday)

I   Jaffe, N. 1993. *The Uninvited Guest and Other Jewish Holiday Tales.* New York: Scholastic. (Jewish holiday tales)

P   Koltach, A. 1992. *The Jewish Child's First Book of Why?* New York: Jonathan David. (Jewish history, Jewish holidays)

I   Lasky, K. 1994. *Days of the Dead.* New York: Hyperion. (Mexican family, holiday)

P, I   Livingston, M. C. 1996. *Festivals.* New York: Holiday House. (Holidays in India)

I   McKissack, P., & McKissack, F. 1994. *Christmas in the Big House, Christmas in the Quarters.* New York: Scholastic. (African American history, Civil War, holidays)

P, I   Miles, C. 1993. *Calvin's Christmas Wish.* New York: Viking. (African American author)

P   Mora, P. 1992. *A Birthday Basket for Tia.* New York: Macmillan. (Hispanic family, holiday)

P   Mora, P. 1994. *Pablo's Tree.* New York: Macmillan. (Hispanic family)

P, I   Newton Chocolate, D. M. 1990. *Kwanzaa.* Chicago: Children's Press. (African American holiday)

P   Newton Chocolate, D. M. 1992. *My First Kwanzaa Book.* New York: Scholastic. (African American holiday)

P, I   Pennington, D. 1994. *Itse Selu: Cherokee Harvest Festival.* Watertown, MA: Charlesbridge. (Cherokee festival)

P   Polacco, P. 1992. *Chicken Sunday.* New York: Philomel. (Russian family, holiday)

P   Polacco, P. 1988. *Rechenka's Eggs.* New York: Philomel. (Russian family, holiday)

P   Portnay, M. A. 1994. *Matzah Ball.* Rockville, MD: Kar-Ben Copies. (Food—Jewish; Jewish holiday)

I   Presilla, M. E. 1994. *Feliz Nochebueno, Feliz Navidad: Christmas Feasts of the Hispanic Carribean.* New York: Holt. (Caribbean Christmas)

P, I   Rattigan, J. K. 1993. *Dumpling Soup.* Boston: Little, Brown. (Holiday, Hawaiian new year)

P   Reddix, V. 1991. *Dragon Kite of Autumn Moon.* New York: Lothrop, Lee & Shepard. (Elderly; Chinese holiday)

P, I   Rhea, M. 1992. *An Ellis Island Christmas.* New York: Viking. (Immigration, holidays)

P, I   Rosen, M. J. 1992. *Elijah's Angel.* San Diego: Harcourt Brace. (Jewish family, Christian holiday)

P   Schotter, R. 1995. *Passover Magic.* Boston: Little, Brown. (Jewish holiday)

P, I Schnur, S. 1995. *The Tie Man's Miracle: A Chanukka Tale.* New York: Morrow. (Jewish tale, Jewish holiday)

P, I Sherman, O., & Schwartz, L. S. 1989. *The Four Questions.* New York: Dial. (Passover story)

P Soto, G. 1993. *Too Many Tamales.* New York: Putnam. (Food—Hispanic)

P Taylor, S. 1980. *Danny Loves a Holiday.* New York: Dutton. (Jewish holiday)

I Walter, M. P. 1995. *Kwanzaa: A Family Affair.* New York: Lothrop, Lee & Shepard. (African American holiday)

P Waters, K., & Slvenz-Low, M. 1990. *Lion Dancer: Ernie Wan's Chinese New Year.* New York: Scholastic. (Chinese holiday)

P Weiss, N. 1992. *The First Night of Hanukkah.* New York: Putnam/Grosset & Dunlap. (Jewish holiday)

I Zapater, B. M. 1992. *Fiesta!* Cleveland, OH: Modern Curriculum Press. (Latin American history, Latin American holidays)

Houses, Homes, and the Homeless

I Ackerson, K. 1991. *The Leaves in October.* New York: Atheneum. (Life in a homeless shelter)

I Bial, R. 1993. *Frontier Home.* Boston: Houghton Mifflin. (Houses and homes)

P Buchanan, K. 1994. *This House Is Made of Mud.* Flagstaff, AZ: Northland. (Houses and homes, Hispanic people)

P, I Bunting, E. 1991. *Fly Away Home.* New York: Clarion. (Homeless)

P Dorros, A. 1992. *This Is My House.* New York: Scholastic. (Houses and homes)

P Emberly, R. 1990. *My House: A Book Written in Two Languages.* Boston: Little, Brown. (Spanish and English languages; houses and homes)

P Eversole, R. H. 1992. *The Magic House.* New York: Orchard. (Houses—different perspectives)

P, I Guzzetti, R. 1996. *The White House.* New York: Simon & Schuster. (Houses and homes)

I Hammond, A. 1991. *The Home We Have Made.* New York: Crown. (Hispanic people, homeless people)

P, I Hathorn, J. 1994. *Way Home.* New York: Crown. (Homeless people)

P Hoberman, A. 1978. *A House Is a House for Me.* New York: Viking. (Houses and homes)

P Jackson, M. 1995. *Homes around the World.* Austin: Steck-Vaughn. (Houses and homes)

I Janeczko, P. B., ed. 1995. *Wherever Home Begins: 100 Contemporary Poems.* New York: Orchard. (Poems, homes)

I   Knight, M. B. 1996. *Talking Walls.* Gardiner, ME: Tilbury. (Houses—different perspectives)

P, I   Lowrey, L. 1995. *Somebody Somewhere Knows My Name.* Minneapolis: Carolrhoda. (Abandoned children, homeless people)

P   McDonald, M. 1996. *My House Has Stars.* New York: Orchard. (Homes—different perspectives)

P   Malone, N. L. 1988. *A Home.* New York: Bradbury. (Houses and homes)

P   Manning, M. 1994. *A Ruined House.* Cambridge, MA: Candlestick Press. (Houses and homes)

P, I   Markin, P. M. 1993. *The Little Painter of Sabana Grande.* New York: Bradbury. (Houses and homes)

I   Monroe, J. G., & Williamson, R. A. 1993. *First Houses: Native Americans' Homes and Sacred Structures.* Boston: Houghton Mifflin. (Houses and homes)

P   Morris, A. 1990. *Houses and Homes.* New York: Lothrop, Lee & Shepard. (Differences and likenesses; houses and homes)

P, I   Rosen, M. J., ed. 1992. *Home: A Collaboration of Thirty Distinguished Authors and Illustrators of Children's Books to Aid the Homeless.* New York: HarperCollins. (Homeless people)

P, I   Ryland, C. 1992. *An Angel for Solomon Singer.* New York: Orchard Books. (Homeless people)

P   Schermbruber, R. 1991. *Charlie's House.* New York: Viking. (South African houses and homes)

P   Shelby, A. 1995. *Homeplace.* New York: Orchard. (Home from 1819 to present)

I   Weatherford, D. 1995. *Foreign and Female: Immigrant Women in America 1840–1930.* New York: Facts on File. (Immigration, gender equity)

P, I   Wallner, A. 1992. *Since 1920.* New York: Doubleday. (Native American family; houses and homes)

P, I   Wolf, B. 1995. *Homeless.* New York: Orchard. (Homeless people)

Jewish History, Culture, and Contributions (Including the Holocaust and World War II)

P, I   Adler, D. A. 1994. *Hilde and Eli: Children of the Holocaust.* New York: Holiday House. (Holocaust)

P, I   Adler, D. A. 1993. *A Picture Book of Anne Frank.* New York: Holiday House. (Jewish history, World War II)

I   Barrie, B. 1990. *Lone Star.* New York: Delacorte. (Jewish history)

P   Ehrlich, A. 1989. *The Story of Hanukkah.* New York: Dial. (Jewish history)

P   Fisher, L. E. 1989. *The Wailing Wall.* New York: Macmillan. (Jewish history)

P, I Fluek, T., & Finkler, L. 1994. *Passover: As I Remember It.* New York: Doubleday. (Jewish history, Jewish holiday)

I Freidman, I. 1982. *Escape or Die: True Stories of Young People Who Survived the Holocaust.* Reading, MA: Addison Wesley. (Jewish history, Holocaust)

P, I Hest, A. 1990. *The Ring and the Window Seat.* New York: Scholastic. (Jewish people, Holocaust)

P Katz, B. 1992. *A Family Hanukkah.* New York: Random House. (Jewish traditions)

P Kimmel, E. 1988. *The Chanukkah Guest.* New York: Holiday House. (Jewish traditions)

P Koltach, A. 1992. *The Jewish Child's First Book of Why?* New York: Jonathan David. (Jewish history, Jewish holidays)

I Leveitin, P. 1993. *Journey to America.* New York: Atheneum. (Jewish history, World War II, immigration)

I Meltzer, M. 1976. *Never to Forget: The Jews of the Holocaust.* New York: Harper & Row. (Jewish people, Holocaust)

I Meltzer, M. 1988. *The Story of How the Gentiles Saved Jews in the Holocaust.* New York: Harper & Row. (Jewish history, Holocaust)

I Perl, L. 1994. *Issac Bashevis Singer: The Life of a Storyteller.* Philadelphia: Jewish Publication Society. (Famous Jewish American, immigration)

P Polacco, P. 1992. *Mrs. Katz and Tush.* New York: Dell. (Elderly; Jewish history; African American history)

P Portnay, M. A. 1994. *Matzah Ball.* Rockville, MD: Kar-Ben Copies. (Food—Jewish; Jewish holiday)

I Potok, C. 1967. *The Chosen.* New York: Simon & Schuster. (Jewish history)

I Sherman, E. 1990. *Independence Avenue.* Philadelphia: Jewish Publication Society. (Jewish history; Jewish immigration—Galveston movement)

P, I Sherman, O., & Swartz, L. S. 1989. *The Four Questions.* New York: Dial. (Passover story)

Languages

P Ancona, G. 1994. *The Pinata Maker: El Pinatero.* San Diego: Harcourt Brace. (Mexican fiestas; Spanish–English language)

P Dorros, A. 1993. *Radio Man.* New York: HarperCollins. (Migrant worker; Hispanic people; Spanish and English languages)

P Emberly, R. 1993. *Let's Go: A Book in Two Languages.* Boston: Little, Brown. (Spanish and English languages)

P Emberly, R. 1990. *My House: A Book Written in Two Languages.* Boston: Little, Brown. (Spanish and English languages; houses and homes)

P Ets, M. H. 1971. *Mojo Means One.* New York: Dial. (African language)

P Feelings, M. 1974. *Jabo Means Hello.* New York: Dial. (African language)

P Gershator, D., & Gershator, P. 1995. *Bread Is for Eating.* New York: Holt. (Food—different perspectives; Spanish and English languages; song)

I Haskins, J. 1992. *Count Your Way through Africa.* Minneapolis: Carolrhoda. (African languages)

I Haskins, J. 1989. *Count Your Way through Canada.* Minneapolis: Carolrhoda. (French language)

I Haskins, J. 1987. *Count Your Way through China.* Minneapolis: Carolrhoda. (Chinese language)

I Haskins, J. 1990. *Count Your Way through Germany.* Minneapolis: Carolrhoda. (German language)

P, I Haskins, J. 1992. *Count Your Way through India.* Minneapolis: Carolrhoda. (Hindi language)

I Haskins, J. 1987. *Count Your Way through Japan.* Minneapolis: Carolrhoda. (Japanese language)

I Haskins, J. 1989. *Count Your Way through Korea.* Minneapolis: Carolrhoda. (Korean language)

I Haskins, J. 1989. *Count Your Way through Mexico.* Minneapolis: Carolrhoda. (Spanish language)

I Haskins, J. 1987. *Count Your Way through Russia.* Minneapolis: Carolrhoda. (Russian language)

I Haskins, J. 1991. *Count Your Way through the Arab World.* Minneapolis: Carolrhoda. (Arabic language)

P Han, S. C. 1994. *Rabbit's Judgment.* New York: Holt. (Korean language)

P Howlett, B. 1993. *I'm New Here.* Boston: Houghton Mifflin. (Spanish language)

P Lee, H. V. 1994. *At the Beach.* New York: Holt. (Mandarin Chinese language)

P Levine, E. 1989. *I Hate English.* New York: Scholastic. (Chinese and English languages)

P, I Mora, F. 1994. *Pablo and Pimiento.* Flagstaff, AZ: Northland. (Migrant workers; Hispanic people; Spanish and English languages)

I Nye, N. S. 1995. *The Tree Is Older Than You Are: A Bilingual Gathering of Poems and Stories from Mexico with Paintings by Mexican Artists.* New York: Simon & Schuster. (Bilingual literature, Mexican poems, Mexican culture)

P Pena, S. C. 1987. *Kikiriki Stories and Poems in English and Spanish for Children.* Houston: Arte Publico. (Puerto Rican poems; Spanish and English languages)

P   Reiser, L. 1993. *Margaret and Margarita.* New York: Greenwillow. (Spanish and English languages)

P   Robinson, M. 1993. *Cock-a-Doodle Doo!: What Does It Sound Like to You?* Stewart, Tabori, & Chang. (Differences and likenesses, languages)

P   Sánchez, I. 1991. *Mis Primeros . . . Números.* New York: Barron's. (Spanish language)

P   Schick, E. 1993. *I Have Another Language: The Language Is Dance.* Louisville, KY: American Printing House for the Blind. (Challenged, languages)

P, I   Spurr, E. 1995. *Lupe & Me.* New York: Gulliver. (Mexican culture; immigration; Spanish and English languages)

P   Stanek, M. 1990. *I Speak English for My Mom.* Niles, IL: Albert Whitman. (Spanish language)

Migrant Workers

P, I   Altman, L. J., & Sanquez, E. O. 1993. *Amelia's Road.* New York: Lee & Low. (Migrant workers, Hispanic people)

I   Ashabranner, B. 1985. *Dark Harvest: Migrant Workers in America.* New York: Putnam. (Migrant workers, Hispanic people)

I   Atkin, B. A. 1993. *Voices from the Field: Children of Migrant Farmworkers Tell Their Stories.* Boston: Little, Brown. (Hispanic migrant workers)

I   Brimner, L. D. 1992. *A Migrant Family.* Minneapolis: Lerner. (Mexican American migrant family)

P   Bunting, E. 1994. *A Day's Work.* New York: Clarion. (Migrant workers, Mexican American family, Mexican American history)

P, I   Covault, R. 1994. *Pablo and Pimiento.* Flagstaff, AZ: Northland. (Migrant workers, Hispanic people)

P, I   DeRuiz, D.C. 1993. *The Causa: The Migrant Farm Workers' Story.* Chatham, NJ: Raintree/Austin: Steck-Vaughn. (Famous Hispanic people—Cesar Chavez and Delores Huerta; social activism; migrant workers)

P   Dorros, A. 1993. *Radio Man.* New York: HarperCollins. (Migrant worker; Hispanic people; Spanish and English languages)

I   Hoyt-Goldsmith, D. 1996. *Migrant Worker: A Boy from the Rio Grande Valley.* New York: Holiday House. (Migrant workers, Hispanic family, social activism)

P   Thomas, J. R. *Lights on the River.* New York: Hyperion. (Migrant workers; Spanish and English languages)

I   White, F. M. 1973. *Cesar Chavez: Man of Courage.* Champaign, IL: Garrard. (Migrant workers, social activism)

P   Williams, S. A. 1992. *Working Cotton.* San Diego: Harcourt Brace Jovanovich. (Migrant workers)

Native American History, Culture, and Contributions

P   Adler, D. A. 1993. *A Picture Book of Sitting Bull.* New York: Holiday House. (Native American history)

P   Aliki. 1976. *Corn Is Maize: The Gift of the Indians.* New York: HarperCollins. (Native Americans)

I   Andrews, E. 1992. *Indians of the Plains.* New York: Facts on File. (Native American history)

P   Baylor, B. 1994. *The Table Where the Rich People Sit.* New York: Scribner's. (Native Americans)

I   Bruchac, J. 1995. *A Boy Called Slow: The True Story of Sitting Bull.* New York: Philomel. (Lakota hero)

I   Bruchac, J. 1996. *Children of the Longhouse.* New York: Dial. (Mohawk culture, peace)

I   Bruchac, J. 1993. *Flying with the Eagle, Racing with the Bear.* Mahwah, NJ: Bridgewater. (Native American stories)

I   Dagliesch, A. 1954. *The Courage of Sarah Noble.* New York: Scribner's. (Native American history)

I   Doherty, C. A., & Doherty, K. M. 1989. *The Apaches and Navajos.* New York: Watts. (Native American history)

I   Driving Hawk Sneve, V. 1995. *The Hopis.* New York: Holiday House. (Hopi history, culture, and contributions)

I   Driving Hawk Sneve, V. 1994. *The Nez Perce.* New York: Holiday House. (Nez Perce creation myth; Nez Perce history, culture, and contributions)

P, I   Eskoomiak, N. 1990. *Artic Memories.* New York: Holt. (Inuit family, Inuit history)

I   Fradin, D. B. 1992. *Hiawatha: Messenger of Peace.* New York: Magaret McElderry. (Native American history—Iroquois)

I   Fritz, J. 1983. *The Double Life of Pocahontas.* New York: Doubleday. (Native American history)

P, I   Gates, F. 1994. *Owl Eyes.* New York: Lothrop. (Mohawk legend)

P, I   Goble, P. 1990. *Dream Wolf.* New York: Bradbury. (Wolves—Native Americans)

P   Himler, R. 1993. *The Navajos: The First Americans Book.* New York: Holiday House. (Native American history)

P   Himler, R. 1993. *The Sioux: The First Americans Book.* New York: Holiday House. (Native American history)

I   Hirschfielder, A. B., & Singer, B. R., eds. 1991. *Rising Voices: Writings of Young Native Americans.* New York: Scribner's. (Native American family, Native American history)

I   Hotze, S. 1988. *A Circle Unbroken*. New York: Clarion. (Stereotyping, prejudice, Native American history)

P   Hoyt-Goldsmith, D. 1993. *Cherokee Summer*. New York: Holiday House. (Native American family)

I   Hoyt-Goldsmith, D. 1991. *Pueblo Storyteller*. New York: Holiday House. (Native American family)

P, I   Hoyt-Goldsmith, D. 1989. *Totem Pole*. New York: Holiday House. (Tsimshian and Klallam Indians)

P, I   Hubbard, J. 1994. *Shooting Back from the Reservation*. New York: New Press. (Photographs of Native American life taken by Native American youth)

I   Hudson, J. 1989. *Sweetgrass*. New York: Philomel. (Blackfoot Indian history, Blackfoot Indian family)

I   Jassem, K. 1978. *Sacajawea*. Mahwah, NJ: Troll. (Native American history)

I   Katz, W. L., & Franklin, P. A. 1993. *Proudly Red and Black: Stories of African and Native Americans*. New York: Atheneum. (African American history, Native American history)

I   Keegan, M. 1991. *Pueblo Boy: Growing Up in Two Worlds*. New York: Dutton. (Pueblo culture)

I   Kendall, R. 1992. *Eskimo Boy: Life in an Inupiaq Village*. New York: Scholastic. (Eskimo culture)

Kent, Z. 1989. *The Story of Geronimo*. Chicago: Children's Press. (Native American history)

P   Kessel, J. 1983. *Squanto and the First Thanksgiving*. Minneapolis: Carolrhoda. (Native American history, Thanksgiving)

P   King, S. 1993. *Shannon: An Ojibway Dancer*. Minneapolis: Lerner. (Ojibway culture)

I   Klausner, J. 1993. *Sequoyah's Gift: A Portrait of the Cherokee Leader*. New York: HarperCollins. (Cherokee history)

I   Lewin, T. 1994. *The Reindeer People*. New York: Macmillan/Simon & Schuster. (Life of the Lapp people)

I   Liptak, K. 1991. *Indians of the Pacific Northwest*. New York: Facts on File. (Native American history)

P, I   Littlechild, G. 1993. *This Land Is My Land*. Emeryville, CA: Children's Book Press. (Native Americans; Columbus—different perspectives)

P, I   Locker, T. 1991. *The Land of the Gray Wolf*. New York: Dial. (Native American history)

P   Lyon, G. E. 1993. *Dreamplace*. New York: Orchard. (Anasazi history)

P   Lyon, G. E. 1992. *Who Came Down That Road?* New York: Orchard. (Native American history; differences and likenesses)

I   McKissack, P. 1984. *The Apache: A New True Book*. Chicago: Children's Press. (Native American history)

P, I   McLerran, A. 1995. *The Ghost Dance.* New York: Clarion. Native American history)

P   Mederias, A. S. 1991. *Dancing with the Indians.* New York: Holiday House. (Family, African American history, Native American history)

I   O'Dell, S., & Hall, E. 1992. *Thunder Rolling in the Mountains.* New York: Dell. (Nez Perce Indians)

P, I   Ortiz, S. 1988. *The People Shall Continue.* Emeryville, CA: Children's Book Press. (Native American history)

I   Osinski, A. 1992. *The Navajo: A New True Book.* Chicago: Children's Press. (Native American history)

I   Penner, L. R. 1994. *The Native American Feast.* New York: Macmillan/Simon & Schuster. (Native American cooking)

P, I   Pennington, D. 1994. *Itse Selu: Cherokee Harvest Festival.* Watertown, MA: Charlesbridge. (Cherokee festival)

I   Peters, R. M. 1992. *Clambake: A Wampanoag Tradition.* Minneapolis: Lerner. (Wampanoag culture)

P   Raczek, L. T. 1995. *The Night the Grandfathers Died.* Flagstaff, AZ: Northland. (Ute culture, elderly)

P, I   Regguinti, G. 1991. *The Sacred Harvest: Ojibway Wild Rice Gathering.* Minneapolis: Lerner. (Ojibway wild rice gathering)

P   Roessel, M. 1993. *Kinaalda: A Navajo Girl Grows Up.* Minneapolis: Lerner. (Navajo culture)

P, I   Sewall, M. 1990. *People of the Breaking Day.* New York: Atheneum. (Wampanoag Indians)

P   Seymour, T. V. N. 1993. *The Gift of the Changing Women.* New York: Holt. (Navajo culture)

P, I   Stroud, V. A. 1994. *Doesn't Fall Off His Horse.* New York: Dial. (Life of a Kiowa boy in the 1890s)

I   Swentzell, R. 1992. *Children of the Clay: A Family of Pueblo Potters.* Minneapolis: Lerner. (Pueblo culture)

I   Tomcheck, A. H. 1992. *The Hopi: A New True Book.* Chicago: Children's Press. (Native American history)

I   Whitehouse, B. 1994. *Sunpainters: Eclipse of the Navajo Sun.* Flagstaff, AZ: Northland. (Navajo culture)

I   Wolfson, E. 1993. *From the Earth to beyond the Sky: Native American Medicine.* Boston: Houghton Mifflin. (Native American medicine men)

Pilgrimages, Immigration, and Migration

P, I   Anderson, J. 1984. *The First Thanksgiving Feast.* Boston: Houghton Mifflin. (Pilgrim—different perspectives)

I   Anzaldua, G. 1993. *Friends from the Other Side.* San Francisco: Children's Book Press. (Mexican American immigration)

I   Bode, J. 1990. *New Kids on the Block: Oral History of Immigrant Teens.* New York: Watts. (Immigration)

P   Bresnick-Perry, R. 1992. *Leaving for America.* San Francisco: Children's Book Press. (Jewish migration)

P, I   Bunting, E. 1988. *How Many Days to America? A Thanksgiving Story.* New York: Clarion. (Haitian pilgrimage)

I   Buss, F. L. 1991. *Journey of the Sparrows.* New York: Lodestar. (Illegal aliens)

P, I   Cech, J. 1991. *Grandmother's Journey.* New York: Bradbury. (Immigration)

P   Cohen, B. 1983. *Molly's Pilgrim.* New York: Lothrop, Lee & Shepard. (Russian pilgrimage)

P, I   Cooney, B. 1990. *Hattie and the Wild Waves: A Story from Brooklyn.* New York: Viking. (Family, immigration)

I   Cooper, M. 1995. *Bound for the Promised Land: The Great Black Migration.* New York: Lodestar. (African American history, migration)

P, I   Feelings, T. 1972. *Black Pilgrimage.* New York: Lothrop. (African American pilgrimage)

I   Freedman, R. 1995. *Immigrant Kids.* New York: Puffin. (Immigration)

I   Graff, N. P. 1993. *Where the River Runs: A Portrait of a Refugee Family.* Boston: Little, Brown. (Cambodian refugees)

P, I   Harvey, B. 1988. *Cassie's Journey: Going West in the 1860's.* New York: Holiday House. (1860 family, migration)

I   Haskins, J. 1982. *The New Americans: Cuban Boat People.* New York: Chelsea House. (Cuban American history, Cuban immigration)

P   Herrald, M. R. 1995. *A Very Important Day.* New York: Morrow. (Immigration)

P, I   Hewett, F. P. 1990. *Hector Lives in the United States Now: The Story of a Mexican–American Child.* Philadelphia: Lippincott. (Immigration, Mexican American family)

I   Ho, M. 1991. *The Clay Marble.* New York: Farrar, Straus, & Giroux. (Refugees— Thailand, Cambodia)

I   Hoobler, D. T., & Hoobler, T. 1995. *The Cuban American Family Album.* New York: Oxford University Press. (Cuban American history, Cuban American immigration)

I   Hoobler, D., & Hoobler, T. 1994. *The Mexican American Family Album.* New York: Oxford University Press. (Mexican American history, Mexican American immigration)

I   Hospital, J. T. 1987. *Dislocations.* Baton Rouge: Lousiana State University. (Immigration)

P, I   Hoyt-Goldsmith, D. 1992. *Hoang Anh: A Vietnamese–American Boy.* New York: Holiday House. (Vietnamese people, immigration)

I   Jacobs, W. J. 1990. *Ellis Island: New Hope in a New Land.* New York: Scribner's. (Immigration)

I   Kalman, E. 1995. *Tchaikovsky Discovers America.* New York: Orchard. (Russian emigres)

P, I   Kid, D. 1991. *Onion Tears.* New York: Orchard. (Vietnamese immigrant)

I   Kitano, H. H. L. 1995. *The Japanese Americans.* New York: Chelsea House. (Japanese American immigration)

P   Kuklin, S. 1992. *How My Family Lives in America.* New York: Bradbury. (African American, Hispanic, and Chinese immigrants)

I   Larsen, R. J. 1989. *The Puerto Ricans in America.* Minneapolis: Lerner. (Puerto Rican immigration)

P, I   Lawrence J. 1993. *The Great Migration: An American Story.* New York: HarperCollins. (Migration)

I   Lehrman, R. 1992. *The Store That Mama Built.* New York: Macmillan. (Jewish immigration)

I   Leveitin, P. 1993. *Journey to America.* New York: Atheneum. (Jewish history, World War II, immigration)

I   Lingard, J. 1990. *Tug of War.* New York: Lodestar. (Immigration)

P, I   Maestro, B. 1996. *Coming to America: The Story of Immigration.* New York: Scholastic. (Immigration)

I   Mayerson, E. W. 1990. *The Cat Who Escaped from Steerage: A Bubbemeiser.* New York: Scribner's. (Jewish history, immigration)

P   Moss, M. 1994. *In America.* New York: Dutton. (Elderly, immigration from Lithuania)

I   Murphy, J. 1993. *Across America on an Emigrant Train.* New York: Clarion. (Emigrants)

Myers, W. D. 1993. *The Great Migration: An American Story.* New York: HarperCollins. (African American history, migration)

I   *Peoples of North America.* New York: Chelsea House. (Series of fifty-one books about immigration, etc.)

I   Perez, N. A. 1988. *Breaker.* Boston: Houghton Mifflin. (Immigration, prejudice)

I   Perl, L. 1994. *Issac Bashevis Singer: The Life of a Storyteller.* Philadelphia: Jewish Publication Society. (Famous Jewish American, immigration)

P, I   Rhea, M. 1992. *An Ellis Island Christmas.* New York: Viking. (Immigration, holidays)

I   Roseblum, R. 1989. *The Old Synagogue.* Philadelphia: Jewish Publication Society. (Jewish history, immigration)

I   Sandler, M. W. 1995. *Immigrants.* New York: HarperCollins. (Immigration—people around the world)

I   Sewall, M. 1995. *Thunder from the Clear Sky.* New York: Atheneum. (Pilgrims—different perspectives)

P   Shefelman, J. 1992. *A Peddler's Dream.* Boston: Houghton Mifflin. (Immigration)

I   Sherman, E. 1990. *Independence Avenue.* Philadelphia: Jewish Publication Society. (Jewish history; Jewish immigration—Galveston movement)

P, I   Spurr, E. 1995. *Lupe & Me.* New York: Gulliver. (Mexican culture, immigration)

I   Takaki, R. 1994. *In the Heart of Filipino America: Immigrants from the Pacific Isles.* New York: Chelsea House. (Filipino American history, Filipino immigrants)

P   Van Leeuwen, J. 1995. *Across the Wide Dark Sea: The Mayflower Journey.* New York: Dial. (Pilgrimages—Pilgrims)

P, I   Waters, K. 1996. *On the Mayflower: Voyage of the Ship's Apprentice & a Passenger Girl.* New York: Scholastic. (Pilgrimages—different perspectives)

P, I   Waters, K. 1989. *Samuel Easton: A Day in the Life of a Pilgrim Boy.* New York: Scholastic. (Pilgrims—different perspectives)

P, I   Waters, K. 1989. *Sarah Morton's Day: A Day in the Life of a Pilgrim Girl.* New York: Scholastic. (Pilgrims—different perspectives)

P, I   Waters, K. 1996. *Tamenum's Day: A Wampanoag Indian Boy in Pilgrim Times.* New York: Scholastic. (Pilgrims—different perspectives)

I   Weatherford, D. 1995. *Foreign and Female: Immigrant Women in America 1840–1930.* New York: Facts on File. (Immigration, gender equity)

I   Yee, P. 1990. *Tales from Gold Mountains: Stories of the Chinese in the New World.* New York: Macmillan. (Immigration, migration)

I   Yep, L. 1993. *Dragons Gate.* New York: Harper. (Chinese immigration)

Poems, Songs from Different Cultures

P   Adoff, A. 1973. *Black Is Brown Is Tan.* New York: Harper. (African American poetry)

P   Bates, K. L. 1993. *America the Beautiful.* New York: Atheneum. (American poem, song)

I   Begay, S. 1995. *Navajo: Visions and Voices across the Mesa.* New York: Scholastic. (Navajo poems)

P, I   Bryan, A. 1974. *Walk Together Children: Black American Spirituals.* New York: Atheneum/Aladdin. (African American songs)

P, I   Clark, A. N. 1991. *In My Mother's House.* New York: Viking Press. (Native American poems)

P, I   Cohn, A. L. 1993. *From Sea to Shining Sea.* New York: Scholastic. (Multicultural songs and stories)

I   Cumpian, C. 1994. *Poems about Latino Americans.* Chicago: Children's Press. (Poems, famous Latino Americans)

I   Delacre, L. 1989. *Arroz Con Leche: Popular Songs and Rhymes from Latin America.* New York: Scholastic. (Latin American songs, Latin American rhymes)

P, I Delacre, L. 1990. *Las Navidades: Popular Christmas Songs from Latin America.* New York: Scholastic. (Latin American songs, Latin American holiday)

P, I Drinking Hawk Sneve, V. 1988. *Dancing Teepees: Poems of American Indian Youth.* New York: Holiday House. (Native American poems)

P, I Ets, M. H. 1971. *Soul Looks Back in Wonder.* New York: Dial. (African American poems)

P Gershator, D., & Gershator, P. 1995. *Bread Is for Eating.* New York: Holt. (Food—different perspectives; Spanish and English languages; song)

P Greenfield, E. 1978. *Honey, I Love.* New York: Dial. (African American poems)

P Greenfield, E. 1988. *Nathaniel Talking.* New York: Crowell. (African American poems)

P, I Greenfield, E. 1991. *Night on Neighborhood Street.* New York: Crowell. (African American poems)

P, I Hudson, W. 1993. *Pass It On: African American Poetry for Children.* New York: Scholastic. (African American poetry)

I Hughes, L. 1994. *The Dream Keeper.* New York: Knopf. (African American poems)

I Janeczko, P. B., ed. 1995. *Wherever Home Begins: 100 Contemporary Poems.* New York: Orchard. (Poems, homes)

P, I Johnson, J. W. 1995. *Lift Ev'ry Voice and Sing.* New York: Scholastic. (African American songs)

P Mattox, C. W. 1989. *Shake It to the One That You Love the Best.* Nashville: Jig (African American songs)

P, I Myers, W. D. 1993. *Brown Angels: An Album of Pictures and Verse.* New York: HarperCollins. (African American poetry)

I Nye, N. S. 1995. *The Tree Is Older Than You Are: A Bilingual Gathering of Poems and Stories from Mexico with Paintings by Mexican Artists.* New York: Simon & Schuster. (Bilingual literature, Mexican poems, Mexican culture)

I Panzer, N. 1994. *Celebrate America in Poetry and Art.* New York: Hyperion. (America's diversity)

P Pena, S. C. 1987. *Kikiriki Stories and Poems in English and Spanish for Children.* Houston: Arte Publico. (Puerto Rican poems; Spanish and English languages)

I Phillips, N., ed. 1995. *Singing American: Poems That Define a Nation.* New York: Viking. (Pueblo and Sioux Indian songs)

I Soto, G. 1992. *Neighbor Odes.* San Diego: Harcourt Brace Jovanovich. (Mexican American poems)

P Spier, P. 1973. *The Star-Spangled Banner.* New York: Doubleday. (Song—national anthem picture book)

P, I Thomas, J. C. 1993. *Brown Honey in Broomwheat Tea.* New York: HarperCollins. (African American poems)

I   Vuong, L. D. 1993. *Sky Legends from Vietnam.* New York: HarperCollins. (Vietnamese stories, poems, and a song)

I   Wood, N. 1995. *Dancing Moons.* New York: Doubleday. (Native American poems)

I   Wood, N. 1993. *Spirit Walker.* New York: Bantam Doubleday Dell. (Native American poems)

P   Wyndham, R. 1968. *Chinese Mother Goose Rhymes.* New York: Putnam. (Chinese rhymes)

Quilt Stories

P, I   Coer, E., & Young, E. 1986. *The Josefina Story Quilt.* New York: Harper & Row. (Quilt stories—Western movement version)

P   Dorros, A. 1991. *Tonight Is Carnival Night.* New York: Dutton. (Quilt story—Peru)

P   Flournoy, V. 1985. *The Patchwork Quilt.* New York: Dial. (Quilt stories—African American family)

P   Hopkinson, D. 1993. *Sweet Clara and the Freedom Quilt.* New York: Knopf. (Quilt story)

P   Johnston, T. 1985. *The Quilt Story.* New York: Putnam. (Quilt story, pioneer version)

I   Kinsley-Warcock, N. 1989. *The Canada Geese Quilt.* New York: Cobblehill. (Quilt story—Canadian)

I   Lyons, M. E. 1993. *Stitching Stars: The Story Quilts of Harriet Powers.* New York: Scribner's. (African American quilt story)

P   Mills, L. 1991. *The Rag Coat.* Boston: Little, Brown. (Appalachian quilt story)

P, I   Paul, A. W. 1991. *Eight Hands Round: A Patchwork Alphabet.* New York: HarperCollins. (Quilt story—U.S. history)

P   Polacco, P. 1988. *The Keeping Quilt.* New York: Simon & Schuster. (Family—quilt)

I   Turner, R. M. 1992. *Faith Ringgold.* Boston: Little, Brown. (Famous African American women, quilts)

Self-Concept

P   Ashley, B. 1991. *Cleversticks.* New York: Crown. (Self-concept, Asian Americans)

P   Baehr, P. 1989. *School Isn't Fair.* New York: Simon & Schuster. (Self-concept)

P   Carle, E. 1984. *The Mixed-Up Chameleon.* New York: Harper. (Self-concept)

P   Carlson, N. 1990. *I Like Me.* New York: Penguin. (Self-concept)

I   Chaikin, M. 1989. *Feathers in the Wind.* New York: Harper & Row. (Jewish people, self-concept)

P   Cogancherry, H. 1990. *All I Am.* New York: Bradbury. (Self-concept)

P   Greenfield, E. 1977. *African Dream.* New York: Harper. (Self-concept, African Americans)

P   Hoffman, M., & Binch, C. 1991. *Amazing Grace.* New York: Dial. (Self-concept, gender equity, African Americans)

P   Hudson, C. W., & Ford, G. F. *Bright Eyes, Brown Skin.* Littleton, MA: Sundance. (Self-concept, African Americans)

I   Jacobs, S. K. 1993. *The Boy Who Loved Morning.* Boston: Little, Brown. (Native American, growing up)

P   Kirk, D. 1994. *Miss Spider's Tea Party.* New York: Scholastic. (Self-concept)

P   Lester, H. 1988. *Tacky the Penguin.* Boston: Houghton Mifflin. (Self-concept)

P   McKee, D. 1989. *Elmer.* New York: Lothrop, Lee & Shepard. (Self-concept)

I   Mendez, P. 1989. *The Black Snowman.* New York: Scholastic. (Self-concept, African Americans, prejudice)

P   Mitchell, R. P. 1993. *Hue Boy.* New York: Dial. (Family, self-concept, Africans)

P   Nikola-Lisa, W. 1995. *Being with You This Way.* New York: Lee & Low. (Self-concept)

P   Payne, L. M. 1993. *Just because I Am.* Minneapolis: Free Spirit. (Self-concept)

P   Pfister, M. 1992. *Rainbow Fish.* New York: North–South. (Self-concept)

P, I   Seuss, Dr. 1990. *Oh, the Places You'll Go.* New York: Random House. (Self-concept)

I   Stevens, J. R. 1993. *Carlos and the Cornfield.* Flagstaff, AZ: Northland. (Hispanic people, self-concept)

P   Tsaitui, Y. 1988. *Anna in Charge.* New York: Viking. (Self-concept)

P   Waber, B. 1966. *You Look Ridiculous: Said the Rhinoceros to the Hippopotamus.* Boston: Houghton Mifflin. (Self-concept)

I   Williams, G. R. 1988. *Blue Tights.* New York: Lodestar. (African Americans, self-concept)

P   Yarbrough, C. 1979. *Cornrows.* New York: Coward-McCann. (Self-concept, African Americans)

P   Young, E. 1987. *I Wish I Were a Butterfly.* San Diego: Harcourt Brace. (Self-concept)

P   Zolotow, C. 1972. *William's Doll.* New York: Harper & Row. (Self-concept, gender equity)

Social Action, Peace

P   Adler, D. A. 1993. *A Picture Book of Frederick Douglass.* New York: Holiday House. (African American history, civil rights, social activism)

P   Adler, D. A. 1989. *A Picture Book of Martin Luther King, Jr.* New York: Scholastic. (African American history, social activism)

P   Adler, D. A. 1993. *A Picture Book of Rosa Parks.* New York: Holiday House. (African American history, civil rights, social activism)

I   Ancona, G. 1990. *Riverkeeper.* New York: Macmillan. (Environment, social activism)

P, I   Blumberg, R. 1993. *Bloomers.* New York: Bradbury. (Women's rights movement, social activism)

I   Brandt, K. 1993. *Rosa Parks: Fight for Freedom.* Mahwah, NJ: Troll. (African American history, social activism)

P, I   Bray, R. L. 1995. *Martin Luther King, Jr.* New York: Greenwillow. (Famous African American, civil rights movement)

I   Bruchac, J. 1996. *Children of the Longhouse.* New York: Dial. (Mohawk culture, peace)

P, I   Codye, C. 1990. *Vilma Martinez.* New York: Raintree/Austin: Steck-Vaughn. (Famous Hispanic women, social actvism)

I   Cone, M. 1992. *Come Back Salmon: How a Group of Dedicated Kids Adopted Pigeon Creek and Brought It Back to Life.* San Francisco: Sierra Club. (Environment, social activism)

I   Curtis, C. P. 1995. *The Watsons Go to Birmingham: 1963.* San Diego: Delacorte. (Civil rights movement)

I   Davis, O. 1992. *Just Like Martin.* New York: Simon & Schuster. (Social activism, Native Americans)

P, I   DeRuiz, D. C. 1993. *The Causa: The Migrant Farm Workers' Story.* Chatham, NJ: Raintree/Austin: Steck-Vaughn. (Famous Hispanic people—Cesar Chavez and Delores Huerta; social activism; migrant workers)

I   Durell, A., & Sacks, M., eds. 1990. *The Big Book for Peace.* New York: Dutton. (Peace)

I   Duvall, L. 1994. *Respecting Our Differences: A Guide to Getting Along in a Changing World.* Minneapolis: Free Spirit. (Peace)

P, I   Earth Works Group 1994. *50 Simple Things Kids Can Do to Recycle.* Berkeley, CA: Earth Works Press. (Ecology, social activism)

I   Ferris, J. 1988. *Go Free or Die: A Story about Harriet Tubman.* Minneapolis: Carolrhoda. (African American history, social activism)

P, I   Fife, D. H. 1991. *The Empty Lot.* San Francisco: Sierra Club. (Environment, social activism)

I   Fritz, J. 1995. *You Want Women to Vote, Lizzie Stanton.* New York: Putnam. (Suffrage campaign)

P, I   Gibbons, G. 1992. *Recycle!: A Handbook for Kids.* Boston: Little, Brown. (Environment, social activism)

I   Greenfield, E. 1973. *Rosa Parks.* New York: Crowell. (African American history, social activism)

P, I   Hamanaka, S. 1994. *Peace Crane.* New York: Morrow. (Hiroshima)

I Hamanaka, S., ed. 1995. *On the Wings of Peace.* New York: Clarion. (Peace)

I Haskins, J. 1992. *I Have a Dream: The Life and Words of Martin Luther King, Jr.* Brookfield, CT: Millbrook. (African American history, social activism)

I Haskins, J. 1993. *The March on Washington.* New York: HarperCollins. (Social activism, discrimination)

I House, P. 1993. *It's Our World, Too!: Stories of Young People Who Are Making a Difference.* Boston: Little, Brown. (Social activism)

I Hoyt-Goldsmith, D. 1996. *Migrant Worker: A Boy from the Rio Grande Valley.* New York: Holiday House. (Migrant worker, Hispanic family, social activism)

I Huff, B. A. 1990. *Greening the City Streets: The Story of Community Gardens.* New York: Clarion. (Environment, social activism)

P Jones, K. 1994. *Happy Birthday, Dr. King!* New York: Simon & Schuster. (African American history, social activism)

I Levine, E. 1993. *Freedom's Children: Young Civil Rights Activists Tell Their Own Stories.* New York: Putnam. (Social activism)

P, I Lewis, B. A. 1995. *The Kid's Guide to Service Projects: Over 500 Service Ideas for Young People Who Want to Make a Difference.* Minneapolis: Free Spirit. (Volunteerism)

P Marzollo, J. 1993. *Happy Birthday, Martin Luther King, Jr.* New York: Scholastic. (African American history, social activism)

P Mattern, J. 1992. *Young Martin Luther King, Jr.: "I Have a Dream."* Mahwah, NJ: Troll. (African American history, social activism)

I McCurdy, M. 1994. *Escape from Slavery: The Boyhood of Frederick Douglass in His Own Words.* New York: Knopf. (African American history, slavery, social activism)

I McGovern, A. 1965. *Runaway Slave: The Story of Harriet Tubman.* New York: Simon & Schuster. (African American history, slavery, social activism)

I McKissack, P. C. 1989. *Jesse Jackson: A Biography.* New York: Scholastic. (African American history, social activism)

I Meltzer, M. 1994. *Who Cares: Millions Do . . . a Book about Altruism.* New York: Walker. (Social activism)

P Mohr, N. 1993. *All for the Better: A Story of El Barrio.* Austin: Raintree Steck-Vaughn. (Puerto Rican contributions, social activism)

I Nelson, T. 1988. *And One for All.* New York: Dell. (Social activism)

I Parker, M. 1990. *What Is Martin Luther King, Jr. Day?* Chicago: Children's Press. (African American history, social activism)

I Robinet, H. G. 1991. *Children of the Fire.* New York: Atheneum. (Slavery, Underground Railroad, social activism)

I Rochelle, B. 1993. *Witnesses to Freedom: Young People Who Fought for Human Rights.* New York: Lodestar. (Social activism)

P, I   Santrey, L. 1983. *Young Frederick Douglass: Fight for Freedom.* Mahwah, NJ: Troll. (African American history, slavery, social activism)

P   Say, A. 1991. *Tree of Cranes.* Boston: Houghton Mifflin. (Family—adoption; peace)

P, I   Schiles, K. 1989. *Peace Begins with You.* San Francisco: Sierra Club. (Peace)

P, I   Schwartz, L. 1994. *How Can You Help?: Creative Volunteer Projects for Kids Who Care.* Armonk, NY: Learning Works. (Social activism, helping the elderly)

I   Spiegel, B. 1992. *The Year They Walked: Rosa Parks and the Montgomery Bus Boycott.* New York: Simon & Schuster. (African American history, social activism)

I   Stevens, B. 1992. *Frank Thompson: Her Civil War Story.* New York: Macmillan. (Social activism)

I   Turner, G. 1989. *Take a Walk in Their Shoes.* New York: Cobblestone. (African American history, social activism)

P, I   Van Allsburg, C. 1990. *Just a Dream.* Boston: Houghton Mifflin. (Environment, social activism)

P, I   Weeks, S. 1995. *Red Ribbon.* New York: HarperCollins. (Social activism—AIDS)

I   White, F. M. 1973. *Cesar Chavez: Man of Courage.* Champaign, IL: Garrard. (Migrant workers, social activism)

I   Whitfield, P. 1989. *Can the Whales Be Saved?: Questions about the Natural World and the Threats to Its Survival Answered by the Natural History Museum.* New York: Viking. (Environment)

P   Winter, J. 1992. *Follow the Drinking Gourd.* New York: Knopf. (African American history, slavery, social activism)

P, I   Zak, M. 1994. *Save My Rainforest.* Volcano, CA: Volcano Press. (Environment, South America)

Stereotyping, Prejudice

I   Ada, A. F. 1993. *My Name Is Maria Isabel.* New York: Atheneum. (Hispanic people, prejudice)

I   Bolenback.1991. *Teammates.* San Diego: Harcourt Brace Jovanovich. (African Americans, stereotyping)

I   Cohn, J. 1995. *The Christmas Menorahs: How a Town Fought Hatred.* New York: Whitman. (Jewish and Christian holidays, prejudice)

P, I   Goble, P. 1990. *Dream Wolf.* New York: Bradbury. (Wolves—Native Americans)

I   Greene, B. 1974. *Phillip Hall Likes Me, I Reckon Maybe.* New York: Dell. (Stereotying, gender equity)

I   Hamanaka, S. 1990. *The Journey: Japanese Americans, Racism, and Renewal.* New York: Orchard. (Japanese American history, World War II, racism)

I   Haskins, J. 1993. *The March on Washington.* New York: HarperCollins. (Social activism, discrimination)

P   Hoffman, M., & Binch, C. 1991. *Amazing Grace.* New York: Dial. (Stereotyping, self-concept, gender equity, African Americans)

I   Hotze, S. 1988. *A Circle Unbroken.* New York: Clarion. (Stereotyping, prejudice, Native American history)

I   Meltzer, M., ed. 1988. *Voices from the Civil War: A Documentary of the Great American Conflict.* New York: Crowell. (Civil War, prejudice)

I   Mendez, P. 1989. *The Black Snowman.* New York: Scholastic. (Self-concept, African Americans, prejudice)

P, I   Mochizuki, K. 1993. *Baseball Saved Us.* New York: Lee & Low. (Japanese American history)

P   Mochizuki, K. 1995. *Heroes.* New York: Lee & Low. (Japanese Americans, stereotyping)

I   Neuberger, A. E. 1995. *The Girl-Son.* Minneapolis: Lerner. (Deconstructing stereotypes)

P   Otey, M. 1990. *Daddy Has a Pair of Striped Shorts.* New York: Farrar, Straus, & Giroux. (Family, stereotyping)

I   Perez, N. A. 1988. *Breaker.* Boston: Houghton Mifflin. (Immigration, prejudice)

P   Say, A. 1982. *The Bicycle Man.* New York: Scholastic. (World War II, stereotyping)

P   Sharmat, M. W. 1980. *Gila Monsters Meet You at the Airport.* New York: Aladdin. (Stereotyping)

I   Siskind, L. 1992. *The Hopscotch Tree.* New York: Bantam. (Prejudice, Jewish people)

I   Springer, N. 1989. *They're Called Wildfire.* New York: Atheneum. (Stereotyping, African Americans)

P   Surat, M. M. 1983. *Angel Child, Dragon Child.* New York: Scholastic. (Stereotyping, Vietnamese Americans)

I   Taylor, M. D. 1980. *Mississippi Bridge.* New York: Dial. (Stereotyping)

I   Taylor, M. D. 1989. *The Road to Memphis.* New York: Dial. (Prejudice)

I   Taylor, M. D. 1976. *Roll of Thunder, Hear My Cry.* New York: Dial. (African American family, prejudice)

I   Turner, A. 1987. *Nettie's Trip South.* New York: Macmillan. (Civil War, prejudice)

I   Van Raven, P. 1989. *Harpoon Island.* New York: Scribner's. (Stereotyping)

I   Woodson, J. 1992. *Maizon at Blue Hill.* New York: Delacorte. (Prejudice)

Tales from Different Cultures

P, I Aardema, V. 1981. *Bringing the Rain to Kapiti Plain.* New York: Dial. (African American tale)

P, I Aardema, V. 1975. *Why Mosquitoes Buzz in People's Ears: A West African Tale.* New York: Dial. (African American tale)

I Aesop. 1997. *Aesop's Fables.* Seattle: University of Washington Press. (Traditional tales)

I Aesop, translated by S. A. Hanford. 1995. *Aesop's Fables.* New York: Puffin. (Traditional tales)

P Anno, M. 1989. *Anno's Aesop: A Book of Fables. Told by Aesop and Mr. Fox.* New York: Orchard. (Traditional tales)

P Ata, T. 1989. *Baby Rattlesnake.* Emeryville, CA: Children's Book Press. (Native American tale)

P, I Bash, B. 1996. *In the Heart of the Village: The World of the Indian Banyan Tree.* Boston: Little, Brown. (Tale from India)

P, I Baumgartner, B. 1994. *Crocodile! Crocodile!: Stories Told around the World.* New York: Dorling Kindersley. (Multicultural tales)

P, I Baylor, B. 1986. *Hawk, I'm Your Brother.* New York: Aladdin/Macmillan. (Native American tale)

I Belting, N. M. 1992. *Moon Was Tired of Walking on Air.* Boston: Houghton Mifflin. (South American Indian tribes myth)

P Bernhard, E. 1993. *Spotted Eagle and Black Crow: A Lakota Legend.* New York: Holiday House. (Lakota legend)

P Bierhorst, J. 1993. *The Woman Who Fell from the Sky: The Iroquois Story of Creation.* New York: Morrow. (Iroquois story of creation)

P Bishop, H., & Wiese, K. 1938. *The Five Chinese Brothers.* New York: Sandcastle. (Chinese tale)

P Brown, M. W. 1961. *Once a Mouse . . . : A Fable Cut in Wood.* New York: Aladdin/Macmillan. (Indian tale)

P Bruchac, J. 1993. *The First Strawberries.* New York: Dial. (Native American tale)

I Bruchac, J. 1993. *Flying with the Eagle, Racing with the Bear.* Mahwah, NJ: Bridgewater. (Native American stories)

I Bruchac, J. 1994. *The Great Ball Game: A Muskogee Story.* New York: Dial. (Muskogee Native American tale)

P, I Bruchac, J., & London, J. 1992. *Thirteen Moons on Turtle's Back: A Native American Year of Moons.* New York: Philomel. (Native American tale)

P, I Bruchac, J., & Ross, G. 1994. *The Girl Who Married the Moon: Tales from Native North America.* Mahwah, NJ: Bridgewater. (Native American tales, gender equity)

P, I   Chief Dan George. 1989. *My Heart Soars.* Blaine, WA: Hancock House. (Native American poems)

Coburn, J. R. 1976. *Beyond the East Wind: Legends and Folktales as told by Duomg Van Quyen.* Thousand Oaks, CA: Burn Hart. (Vietnamese legends and tales)

I   Coburn, J. R. 1979. *Encircled Kingdom: Legends and Folktales from Laos.* Thousand Oaks, CA: Burn Hart. (Laotian legends and tales)

I   Coburn, J. R. 1978. *Khmers, Tigers, and Talismans: From the History and Legends of Mysterious Cambodia.* Thousand Oaks, CA: Burn Hart. (Cambodian legends and tales)

P   Cohlene, T. 1990. *Turquoise Boy: A Navajo Legend.* Vero Beach, FL: Rourke Corporation. (Navajo legend)

P   Crowder, J. 1986. *Tonibah and the Rainbow.* Bernalillo, NM: Upper Strata Ink. (Native American tale)

P, I   Dayrell, E. 1991. *Why the Sun and the Moon Live in the Sky.* New York: Scholastic. (Native American tale)

I   DeArmond, D. 1990. *The Boy Who Found the Light: Eskimo Folktales.* San Francisco: Sierra Club/Boston: Little, Brown. (Eskimo folktales)

P, I   DeArmond, D. 1987. *The Seal Oil Lamp.* San Francisco: Sierra Club/Boston: Little, Brown. (Eskimo tale)

P   Demi. 1990. *The Empty Pot.* New York: Holt. (Chinese tale)

P   Demi. 1997. *One Grain of Rice: A Mathematical Folktale.* New York: Scholastic. (Tale from India)

P   dePaola, T. 1989. *The Legend of the Bluebonnet: An Old Tale of Texas.* New York: Scholastic. (Native American tale)

P   dePaola, T. 1988. *The Legend of the Indian Paintbrush.* New York: Putnam. (Native American tale)

P   dePaola, T. 1989. *Strega Nona.* New York: Simon & Schuster. (Italian American tale)

P, I   DeSpain, P. 1933. *Thirty-Three Multicultural Tales to Tell.* Little Rock, AR: August House. (Multicultural tales)

P   Dewey, A. 1993. *The Narrow Escapes of Davy Crockett: From a Bear, a Boa Constrictor, a Hoop Snake, an Elk, Eagles, Rattlesnakes, Wildcats, Trees, Tornadoes. . . .* New York: Mulberry Books. (American tall tales)

P   Dixon, A. 1992. *How Raven Brought Light to People.* New York: Margaret McElderry. (Tlingit Indian legend)

I   Driving Hawk Sneve, V. 1994. *The Nez Perce.* New York: Holiday House. (Nez Perce creation myth; Nez Perce history, culture, and contributions)

I   Esbensen, B. J. 1989. *Ladder to the Sky: How the Gift of Healing Came to the Ojibway Nation.* Boston: Little, Brown. (Ojibway nation tale)

P   Fleischman, S. 1992. *Mr. Brown's Wonderful One-Acre Farm: Three Tall Tales.* New York: Greenwillow. (Humorous tales)

P, I   Gates, F. 1994. *Owl Eyes.* New York: Lothrop. (Mohawk legend)

I   Geras, A. 1990. *My Grandmother's Stories: A Collection of Jewish Folk Tales.* New York: Knopf. (Jewish tales)

P, I   Ginsburg, M. 1988. *The Chinese Mirror.* New York: Harcourt Brace Jovanovich. (Chinese tales)

P   B. Glesson. 1997. *Pecos Bill.* New York: Simon & Schuster. (American tale)

I   Goble, P. 1994. *Adopted by the Tigers.* New York: Bradbury/Simon & Schuster. (Lakota Indian tale)

P, I   Goble, P. 1988. *Beyond the Ridge.* New York: Bradbury. (Plains Indian tale)

P   Goble, P. 1978. *The Girl Who Loved Wild Horses.* New York: Aladdin/Macmillan. (Native American tale)

P   Goble, P. 1987. *Ikotomi and the Boulder: A Plains Indian Story.* New York: Orchard. (Plains Indian tale)

P   Goble, P. 1993. *The Lost Children: The Boys Who Were Neglected.* New York: Bradbury. (Blackfoot legend)

P   Goble, P. 1992. *Love Flute.* New York: Bradbury. (Plains Indian love story)

P   Goble, P. 1991. *Star Boy.* New York: Aladdin/Macmillan. (Native American tale)

P   Gonzales, L. M. 1994. *The Bossy Gallito.* New York: Scholastic. (Cuban folktale, retold in Spanish and Engish)

I   Greene, E. 1993. *The Legend of the Cranberry: A Paleo Indian Tale.* New York: Simon & Schuster. (Native American tale)

P, I   Grifalconi, A. 1986. *The Village of Round and Square Houses.* Boston: Little, Brown. (African American tales)

P   Grover, M. 1995. *The Amazing & Incredible Counting Stories: A Number of Tall Tales.* San Diego: Harcourt. (Modern tales)

P, I   Guthrie, D. W. 1993. *Nobiah's Well: A Modern African Folktale.* Nashville, TN: Ideals. (African American tale)

P, I   Hamilton, V. 1995. *Her Stories: African American Folktales, Fairy Tales, and True Tales.* New York: Blue Sky. (Tales from different cultures, gender equity)

I   Hamilton, V. 1985. *The People Could Fly: American Black Folktales.* New York: Knopf. (African American tales)

P   Han, S. C. 1994. *Rabbit's Judgment.* New York: Holt. (Korean tale, Korean language)

P, I   Hodges, M. 1994. *Hidden in the Sand.* New York: Scribner's. (India and Buddha tale)

P   Hogan, P. 1997. *Johnny Appleseed: A Tall Tale.* Mahwah, NJ: Troll. (American tale)

P, I   Jacobs, J., ed. 1994. *Indian Fairy.* New York: Dover. (Tales from India)

I   Jaffe, N. 1993. *The Uninvited Guest and Other Jewish Holiday Tales.* New York: Scholastic. (Jewish holiday tales)

P, I   Jaffrey, M. 1985. *Seasons of Splendor: Tales, Myths, and Legends from India.* New York: Macmillan. (Indian tales, myths, and legends)

P   Jennings, P. 1992. *Strawberry Thanksgiving.* Cleveland: Modern Curriculum Press. (Native American tales)

P   Jensen, P. 1995. *Paul Bunyan and His Blue Ox.* Mahwah, NJ: Troll. (American tall tales)

P   Jensen, P. 1997. *The Legend of Sleepy Hollow.* Mahwah, NJ: Troll. (American tall tales)

P   Jensen, P., & Litzinger, R. 1995. *John Henry and His Mighty Hammer.* Mahwah, NJ: Troll. (American tall tales)

P   Keams, G. 1995. *Grandmother Spider Brings the Sun.* Flagstaff, AZ: Northland. (Cherokee creation story)

P, I   Keats, E. J. 1965. *John Henry.* New York: Pantheon. (African American tall tale)

P   Kellogg, S. 1994. *Paul Bunyan.* New York: Mulberry Books. (American tall tales)

P   Kellogg, S. 1992. *Pecos Bill.* New York: Mulberry Books. (American tall tales)

P, I   Kesey, K. 1991. *The Sea Lion.* New York: Puffin. (Pacific Northwest Native American tale)

P   Kimmel, E. *Hershel and the Hanukkah Goblins.* New York: Holiday House. (Jewish tale)

I   King, S. 1993. *Shannon: an Ojibway Dancer.* Minneapolis: Lerner. (Ojibway family)

P, I   Kipling, R. 1987. *The Jungle Book.* New York: Puffin. (Tales from India)

I   Kipling, R. 1865–1936. *The Jungle Book: The Mowgli Stories.* New York: Arcade. (Tales from India)

P   Kipling, R. 1997. *Rikki-Tikki-Tavi.* New York: Morrow. (Tales from India)

P, I   Kipling, R.; Ashachik, D.; & Hannon, H. 1992. *The Jungle Book.* Mahwah, NJ: Troll. (Tales from India)

P   Laan, N. V. 1993. *A Blackfoot Legend: Buffalo Dance.* Boston: Little, Brown. (Blackfoot legend)

P   Larry, C. 1993. *Peboan and Seeqwun.* New York: Farrar, Straus, & Giroux. (Ojibway tale)

P, I   Lattimore, D. N. 1988. *Why There Is No Arguing in Heaven: A Mayan Myth.* New York: Harper. (Maya creation story)

P, I   Lester, H. 1994. *John Henry.* New York: Dial. (African American tall tale)

P, I   Lester, J. 1989. *How Many Spots Does a Leopard Have?: And Other Tales.* New York: Scholastic. (African- and Jewish-based tales)

P, I Lewis, R. 1991. *All of You Was Singing*. New York: Atheneum. (Aztec myth)

P Martin, R. 1997. *The Monkey Bridge*. Knopf. (Tale from India)

P Martin, R., & Anderson, B. 1998. *The Brave Little Parrot*. New York: Putnam. (Tale from India)

I Mayo, G. 1988. *Earthmaker's Tales: North American Indian Stories about Earth's Happenings*. New York: Walker. (North American Indian tales)

P McDermott, G. M. 1972. *Anansi the Spider*. New York: Scholastic. (African American tale)

P McDermott, G. M. 1993. *Raven: A Trickster Tale from the Pacific Northwest*. New York: Scholastic. (Native American tale)

P McGovern, A. 1986. *Stone Soup*. New York: Scholastic. (French folklore)

I McKissack, P. C. 1992. *The Dark Thirty: Southern Tales of the Supernatural*. New York: Knopf. (Southern tales)

P Munsch, R. 1980. *The Paper Bag Princess*. Toronto: Annick Press. (Fairy tale—gender equity)

P, I Murphy, C. R. 1993. *The Prince and the Salmon People*. New York: Rizzoli. (Native American tale)

P Nieves, E. R. 1994. *Juan Bobo: Four Folktales from Puerto Rico*. New York: HarperCollins. (Puerto Rican folktales)

P, I Osborne, M. P. 1991. *American Tall Tales*. New York: Knopf. (American tall tales)

I Osborne, M. P. 1993. *Mermaid Tales from around the World*. New York: Scholastic. (Tales—different perspectives)

P, I Osofsky, A. 1992. *Dreamcatcher*. New York: Orchard. (Native American tale)

P Oughton, J. 1992. *How the Stars Fell into the Sky*. Boston: Houghton Mifflin. (Navajo folktale)

P, I Oughton, J. 1994. *The Magic Weaver of Rugs: A Tale of the Navajo*. Boston: Houghton Mifflin. (Navajo tale)

P, I Pan Cai Ying. 1988. *Monkey Creates Havoc in Heaven*. New York: Viking. (Chinese tale)

P, I Peterson, P. 1993. *Inunguak the Little Greenlander*. New York: Lothrop. (Inuit legend)

I Phelps, E. J. 1981. *The Maid of the North: Feminist Folk Tales from around the World*. New York: Holt. (Folktales—gender equity)

I Phillips, N. 1995. *The Illustrated Book of World Myths: Tales and Legends of the World*. New York: DK. (Tales from different cultures)

P, I Polacco, P. 1993. *Babushka Baba Yaga*. New York: Philomel. (Russian tale)

P   Rajpust, M. 1997. *The Peacock's Pride.* New York: Disney Press. (Tale from India)

P, I   Rucki, A. 1992. *Turkey's Gift to the People.* Flagstaff, AZ: Northland. (Native American tale)

P, I   San Souci, R. D. 1993. *Cut from the Same Cloth: American Women of Myth, Legend, and Tall Tales.* New York: Philomel. (American tall tales, gender equity)

I   San Souci, R. D. 1995. *Larger Than Life: The Adventures of American Legendary Heroes.* New York: Doubleday. (American tall tales)

P, I   San Souci, R. D. 1988. *The Talking Egg: A Folktale from the American South.* New York: Dial. (Creole version of *Cinderella*)

P, I   Schnur, S. 1995. *The Tie Man's Miracle: A Chanukka Tale.* New York: Morrow. (Jewish tale, Jewish holiday)

I   Schwartz, H., & Rush, B. 1991. *The Diamond Tree: Jewish Tales from Around the World.* New York: HarperCollins. (Jewish tales)

P   Seeger, P. 1994. *Abiyoyo.* New York: Aladdin. (Modern African American tale)

P   Shepard, A. 1995. *The Gifts of Wali Dad: A Tale of India and Pakistan.* New York: Atheneum. (Tale from India)

P   Shepard, A. 1992. *Savitri: A Tale of Ancient India.* New York: Philomel. (Tale from India)

P, I   Shetterly, S. H. 1991. *Raven's Light: A Myth from the People of the Northwest Coast.* New York: Atheneum. (Native American creation myth)

P   Snyder, D. 1988. *The Boy of the Three-Year Nap.* Boston: Houghton Mifflin. (Asian American tale)

P   Souhami, J. 1997. *Rama and the Demon King: An Ancient Tale from India.* New York: DK. (Tale from India)

P, I   Stevens, J. 1993. *Coyote Steals the Blanket.* New York: Holiday House. (Ute tale)

P, I   Stevenson, J. 1977. *"Could Be Worse."* New York: Mulberry Books. (Elderly version of "It Could Always Be Worse")

I   Stoutenburg, A., & Powers, R. M. 1976. *American Tall Tales.* New York: Viking. (American tall tales)

P, I   Straight, S. 1990. *Aquaboogie.* Minneapolis: Milkweed. (African American tale)

I   Thomas, J. C. 1992. *When the Nightingale Sings.* New York: HarperCollins. (Modern African American *Cinderella*-like story)

P   Tran, K. 1987. *The Little Weaver of Thai-Shen Village.* San Francisco: Children's Book Press. (Vietnamese American tale)

P   Uchida, Y. 1993. *The Magic Purse.* New York: Margaret McElderry. (Japanese folktale)

P   Uchida, Y. 1994. *The Wise Old Women.* New York: Margaret McElderry. (Japanese folktale)

P   Va, L. 1991. *A Letter to King.* New York: HarperCollins. (Chinese tale, Chinese and English languages)

P   Van Laan, N. 1991. *The Legend of El Dorado: A Latin American Tale.* New York: Knopf. (Latin American tale)

P, I   Volkmer, J. A. *Song of Chrimia: A Guatemalan Folktale/La Musica de la Chrimia: Folktale Guatemalteco.* Minneapolis: Carolrhoda. (Guatemalan folktale)

I   Vuong, L. D. 1993. *The Golden Carp and Other Tales of Vietnam.* New York: Lothrop. (Vietnamese tales)

I   Walker, P. R. 1993. *Big Men, Big Country: A Collection of American Tall Tales.* New York: Harcourt Brace. (American tall tales)

P   Wolf, G. 1996. *The Very Hungry Lion: A Folktale.* Toronto: Annick Press. (Tale from India)

P, I   Yep, L. 1993. *The Shell Woman and the King: A Chinese Folktale.* New York: Dial. (Chinese folktale)

P, I   Yolen, J. 1986. *Favorite Folktales from Around the World.* New York: Pantheon. (Multicultural tales)

P   Young, E. 1995. *Night Visitors.* New York: Philomel. (Chinese folktale)

P   Young, E. 1992. *Seven Blind Mice.* New York: Philomel. (Indian tale, different perspectives)

Vietnamese/Vietnamese American History, Culture, and Contributions

I   Ashabranner, B. 1988. *Always to Remember: The Story of the Vietnam Veterans Memorial.* New York: Dodd, Mead/Putnam. (Vietnamese American history)

P, I   Bunting, E. 1990. *The Wall.* New York: Clarion. (Vietnamese history)

P   Garland, S. 1994. *The Lotus Seed.* San Diego: Harcourt Brace Jovanovich. (Vietnamese culture)

I   Hoobler, D., & Hoobler, T. 1990. *Vietnam, Why We Fought: An Illustrated History.* New York: Knopf. (Vietnamese history)

P, I   Hoyt-Goldsmith, D. 1992. *Hoang Anh: A Vietnamese–American Boy.* New York: Holiday House. (Vietnamese people, immigration)

P   Keller, H. 1994. *Grandfather's Dream.* New York: Greenwillow. (Elderly; Vietnamese history)

P, I   Kid, D. 1991. *Onion Tears.* New York: Orchard. (Vietnamese people, immigration)

         Nhuong, H. Q. 1982. *The Land I Lost: Adventures of a Boy in Vietnam.* New York: Harper. (Vietnamese people)

I   Paterson, K. 1989. *Park's Quest.* New York: Puffin. (Vietnamese people)

Wolves, Foxes, and Coyotes—Folktales and True Stories

P, I   Crawford, E. D. 1983. *The Little Red Cap.* New York: Morrow. (Version of *Little Red Riding Hood*)

P, I   Dove, M. 1990. *Coyote Stories.* Lincoln: University of Nebraska Press. (Native American tales)

P, I   Emberly, M. 1990. *Ruby.* Boston: Little, Brown. (Version of *Little Red Riding Hood*)

I   George J. C. 1972. *Julie of the Wolves.* New York: Harper. (Wolves; Native American)

P, I   Goble, P. 1990. *Dream Wolf.* New York: Bradbury. (Wolves; Native Americans)

P, I   Hayes, J. 1990. *Coyote and: Native American Folk Tales.* Santa Fe, NM: Mariposa. (Native American tales)

P   Hooks, W. H. 1989. *The Three Little Pigs and the Fox.* New York: Macmillan. (Appalachian version of *The Three Little Pigs*)

P, I   Ling, M. 1991. *Eyewitness Juniors: Amazing Wolves, Dogs, & Foxes.* New York: Knopf. (True stories about wolves, dogs, and foxes)

P, I   London, J. 1993. *The Eyes of the Gray Wolf.* San Francisco: Chronicle. (True story about wolves)

P   London, J. 1996. *Red Wolf Country.* New York: Dutton. (Wolves—different perspectives)

P   Mathers, P. 1991. *Borreguita and the Coyote.* New York: Knopf. (Mexican tale)

P   McKissack, P. 1986. *Flossie and the Fox.* New York: Dial. (African American version of *The Three Little Pigs*)

P   Montresor, B. 1991. *Little Red Riding Hood.* New York: Doubleday. (Classic fairy tale)

P, I   Nolan, D. 1988. *Wolf Child.* New York: Macmillan. (Wolves)

P, I   Patent, D. H. 1990. *Gray Wolf, Red Wolf.* New York: Clarion. (True story about wolves)

P, I   Scieszka, J. 1989. *The True Story of the 3 Little Pigs by A. Wolf.* New York: Viking. (The wolf's version of *The Three Little Pigs*)

P, I   Scieszka, J. and L. Smith. 1992. *The Stinky Cheese Man and Other Fairly Stupid Tales.* New York: Viking. (Humorous folktales and fairy tales)

P, I   Trivias, E., & Oxenbury, H. 1993. *The Three Little Wolves and the Big Bad Pig.* New York: Margaret McElderry. (Humorous version of *The Three Little Pigs*)

P   Young, E. 1989. *Lon Po Po.* New York: Philomel. (Chinese *Little Red Riding Hood*)

AUTHOR BOOK LIST

The following list organizes books alphabetically by author. The designatiuon "P" and "I" indicate books suitable for children at the primary and/or intermediate levels.

P, I   Aardema, V. 1981. *Bringing the Rain to Kapiti Plain.* New York: Dial. (African American tale)

P, I   Aardema, V. 1975. *Why Mosquitoes Buzz in People's Ears: A West African Tale.* New York: Dial. (African American tale)

P   Ackerson, K. 1993. *By the Dawn's Early Light.* New York: Atheneum. (African American family)

I   Ackerson, K. 1991. *The Leaves in October.* New York: Atheneum. (Life in a homeless shelter)

I   Ackerson, K. 1994. *The Night Crossing.* New York: Random House. (Jewish people, Holocaust)

I   Ada, A. F. 1993. *My Name Is Maria Isabel.* New York: Atheneum. (Hispanic, prejudice)

I   Atkins, J. 1995. *Aani and the Tree Huggers.* New York: Lee & Low. (India, Environment)

P, I   Adler, D. A. 1994. *Hilde and Eli: Children of the Holocaust.* New York: Holiday House. (Holocaust)

P, I   Adler, D. A. 1995. *One Yellow Daffodil: A Hanukkah Story.* New York: Gulliver. (Jewish holiday)

P   Adler, D. A. 1995. *A Picture Book of Abraham Lincoln.* New York: Holiday House. (African American history)

P, I   Adler, D. A. 1993. *A Picture Book of Anne Frank.* New York: Holiday House. (Jewish history, World War II)

P   Adler, D. A. 1991. *A Picture Book of Christopher Columbus.* New York: Holiday House. (Columbus—different perspectives)

P   Adler, D. A. 1993. *A Picture Book of Frederick Douglass.* New York: Holiday House. (African American history, civil rights, social activism)

P   Adler, D. A. 1990. *A Picture Book of Helen Keller.* New York: Holiday House. (Challenged—blind and deaf)

P   Adler, D. A. 1989. *A Picture Book of Martin Luther King, Jr.* New York: Scholastic. (African American history, social activism)

P   Adler, D. A. 1993. *A Picture Book of Sitting Bull.* New York: Holiday House. (Native American history)

P   Adler, D. A. 1994. *A Picture Book of Sojourner Truth.* New York: Holiday House. (African American history)

I   Adler, D. A. 1989. *We Remember the Holocaust.* New York: Holt. (Holocaust)

P   Adoff, A. 1982. *All Colors of the Race.* New York: Lothrop. (Biracial people)

P   Adoff, A. 1973. *Black Is Brown Is Tan.* New York: Harper. (African American poetry)

P   Adoff, A., & Pinkney, J. 1991. *In for the Winter, Out for the Spring.* San Diego: Harcourt Brace. (African Americans, changing seasons)

I   Aesop. 1997. *Aesop's Fables.* Seattle: University of Washington Press. (Traditional tales)

I   Aesop, translated by S. A. Hanford. 1995. *Aesop's Fables.* New York: Puffin. (Traditional tales)

I   Alexander, S. H. 1990. *Mom Can't See Me.* New York: Macmillan. (Challenged—blind; family)

P   Alexandra, M. 1992. *Where Does the Sky End, Grandpa?* San Diego: Harcourt Brace Jovanovich. (Family, elderly)

P   Aliki. 1976. *Corn Is Maize: The Gift of the Indians.* New York: HarperCollins. (Food—different perspectives, Native Americans)

P   Aliki. 1992. *I'm Growing!* New York: HarperCollins. (Indian)

P, I   Allen, J. 1992. *Tiger.* Cambridge, MA: Candlewick. (Environment, South China)

P, I   Altman, L. J., & Sanquez, E. O. 1993. *Amelia's Road.* New York: Lee & Low. (Migrant workers, Hispanic people)

P   Ancona, G. 1994. *The Pinata Maker: El Pinatero.* San Diego: Harcourt. (Mexican fiestas, Spanish–English language)

I   Ancona, G. 1990. *Riverkeeper.* New York: Macmillan. (Environment, social activism)

P, I   Anderson, J. 1984. *The First Thanksgiving Feast.* Boston: Houghton Mifflin. (Pilgrims—different perspectives)

I   Andrews, E. 1992. *Indians of the Plains.* New York: Facts on File. (Native American history and contributions)

P   Andrews, J. 1991. *The Auction.* New York: Macmillan. (Elderly)

P, I   Anholt, L. 1992. *The Forgotten Forest.* San Francisco: Sierra Club. (Environment)

P   Anno, M. 1989. *Anno's Aesop: A Book of Fables Told by Aesop and Mr. Fox.* New York: Orchard. (Traditional tales)

I   Anzaldua, G. 1993. *Friends from the Other Side.* San Francisco: Children's Book Press. (Mexican American immigration)

P, I   Appelbaum, D. 1993. *Giants in the Land.* Boston: Houghton Mifflin. (Environment)

I   Armstrong, J. 1992. *Steal Away to Freedom.* New York: Scholastic. (African Americans, slavery)

I   Armstrong, W. H. 1969. *Sounder.* New York: Harper. (Family, African Americans)

P   Asch, F. 1993. *The Earth and I.* San Diego: Harcourt Brace. (Environment)

I   Ashabranner, B. 1988. *Always to Remember: The Story of the Vietnam Veterans Memorial.* New York: Dodd, Mead/Putnam. (Vietnamese American history)

I   Ashabranner, B. 1985. *Dark Harvest: Migrant Workers in America.* New York: Putnam. (Migrant workers, Hispanic people)

P, I   Ashby, R., & Ohrn, D. G. 1995. *Herstory: Women Who Changed the World.* New York: Viking. (Famous women)

P   Ashe-Moutoussamy, J. 1993. *Daddy and Me: A Photo Story of Arthur Ashe and His Daughter, Camera.* New York: Knopf. (Famous African American, family dealing with AIDS)

P   Ashley, B. 1991. *Cleversticks.* New York: Crown. (Self-concept, Asian Americans)

P   Ata, T. 1989. *Baby Rattlesnake.* Chicago: Children's Press. (Native American tale)

I   Atkin, B. A. 1993. *Voices from the Fields: Children of Migrant Farmworkers Tell Their Stories.* Boston: Little, Brown. (Hispanic migrant workers)

I   Bachrach, S. D. 1994. *Tell Them We Remember: The Story of the Holocaust.* Boston: Little, Brown. (Holocaust)

P   Baehr, P. 1989. *School Isn't Fair.* New York: Simon & Schuster. (Self-concept)

P   Baer, E. 1990. *This Is the Way We Go to School: A Book about Children around the World.* New York: Scholastic. (Differences and likenesses)

P, I   Bahr, M. 1992. *The Memory Box.* Morton Grove, IL: Albert Whitman. (Challenged—Alzheimers; family)

I   Baile, A. *Little Brother.* New York: Viking. (Cambodian family)

P, I   Baker, J. 1991. *Window.* New York: Greenwillow. (Environment)

I   Balgassi, H. 1996. *Peacebound Trains.* New York: Clarion. (Korean War story)

P   Bang, M. 1985. *The Paper Crane.* New York: Mulberry Books. (Asian Americans)

P   Banish, R. 1992. *A Forever Family: A Child's Story about Adoption.* New York: Harper. (Family)

P   Bannerman, H. 1996. *The Story of Little Babaji.* New York: HarperCollins. (Indian history, culture, contributions)

P   Barrett, M. B. 1994. *Sing to the Stars.* Boston: Little, Brown. (Challenged—blind)

I   Barrie, B. 1990. *Lone Star.* New York: Delacorte. (Jewish history)

P, I   Bash, B. 1996. *In the Heart of the Village: The World of the Indian Banyan Tree.* Boston: Little, Brown. (Tale from India)

P   Bates, K. L. 1993. *America the Beautiful.* New York: Atheneum. (American poem, song)

P, I   Baumgartner, B. 1994. *Crocodile! Crocodile!: Stories Told around the World.* New York: DK. (Multicultural tales)

P   Baylor, B. 1989. *Amigo.* New York: Aladdin/Macmillan. (Hispanic people)

P, I   Baylor, B. 1986. *Hawk, I'm Your Brother.* New York: Aladdin/Macmillan. (Native American tale)

P   Baylor, B. 1994. *The Table Where the Rich People Sit.* New York: Scribner's. (Native Americans)

I   Beatty, P. 1991. *Jayhawker.* New York: Morrow. (Civil War, slavery)

I   Beatty, P. 1992. *Who Comes with Cannons?* New York: Morrow. (Underground Railroad)

I   Begay, S. 1995. *Navajo: Visions and Voices across the Mesa.* New York: Scholastic. (Navajo poems)

P   Behrens, J. 1978. *Fiesta! Cinco de Mayo.* Chicago: Children's Press. (Holiday, Hispanic)

P   Behrens, J. 1982. *Gung Hay Fat Choy!* Chicago: Children's Press. (Asian American holiday)

P   Behrens, J. 1983. *Hanukkah.* Chicago: Children's Press. (Jewish holiday)

I   Bell, C. 1990. *Perez Family.* New York: Norton. (Cuban American family)

P   Belton, S. 1994. *May'naise Sandwiches & Sunshine Tea.* New York: Simon & Schuster. (Importance of family)

I   Bentley, J. 1990. *Harriet Tubman.* New York: Watts. (African American history)

P   Berenzy, A. 1989. *A Frog Prince.* New York: Holt. (Classic fairy tale)

P   Bernhard, E. 1993. *Spotted Eagle and Black Crow: A Lakota Legend.* New York: Holiday House. (Lakota legend)

P   Bernier-Grand, C. T. 1995. *Poets of Puerto Rico: Don Luis Munoz Marin.* Chicago: Orchard. (Famous Puerto Rican)

P, I   Berry, J. 1993. *Every Kid's Guide to Saving the Earth.* Nashville: Ideals. (Environment)

I   Bial, R. 1993. *Amish Home.* Boston: Houghton Mifflin. (Amish family)

I   Bial, R. 1993. *Frontier Home.* Boston: Houghton Mifflin. (Houses and homes)

I   Bial, R. 1995. *The Underground Railroad.* Boston: Houghton Mifflin. (African American history, Underground Railroad)

P   Bierhorst, J. 1993. *The Woman Who Fell from the Sky: The Iroquois Story of Creation.* New York: Morrow. (Iroquois story of creation)

P, I   Birdseed, T. *A Song of Stars.* New York: Holiday House. (Japanese and Chinese tale)

P   Bishop, H., & Wiese, K. 1938. *The Five Chinese Brothers.* New York: Sandcastle. (Chinese tale)

I   Bishop, R. S. 1991. *Presenting Walter Dean Myers.* Boston: Dwanye. (African American)

P, I   Black, S. 1994. *Upside Down Tales: Hansel and Gretel and The Witch's Tale.* New York: Carol Publishing Group. (Classic and witch's versions of *Hansel and Gretel*)

P, I   Blackmore, V. 1984. *Why Corn Is Golden: Stories about Plants.* Boston: Little, Brown. (Food—different perspectives; Mexican tales)

P, I   Blashfield, J. F. 1996. *Women Inventors.* Minneapolis: Capstone Press. (Woman inventors)

P, I   Blumberg, R. 1993. *Bloomers.* New York: Bradbury. (Women of the women's rights movement, social activism)

I   Bode, J. 1990. *New Kids on the Block: Oral History of Immigrant Teens.* New York: Watts. (Immigration)

I   Bogart, M., ed. 1989. *African American Biographies.* Englewood Cliffs, NJ: Globe. (Famous African American women)

I   Bolenback.1991. *Teammates.* San Diego: Harcourt Brace Jovanovich. (Stereotyping)

P, I　Bond, R. 1995. *Binya's Blue Umbrella.* Honesdale, PA: Boyds Mill Press. (Indian history, culture, and contributions)

P　Bond, R. 1996. *Cherry Tree.* Honesdale, PA: Boyds Mill Press. (Indian history, culture, and contributions)

P　Bonnici, P. 1984. *The Festival.* Minneapolis: Carolrhoda. (East Indian festival)

I　Borton de Tevino, E. 1989. *El Guero: An Adventure Story.* New York: Farrar, Straus, & Giroux. (Mexican history)

I　Bosse, M. 1995. *Tusk and Stone.* New York: Puffin. (Indian history, culture, and contributions)

P　Bowen, B. 1991. *Antler, Bear, Canoe: A Northlands Alphabet Book.* Boston: Little, Brown. (Environment)

P　Brady, A. A. 1995. *Kwanzaa Karamu: Cooking and Crafts for a Kwanzaa Feast.* Minneapolis: Carolrhoda. (African American holiday, food)

I　Brandt, K. 1993. *Rosa Parks: Fight for Freedom.* Mahwah, NJ: Troll. (African American history, social activism)

I　Brashler, W. 1994. *The Story of Negro League Baseball.* New York: Ticknor & Fields. (Famous African Americans)

P, I　Bray, R. L. 1995. *Martin Luther King, Jr.* New York: Greenwillow. (Famous African American, civil rights movement)

I　Brenner, B. 1991. *If You Were There in 1492.* New York: Bradbury. (Columbus—different perspectives)

P　Bresnick-Perry, R. 1992. *Leaving for America.* San Francisco: Children's Book Press. (Jewish migration)

P, I　Briggs, R. 1970. *Jim and the Beanstalk.* New York: Coward-McCann. (Elderly, fairy tale)

I　Brimner, L. D. 1992. *A Migrant Family.* Minneapolis: Lerner. (Mexican American migrant family)

P　Brown, M. 1982. *Shadow.* New York: Aladdin/Macmillan. (African Americans)

P　Brown, M. W. 1961. *Once a Mouse . . . . : A Fable Cut in Wood.* New York: Aladdin/Macmillan. (Indian tale)

I　Bruchac, J. 1995. *A Boy Called Slow: The True Story of Sitting Bull.* New York: Philomel. (Lakota hero)

I　Bruchac, J. 1996. *Children of the Longhouse.* New York: Dial. (Mohawk culture, peace)

I　Bruchac, J. 1993. *The First Strawberries.* New York: Dial. (Native American tale)

I　Bruchac, J. 1993. *Flying with the Eagle, Racing with the Bear.* Mahwah, NJ: Bridgewater. (Native American stories)

I　Bruchac, J. 1994. *The Great Ball Game: A Muskogee Story.* New York: Dial. (Muskogee Native American tale)

P, I　Bruchac, J., & London, J. 1992. *Thirteen Moons on Turtle's Back: A Native American Year of Moons.* New York: Philomel. (Native American tale)

P, I   Bruchac, J., & Ross, G. 1994. *The Girl Who Married the Moon: Tales from Native North America.* Mahwah, NJ: Bridgewater. (Native American tales, gender equity)

P, I   Bryan, A. 1974. *Walk Together Children: Black American Spirituals.* New York: Atheneum/Aladdin. (African American songs)

P   Buchanan, K. 1994. *This House Is Made of Mud.* Flagstaff, AZ: Northland. (Houses and homes, Hispanic people)

P   Buckley, H. E. 1994. *Grandfather and I.* New York: Lothrop, Lee & Shepard. (Family, elderly)

P   Buckley, H. E. 1994. *Grandmother and I.* New York: Lothrop, Lee & Shepard. (Family, elderly)

I   Bullock, S. 1993. *Free at Last: A History of the Civil Rights Movement and Those Who Died in the Struggle.* New York: Oxford University Press. (African American history, civil rights)

P   Bunting, E. 1994. *A Day's Work.* New York: Clarion. (Migrant workers, Mexican American family, Latino history)

P   Bunting, E. 1991. *Fly Away Home.* New York: Clarion. (Homeless people)

P, I   Bunting, E. 1988. *How Many Days to America? A Thanksgiving Story.* New York: Clarion. (Haitian pilgrimage)

P, I   Bunting, E. 1994. *Smoky Nights.* San Diego: Harcourt Brace. (Los Angeles riots)

I   Bunting, E. 1990. *Terrible Things: An Allegory of the Holocaust.* Philadelphia: Jewish Publication Society. (Jewish history, Holocaust)

P, I   Bunting, E. 1990. *The Wall.* New York: Clarion. (Vietnamese history)

I   Burns, K., & Miles, W. 1995. *Black Stars in Orbit: NASA's African American Astronauts.* New York: Gulliver. (Famous black Americans)

I   Buss, F. L. 1991. *Journey of the Sparrows.* New York: Lodestar. (Illegal aliens)

P   Cairo, S.; Cairo, J.; & Cairo, T. 1985. *Our Brother Has Down's Syndrome.* Toronto: Annick Press. (Family; challenged—Down syndrome)

P, I   Calmenson, S. 1989. *The Principal's New Clothes.* New York: Scholastic. (Fairy tale—modern version of *The Emperor's New Clothes*)

P   Cameron, A. 1988. *The Most Beautiful Place in the World.* New York: Random House. (Extended family)

P   Cannon, J. 1993. *Stellaluna.* San Diego: Harcourt Brace. (Differences and likenesses)

P   Carle, E. 1984. *The Mixed-Up Chameleon.* New York: Harper. (Self-concept)

P   Carlson, N. 1990. *I Like Me.* New York: Penguin. (Self-concept)

P   Carlstom, N. W. 1987. *Wild Wild Sunflower Child Anna.* New York: Macmillan. (African American family)

P   Castaneda, O. S. 1993. *Abuela's Weave.* New York: Lee & Low. (Family, elderly)

I   Castaneda, O. S. 1993. *Among the Volcanoes.* New York: Lodestar. (Maya family)

P, I   Cech, J. 1991. *Grandmother's Journey.* New York: Bradbury. (Family, immigration)

I   Chaikin, M. 1990. *Feathers in the Wind.* New York: Harper & Row. (Jewish people, self-concept)

P   Chen-Lee, C. 1993. *Almond Cookies and Dragon Well Tea.* Chicago: Polychrome. (Chinese culture)

P   Cherry, L. 1995. *The Great Kapok Trees.* New York: Dial. (Environment, Latinos)

P, I   Chief Dan George. 1989. *My Heart Soars.* Blaine, WA: Hancock House. (Native American poems)

P, I   Chief Jake Swamp. 1995. *Giving Thanks: A Native American Good Morning Message.* New York: Lee & Low. (Iroquois thanksgiving address, environment)

I   Childress, A. 1981. *Rainbow Jordon.* New York: Avon. (Family—foster homes; neglect)

P   Chin, K. 1995. *Sam and the Lucky Money.* New York: Lee & Low. (Chinese New Year)

P   Chocolate, D. 1995. *On the Day I Was Born.* New York: Scholastic. (African American cultures)

P, I   Christiansen, C. B. 1994. *I See the Moon.* New York: Atheneum. (Family, adoption)

I   Christiansen, C. B. 1989. *My Mother's House, My Father's House.* New York: Atheneum. (Family)

I   Chui, C. 1996. *Lives of Notable Asian Americans: Literature and Education.* New York: Chelsea House. (Famous Asian Americans, Asian American culture)

P, I   Clark, A. N. 1991. *In My Mother's House.* New York: Viking. (Native American poems)

P   Clifton, L. 1983. *Everett Anderson's Goodbye.* New York: Holt. (Elderly, death)

P, I   Climo, S. 1989. *The Egyptian Cinderella.* New York: HarperCollins. (Egyptian version of *Cinderella*)

I   Climo, S. 1993. *The Korean Cinderella.* New York: HarperCollins. (Korean version of *Cinderella*)

I   Coburn, J. R. 1976. *Beyond the East Wind: Legends and Folktales As Told by Duomg Van Quyen.* Thousand Oaks, CA: Burn Hart. (Vietnamese legends and tales)

I   Coburn, J. R. 1979. *Encircled Kingdom: Legends and Folktales from Laos.* Thousand Oaks, CA: Burn Hart. (Laotian legends and tales)

I   Coburn, J. R. 1978. *Khmers, Tigers, and Talismans: From the History and Legends of Mysterious Cambodia.* Thousand Oaks, CA: Burn Hart. (Cambodian legends and tales)

P, I   Codye, C. 1990. *Vilma Martinez.* Chatham, NJ: Raintree/Austin: Steck-Vaughn. (Famous Hispanic women, social activism)

P, I   Coeer, E. 1993. *Sadako.* New York: Putnam. (Hiroshima, Japanese people)

I   Coeer, E. 1977. *Sadako and the Thousand Cranes.* New York: Putnam. (Hiroshima, Japanese people)

P, I   Coer, E., & Young, E. 1986. *The Josefina Story Quilt.* New York: Harper & Row. (Quilt stories—Western movement version)

P   Cogancherry, H. 1990. *All I Am.* New York: Bradbury. (Self-concept)

P   Cohen, B. 1994. *Make a Wish, Molly.* New York: Doubleday. (Jewish holiday)

P   Cohen, B. 1983. *Molly's Pilgrim.* New York: Lothrop, Lee & Shepard. (Russian pilgrimage)

P   Cohlene, T. 1990. *Turquoise Boy: A Navajo Legend.* Vero Beach, FL: Rourke Corporation. (Navajo legend)

P, I   Cohn, A. L. 1993. *From Sea to Shining Sea.* New York: Scholastic. (Multicultural songs and stories)

I   Cohn, J. 1995. *The Christmas Menorahs: How a Town Fought Hatred.* New York: Whitman. (Jewish and Christian holidays, prejudice)

P, I   Cole, B. 1992. *Prince Cinders.* New York: Putnam. (Gender-equity version of *Cinderella*)

P   Cole, J. 1995. *How I Was Adopted.* New York: Morrow. (Families—adoption)

P, I   Coles, R. 1995. *The Story of Ruby Bridges.* New York: Scholastic. (African American history)

I   Collier, J. L., & Collier, C. 1981. *Jump Ship to Freedom.* New York: Delacorte. (Civil War, slavery)

I   Collier, J. L., & Collier, C. 1994. *With Every Drop of Blood: A Novel of the Civil War.* New York: Delacorte. (Civil War, slavery)

P   Condra, E. 1994. *See the Ocean.* Nashville: Ideals. (Family; challenged—blind; environment)

I   Cone, M. 1992. *Come Back Salmon: How a Group of Dedicated Kids Adopted Pigeon Creek and Brought It Back to Life.* San Francisco: Sierra Club. (Environment, social activism)

P   Conrad, P. 1991. *Pedro's Journal.* New York: Scholastic. (Columbus—different perspectives)

P, I   Cooney, B. 1990. *Hattie and the Wild Waves: A Story from Brooklyn.* New York: Viking. (Family, immigration)

I   Cooper, M. 1995. *Bound for the Promised Land: The Great Black Migration.* New York: Lodestar. (African American history, migration)

P   Cooper, M. 1993. *I Got a Family.* New York: Holt. (Extended family)

P, I   Copsey, S. E., with A. Kindersley. *Children Just Like Me.* New York: DK. (Differences and likenesses)

P, I   Covault, R. M. 1994. *Pablo and Pimiento.* Flagstaff, AZ: Northland. (Migrant workers; Hispanic people; Spanish and English languages)

P   Cowcher, H. 1988. *Rain Forest.* New York: Farrar, Straus, & Giroux. (Environment)

P   Cowen-Fletcher, J. 1993. *Mama Zooms.* New York: Scholastic. (Family, challenged)

I   Cox, C. 1993. *The Forgotten Heroes: The Story of the Buffalo Soldiers.* New York: Scholastic. (African American history)

P, I   Crawford, E. D. 1983. *The Little Red Cap.* New York: Morrow. (Version of *Little Red Riding Hood*)

P   Crowder, J. 1986. *Tonibah and the Rainbow.* Bernalillo, NM: Upper Strata Ink. (Native American tale)

I   Cumpian, C. 1994. *Poems about Latino Americans.* San Francisco: Children's Press. (Poems, famous Latino Americans)

I   Cunningham, L. 1989. *Sleeping Arrangements.* New York: Knopf. (Holocaust, Jewish people).

I   Curtis, C. P. 1995. *The Watsons Go to Birmingham: 1963.* San Diego: Delacorte. (Civil rights movement)

P, I   Czernecki, S., & Rhodes, T. 1992. *Pancho's Pinata.* New York: Hyperion. (Holiday, Hispanic family)

I   Dagliesch, A. 1954. *The Courage of Sarah Noble.* New York: Scribner's. (Native American history)

P, I   Daly, N. 1995. *My Dad.* New York: Margaret McElderry. (Family—alcoholism)

P   Daly, N. 1985. *Not So Fast Songololo.* New York: Puffin. (Family, elderly)

I   Das, P. 1996. *I Is for India.* Englewood Cliffs, NJ: Silver Burdett. (Indian history, culture, contributions)

I   Davis, D. 1994. *My Brother Has AIDS.* New York: Atheneum. (Challenged—AIDS)

I   Davis, D. 1989. *The Secret of the Seal.* New York: Crown. (Environment, Inuit family)

I   Davis, O. 1992. *Just Like Martin.* New York: Simon & Schuster. (Social activism, Native Americans)

P, I   Dayrell, E. 1991. *Why the Sun and the Moon Live in the Sky.* New York: Scholastic. (Native American tale)

I   DeArmond, D. 1990. *The Boy Who Found the Light: Eskimo Folktales.* San Francisco: Sierra Club/Boston: Little, Brown. (Eskimo folktales)

P, I   DeArmond, D. 1989. *The Seal Oil Lamp.* San Francisco: Sierra Club/Boston: Little, Brown. (Eskimo tale)

I   Delacre, L. 1989. *Arroz Con Leche: Popular Songs and Rhymes from Latin America.* New York: Scholastic. (Latin American songs, Latin American rhymes)

P, I   Delacre, L. 1990. *Las Navidades: Popular Christmas Songs from Latin America.* New York: Scholastic. (Latin American songs)

P   Delacre, L. 1993. *Vejigante/Masquerader.* New York: Scholastic. (Latin American holiday)

P   Demi. 1990. *The Empty Pot.* New York: Holt. (Chinese tale)

P   Demi. 1997. *One Grain of Rice: A Mathematical Folktale.* New York: Scholastic. (Tale from India)

P, I   DenBoer, H. 1994. *Please Don't Cry, Mom.* Minneapolis: Carolrhoda. (Family; challenged—depression)

P   dePaola, T. 1989. *The Legend of the Bluebonnet: An Old Tale of Texas.* New York: Scholastic. (Native American tale)

P   dePaola, T. 1988. *The Legend of the Indian Paintbrush.* New York: Putnam. (Native American tale)

P   dePaola, T. 1978. *Nana Upstairs & Nana Downstairs.* New York: Puffin. (Elderly, death)

P   dePaola, T. 1989. *Strega Nona.* New York, Simon & Schuster. (Italian American tale)

P, I   DeRuiz, D. C. 1993. *The Causa: The Migrant Farm Workers' Story.* Chatham, NJ: Raintree/Austin: Steck-Vaughn. (Famous Hispanic people—Cesar Chavez and Delores Huerta; social activism; migrant workers)

P, I   DeSpain, P. 1933. *Thirty-Three Multicultural Tales to Tell.* Little Rock, AR: August House. (Multicultural tales)

P   Dewey, A.1993. *The Narrow Escapes of Davy Crockett: From a Bear, a Boa Constrictor, a Hoop Snake, an Elk, Eagles, Rattlesnakes, Wildcats, Trees, Tornadoes. . . .* New York: Mulberry Books (American tall tales)

P   Dionetti, M. 1991. *Coal Mine Peaches.* New York: Orchard. (Elderly, migrant workers, Italians)

P, I   Di Salvo-Ryan, F. D. 1992. *Uncle Willie and the Soup Kitchen.* New York: Morrow. (Family, hunger)

P   Dixon, A. 1992. *How Raven Brought Light to People.* New York: Margaret McElderry. (Tlingit Indian legend)

I   Doctor, B. A. 1992. *Malcolm X for Beginners.* New York: Writers and Readers. (Famous African American, civil rights)

I   Doherty, C. A., & Doherty, K. M. 1989. *The Apaches and Navajos.* New York: Watts. (Native American history)

P   Doherty, C. A., & Doherty, K. M. 1991. *Nine Days until Christmas: A Mexican Story.* New York: Puffin. (Mexican holiday)

P   Dooley, N. 1991. *Everybody Cooks Rice.* Minneapolis, MN: Carolrhoda. (Differences and likenesses)

I   Dorris, M. 1992. *Morning Girl.* New York: Hyperion. (Taino Indian family)

I   Dorris, M. 1987. *Yellow Raft in Blue Water.* New York: Warner. (Native American women)

P   Dorros, A. 1991. *Abuela.* New York: Dutton. (Elderly; Hispanic people)

P   Dorros, A. 1993. *Radio Man.* New York: HarperCollins. (Migrant worker; Hispanic people; Spanish and English languages)

P   Dorros, A. 1992. *This Is My House.* New York: Scholastic. (Houses and homes)

P   Dorros, A. 1991. *Tonight Is Carnival.* New York: Dutton. (South American quilts)

P, I   Dove, M. 1990. *Coyote Stories.* Lincoln: University of Nebraska Press. (Native American tales)

I   Drimmer, F. 1988. *Born Different: Amazing Stories of Very Special People.* New York: Atheneum. (Family, challenged)

P, I   Driving Hawk Sneve, V. 1988. *Dancing Teepees: Poems of American Indian Youth.* New York: Holiday House. (Native American poems)

I   Driving Hawk Sneve, V. 1995. *The Hopis.* New York: Holiday House. (Hopi history, culture, and contributions)

I   Driving Hawk Sneve, V. 1994. *The Nez Perce.* New York: Holiday House. (Nez Perce creation myth; Nez Perce history, culture, and contributions)

I   Drucknor, M., & Halperin, M. 1993. *Jacob's Rescue: A Holocaust Story.* New York: Bantam Doubleday Dell. (Holocaust)

P   Dupree, R. 1993. *The Wishing Chair.* Minneapolis: Carolrhoda. (African American history, African American family)

P, I   Durell, A.; Patterson, K.; & George, J. C., eds. 1992. *The Big Book for Our Planet.* New York: Dutton. (Environment)

I   Durell, A., & Sacks, M., eds. 1990. *The Big Book for Peace.* New York: Dutton. (Peace)

I   Duvall, L. 1994. *Respecting Our Differences: A Guide to Getting Along in a Changing World.* Minneapolis: Free Spirit. (Peace)

P, I   Dyson, J. 1991. *Westward with Columbus: Set Sail on the Voyage That Changed the World.* New York: Scholastic. (Columbus)

P, I   Earth Works Group 1994. *50 Simple Things Kids Can Do to Recycle.* Berkeley, CA: Earth Works Press. (Environment, social activism)

P   Ehrlich, A. 1989. *The Story of Hanukkah.* New York: Dial. (Jewish history)

P   Eisen, A. 1992. *Treasury of Children's Literature.* Boston: Houghton Mifflin. (Anthology of tales)

P   Eisenberg, P. R. 1992. *You're My Nikki.* New York: Dial. (African American family)

P, I   Emberly, M. 1990. *Ruby.* Boston: Little, Brown (Version of *Little Red Riding Hood*)

P   Emberly, R. 1993. *Let's Go: A Book in Two Languages.* Boston: Little, Brown. (Spanish and English languages)

P   Emberly, R. 1990. *My House: A Book Written in Two Languages.* Boston: Little, Brown. (Spanish and English languages; houses and homes)

I   Esbensen, B. J. 1989. *Ladder to the Sky: How the Gift of Healing Came to the Ojibway Nation.* Boston: Little, Brown. (Ojibway nation tale)

P, I   Eskoomiak, N. 1990. *Arctic Memories.* New York: Holt. (Inuit family, Inuit history)

P   Ets, M. H. 1963. *Gilberto and the Wind.* New York: Viking. (Hispanic people)

P, I   Ets, M. H. 1971. *Mojo Means One.* New York: Dial. (Language, African Americans)

P, I   Ets, M. H. 1971. *Soul Looks Back in Wonder.* New York: Dial. (African American poems)

P, I   Everett, G. 1992. *Li'l Sis and Uncle Willie: A Story Based on the Life and Paintings of William H. Johnson.* New York: Rizzoli. (Famous African Americans)

P   Eversole, R. H. 1992. *The Magic House.* New York: Orchard. (Houses—different perspectives)

I   Evitts, W. J. 1985. *Captive Bodies, Free Spirits: The Story of Southern Slavery.* San Francisco: Children's Book Press. (Slavery)

P, I   Fabers, D. 1991. *The Amish.* New York: Doubleday. (Amish family)

P, I   Feelings, M. 1974. *Jabo Means Hello.* New York: Dial. (African American language)

P, I   Feelings, M. 1995. *The Middle Passage: White Ships/Black Cargo.* New York: Dial. (African American history, slavery)

I   Feelings, T. 1972. *Black Pilgrimage.* New York: Lothrop. (African American pilgrimage)

I   Ferris, J. 1988. *Go Free or Die: A Story about Harriet Tubman.* Minneapolis: Carolrhoda. (African American history, social activism)

P, I   Ferris, J. 1988. *Walking the Road to Freedom: A Story about Sojourner Truth.* Minneapolis: Carolrhoda. (African American history)

I   Ferris, J. 1994. *What I Was Singing: The Story of Marian Anderson.* Minneapolis: Carolrhoda. (Famous African American woman)

P, I   Fife, D. H. 1991. *The Empty Lot.* San Francisco: Sierra Club. (Environment, social activism)

P   Fisher, L. E. 1989. *The Wailing Wall.* New York: Macmillan. (Jewish history)

P   Fleischman, S. 1992. *Mr. Brown's Wonderful One-Acre Farm: Three Tall Tales.* Greenwillow. (Humorous tales)

I   Fleishman, P. 1993. *Bull Run.* New York: HarperCollins. (Civil War—different perspectives)

I   Fleming, S. 1986. *Exile of Sergeant Nem: A Novel.* Chapel Hill, NC: Algonquin. (Vietnamese Americans)

P   Fleming, V. 1993. *Be Good to Eddie Lee.* New York: Philomel Books. (Stereotyping, challenged)

P   Flora. 1989. *Feathers Like a Rainbow: An Amazon Indian Tale.* New York: Harper. (Amazon Indian tale)

P   Flournoy, V. 1985. *The Patchwork Quilt.* New York: Dial. (Quilt stories—African American family)

P, I   Fluek, T., & Finkler, L. 1994. *Passover: As I Remember It.* New York: Doubleday. (Jewish history, Jewish holiday)

I   Foster, J. 1991. *Cartons, Cans, and Orange Peels: Where Does Your Garbage Go?* New York: Clarion. (Environment)

I   Fox, P. 1973. *The Slave Dancer.* New York: Bradbury. (Slavery)

I   Fradin, D. B. 1992. *Hiawatha: Messenger of Peace.* New York: Margaret McElderry. (Native American history—Iroquois)

I   Fradin, D. B., & Fradin, J. B. 1995. *Puerto Rico.* Danbury, CT: Children's Press. (Puerto Rican history, Puerto Rican culture)

P, I   Frasier, D. 1991. *On the Day That You Were Born.* San Diego: Harcourt Brace Jovanovich. (Environment)

I   Frank, A. 1967. *Anne Frank: The Diary of a Young Girl.* New York: Doubleday. (Holocaust, Jewish people)

P   Franklin, K. L. 1992. *The Old, Old Man and the Very Little Boy.* New York: Atheneum. (African family, elderly)

I   Freedman, R. 1995. *Immigrant Kids.* New York: Puffin. (Immigration)

P   Freeman, D. 1968. *Corduroy.* New York: Viking. (African African family)

P   Freeman, D. 1983. *A Pocket for Corduroy.* New York: Penguin. (African American family)

I   Freeman, F. B. 1971. *Two Tickets to Freedom: The True Story of Ellen and William Craft, Fugitive Slaves.* New York: Peter Bedrick. (Slavery)

P   Freidman, F. B. 1984. *How My Parents Learned to Eat.* Boston: Houghton Mifflin. (Biracial family)

I   Freidman, I. 1982. *Escape or Die: True Stories of Young People Who Survived the Holocaust.* Reading, MA: Addison Wesley. (Jewish history, Holocaust)

P, I   French, F. 1992. *Snow White in New York.* New York: Oxford University Press. (Fairy tale—modern version of *Snow White*)

I   Fritz, J. 1983. *The Double Life of Pocahontas.* New York: Doubleday. (Native American history)

I   Fritz, J. 1982. *Homesick: My Own Story.* New York: Putnam. (Chinese history)

I   Fritz, J. 1995. *You Want Women to Vote, Lizzie Stanton.* New York: Putnam. (Suffrage campaign)

I   Gallico, P. 1940. *The Snow Goose.* New York: Knopf. (World War II)

I   Garcia, G. 1995. *Spirit of the Maya: A Boy Explores His People's Mysterious Past.* New York: Simon & Schuster. (Maya culture)

P, I   Garcia, M. 1987. *The Adventures of Connie and Diego.* San Francisco: Children's Book Press. (Hispanic and biracial people)

P   Garland, S. 1994. *The Lotus Seed.* San Diego: Harcourt Brace Jovanovich. (Vietnamese culture)

P, I   Gates, F. 1994. *Owl Eyes.* New York: Lothrop. (Mohawk legend)

I   Gay, K. 1988. *Changing Families: Meeting Today's Challenges.* Springfield, NJ: Enslow. (Families—different perspectives)

I   George J. C. 1994. *Julie.* New York: Harper. (Julie of the Wolves returns to modern life)

I   George J. C. 1972. *Julie of the Wolves.* New York: Harper. (Wolves, Native Americans)

I   George, J. C. 1990. *One Day in the Tropical Rain Forest.* New York: HarperCollins. (Environment)

I   Geras, A. 1990. *My Grandmother's Stories: A Collection of Jewish Folk Tales.* New York: Knopf. (Jewish tales)

I   Gernard, R. 1988. *The Cuban Americans.* New York: Chelsea House. (Cuban American history)

P   Gershator, D., & Gershator, P. 1995. *Bread Is for Eating.* New York: Holt. (Food—different perspectives; Spanish and English languages, song)

P, I   Gibbons, G. 1992. *Recycle!: A Handbook for Kids.* Boston: Little, Brown. (Environment, social activism)

P, I   Ginsburg, M. 1988. *The Chinese Mirror.* San Diego: Harcourt Brace Jovanovich. (Chinese tales)

P, I   Girard, L. W. 1989. *We Adopted You, Benjamin Koo.* Morton Grove, IL: Albert Whitman. (Family—adoption)

I   Gleiter, J. 1989. *Diego Rivera.* Milwaukee: Raintree. (Hispanic people).

P   Glesson, B. 1997. *Pecos Bill.* New York: Simon & Schuster. (American tale)

I   Goble, P. 1994. *Adopted by the Tigers.* New York: Bradbury/Simon & Schuster. (Lakota Indian tale)

P, I   Goble, P. 1988. *Beyond the Ridge.* New York: Bradbury. (Plains Indian tale)

P, I   Goble, P. 1990. *Dream Wolf.* New York: Bradbury. (Wolves—Native Americans)

P   Goble, P. 1978. *The Girl Who Loved Wild Horses.* New York: Aladdin/Macmillan. (Native American tale)

P   Goble, P. 1988. *Ikotomi and the Boulder: A Plains Indian Story.* New York: Orchard. (Plains Indian tale)

P   Goble, P. 1993. *The Lost Children: The Boys Who Were Neglected.* New York: Bradbury. (Blackfoot legend)

P   Goble, P. 1992. *Love Flute.* New York: Bradbury. (Plains Indian love story)

P   Goble, P. 1991. *Star Boy.* New York: Aladdin/Macmillan. (Native American tale)

I   Godden, R. 1993. *Great Grandmother's House.* New York: Greenwillow. (Japanese family, elderly)

P   Godden, R. 1997. *Premlata and the Festival of Lights.* New York: Greenwillow. (Indian holiday)

I   Golenbook, P. 1990. *Teammates.* New York: Trumpet Club. (African Americans, stereotyping)

P   Gonzales, L. M. 1994. *The Bossy Gallito.* New York: Scholastic. (Cuban folktale retold in Spanish and English)

P, I   Gordon, G. 1993. *My Two Worlds.* New York: Clarion. (Dominican Republic Christmas)

I Graff, N. P. 1993. *Where the River Runs: A Portrait of a Refugee Family.* Boston: Little, Brown. (Cambodian refugee)

P, I Granowsky, A. 1993. *Point of View Stories: Cinderella and That Awful Cinderella.* Austin: Steck-Vaughn. (Classic and stepsisters' versions of *Cinderella*)

P, I Granowsky, A. 1993. *Point of View Stories: Peter Pan: The Classic Tale and Grow Up, Peter Pan!* Austin: Steck-Vaughn. (Classic and So-and-So's versions of *Peter Pan*)

P, I Granowsky, A. 1993. *Point of View Stories: Snow White: The Classic Tale and The Unfairest of Them All.* Austin: Steck-Vaughn. (Classic and stepmother's versions of *Snow White*)

P Gray, N. 1988. *A Balloon for Grandad.* New York: Orchard. (Elderly)

I Greenberg, K. E. 1992. *Magic Johnson: Champion with a Cause.* Minneapolis: Lerner. (Famous African American)

I Greene, B. 1974. *Phillip Hall Likes Me, I Reckon Maybe.* New York: Dell. (Stereotyping, gender equity)

I Greene, E. 1993. *The Legend of the Cranberry: A Paleo Indian Tale.* New York: Simon & Schuster. (Native American tale)

P Greenfield, E. 1980. *Alesia.* New York: Philomel. (Challenged—wheelchair)

P Greenfield, E. 1991. *First Pink Light.* New York: Crowell. (African American family)

P Greenfield, E. 1988. *Grandpa's Face.* New York: Philomel. (Family, elderly)

P Greenfield, E. 1978. *Honey, I Love.* New York: Dial. (African American poems).

P Greenfield, E. 1988. *Nathaniel Talking.* New York: Crowell. (African American poems)

P, I Greenfield, E. 1991. *Night on Neighborhood Street.* New York: Crowell. (African American poems)

P, I Greenfield, E. 1973. *Rosa Parks.* New York: Crowell. (African American history, social activism)

P Greenfield, E. 1974. *She Come Bringing Me That Baby Girl.* Philadelphia: Lippincott. (African American family)

P Greenfield, E. 1993. *William and the Good Old Days.* New York: HarperCollins. (Elderly, death, African Americans)

I Greenfield, H. 1993. *The Hidden Children.* New York: Ticknor & Fields. (Holocaust)

P Griese, A. 1995. *Anna's Athabaskan Summer.* New York: Boyds Mills Press. (Native Americans, life cycle)

P, I Grifalconi, A. 1986. *The Village of Round and Square Houses.* Boston: Little, Brown. (African American tales)

P Grossman, P. 1994. *Saturday Market.* New York: Lothrop, Lee & Shepard. (Hispanic)

P Grover, M. 1995. *The Amazing & Incredible Counting Stories: A Number of Tall Tales.* San Diego, CA: Harcourt. (Modern tales)

P, I   Guthrie, D. W. 1993. *Nobiah's Well: A Modern African Folktale.* Nashville: Ideals. (African American tale)

P, I   Guzzetti, R. 1996. *The White House.* New York: Simon & Schuster. (Houses and homes)

P   Haggerty, M. E. 1993. *A Crack in the Wall.* New York: Lee & Low. (Family, holiday, Hispanic people)

I   Haldane, S. 1991. *Helping Hands: How Monkeys Assist People Who Are Disabled.* New York: Dutton. (Challenged)

I   Hall, L. 1990. *Halsey's Pride.* New York: Scribner's. (Challenged—epileptic)

P   Hallinan, P. K. 1992. *For the Love of Earth.* Nashville: Ideals. (Environment)

P   Hamanaka, S. 1994. *All the Colors of the Earth.* New York: Morrow. (Differences and likenesses)

I   Hamanaka, S. 1990. *The Journey: Japanese Americans, Racism, and Renewal.* New York: Orchard. (Japanese American history, World War II, racism)

P, I   Hamanaka, S. 1994. *Peace Crane.* New York: Morrow. (Hiroshima)

I   Hamanaka, S., ed. 1995. *On the Wings of Peace.* New York: Clarion. (Peace)

P, I   Hamilton, V. 1995. *Her Stories: African American Folktales, Fairy Tales, and True Tales.* New York: Blue Sky. (Tales from different cultures, gender equity)

I   Hamilton, V. 1988. *In the Beginning: Creation Stories from around the World.* San Diego: Harcourt Brace Jovanovich. (Tales—different perspectives)

I   Hamilton, V. 1993. *Many Thousand Gone: African Americans from Slavery to Freedom.* New York: Knopf. (African American history, slavery)

I   Hamilton, V. 1985. *The People Could Fly: American Black Folktales.* New York: Knopf. (African American tales)

I   Hammond, A. 1991. *The Home We Have Made.* New York: Crown. (Hispanic people, homeless people)

P   Han, S. C. 1994. *Rabbit's Judgment.* New York: Holt. (Korean tale)

I   Hansen, J. 1988. *Out from This Place.* New York: Walker. (Civil War, slavery)

P   Harness, C. 1995. *Papa's Christmas Gift: Around the World the Night before Christmas.* New York: Simon & Schuster. (Christmas around the World)

I   Harness, C. 1996. *Young Abe Lincoln: The Frontier Days, 1809–1837.* Washington, DC: National Geographic Society. (Slavery)

P, I   Harshman, M. 1995. *The Storm.* New York: Cobblehill. (Challenged—wheelchair)

P, I   Harvey, B. 1988. *Cassie's Journey: Going West in the 1860's.* New York: Holiday House. (1860 family, migration)

I   Haskins, J. 1992. *Against All Opposition: Black Explorers in America.* New York: Walker. (African American history; Columbus—different perspectives)

I   Haskins, J. 1996. *Black Eagles: African Americans in Aviation.* New York: Scholastic. (Famous African Americans)

I Haskins, J. 1992. *Count Your Way through Africa.* Minneapolis: Carolrhoda. (African languages)

I Haskins, J. 1989. *Count Your Way through Canada.* Minneapolis: Carolrhoda. (French language)

I Haskins, J. 1987. *Count Your Way through China.* Minneapolis: Carolrhoda. (Chinese language)

I Haskins, J. 1990. *Count Your Way through Germany.* Minneapolis: Carolrhoda. (German language)

I Haskin, J. 1987. *Count Your Way through Japan.* Minneapolis: Carolrhoda. (Japanese language)

I Haskins, J. 1989. *Count Your Way through Korea.* Minneapolis: Carolrhoda. (Korean language)

I Haskins, J. 1989. *Count Your Way through Mexico.* Minneapolis: Carolrhoda. (Spanish language)

I Haskins, J. 1987. *Count Your Way through Russia.* Minneapolis: Carolrhoda. (Russian language)

I Haskins, J. 1991. *Count Your Way through the Arab World.* Minneapolis: Carolrhoda. (Arabic language)

I Haskins, J. 1993. *Get On Board: The Story of the Underground Railroad.* New York: Scholastic. (Underground Railroad)

I Haskins, J. 1992. *I Have a Dream: The Life and Words of Martin Luther King, Jr.* Brookfield, CT: Millbrook. (African American history, social activism)

I Haskins, J. 1989. *India under Indira and Ravij Gandi.* Springfield, NJ: Enslow. (Indian history, culture, contributions)

I Haskins, J. 1993. *The March on Washington.* New York: HarperCollins. (Social activism, discrimination)

I Haskins, J. 1982. *The New Americans: Cuban Boat People.* New York: Chelsea House. (Cuban American history, Cuban immigration)

I Haskins, J. 1991. *Outward Dreams: Black Inventors and Their Inventions.* New York: Walker. (Famous African Americans)

P, I Hathorn, J. 1994. *Way Home.* New York: Crown. (Homeless)

P Havill, J. 1993. *Jamaica and Brianna.* Boston: Houghton Mifflin. (African Americans)

P Havill, J. 1986. *Jamaica's Find.* Boston: Houghton Mifflin. (African Americans)

P Havill, J. 1986. *Jamaica Tag Along.* Boston: Houghton Mifflin. (African American family)

P, I Havill, J. 1993. *Sato and the Elephants.* New York: Lothrop. (Environment)

P, I Hayes, J. 1990. *Coyote & Native American Folk Tales.* Sante Fe: Mariposa. (Native American tales)

P   Hazen, B. 1985. *Why Are People Different?* Racine, WI: Western. (African Americans, elderly)

P, I Heide, P. H., & Gilland, J. H. 1990. *The Day of Ahmed's Secret.* New York: Lothrop. (Cairo)

P   Heins, P. 1974. *Snow White.* Boston: Little, Brown. (Classic fairy tale)

P   Herrald, M. R. 1995. *A Very Important Day.* New York: Morrow. (Immigration)

I   Hesse, K. 1993. *Lester's Dog.* New York: Crown. (Challenged—hearing impaired)

I   Hesse, K. 1964. *Letters from Rifka.* New York: Puffin. (Jewish people, Holocaust)

P   Hesse, K. 1993. *Poppy's Chair.* New York: Macmillan. (Family, elderly, death)

P   Hest, A. 1989. *The Midnight Eaters.* New York: Simon & Schuster. (Family, elderly)

P, I Hest, A. 1990. *The Ring and the Window Seat.* New York: Scholastic. (Jewish family, Holocaust)

I   Hewett, F. P. 1990. *Hector Lives in the United States Now: The Story of a Mexican American Child.* Philadelphia: Lippincott. (Immigration, Mexican American family)

I   Hijuelos, O. 1989. *Mambo Kings Play Songs of Love: A Novel.* New York: Farrar, Straus, & Giroux. (Cuban Americans)

I   Hill, D. 1994. *See Ya, Simon.* New York: Dutton. (Challenged—muscular dystrophy)

I   Hillerman, T. 1985. *Ghostway.* New York: Harper & Row. (Native Americans)

P   Himler, R. 1993. *The Navajos: The First Americans Book.* New York: Holiday House. (Native American history)

P   Himler, R. 1993. *The Sioux: The First Americans Book.* New York: Holiday House. (Native American history)

P   Hines, A. G. 1986. *Daddy Makes the Best Spaghetti.* New York: Clarion. (Family, gender equity)

I   Hirschfielder, A. B., & Singer, B. R., eds. 1991. *Rising Voices: Writings of Young Native Americans.* New York: Scribner's. (Native American family, Native American history)

I   Ho, M. 1991. *The Clay Marble.* New York: Farrar, Straus, & Giroux. (Refugees—Thailand, Cambodia)

P   Hoberman, A. 1978. *A House Is a House for Me.* New York: Viking. (Houses and homes)

P, I Hodges, M. 1994. *Hidden in the Sand.* New York: Scribner's. (India and Buddha tale)

P   Hoffman, M., & Binch, C. 1991. *Amazing Grace.* New York: Dial. (Self-concept, gender equity, African Americans)

P   Hoffman, M., & Binch, C. 1995. *Boundless Grace.* New York: Dial. (Family, African Americans)

P   Hogan, P. 1997. *Johnny Appleseed: A Tall Tale.* Mahwah, NJ: Troll. (American tall tale)

I   Hoobler, D., & Hoobler, T. 1994. *The Chinese American Family Album.* New York: Oxford University Press. (Chinese American culture)

I   Hoobler, D., & Hoobler, T. 1995. *The Cuban American Family Album.* New York: Oxford University Press. (Cuban American history, Cuban American immigration)

I   Hoobler, D., & Hoobler, T. 1995. *The Japanese American Family Album.* New York: Oxford University Press. (Japanese American culture)

I   Hoobler, D., & Hoobler, T. 1994. *The Mexican American Family Album.* New York: Oxford University Press. (Mexican American history, Mexican American immigration)

I   Hoobler, D., & Hoobler, T. 1990. *Vietnam, Why We Fought: An Illustrated History.* New York: Knopf. (Vietnamese history)

I   Hooks, W. H. 1990. *The Ballad of Belle Dorcas.* New York: Knopf. (African American history, slavery)

I   Hooks, W. H. 1988. *A Flight of Dazzle Angels.* New York: Macmillan. (Challenged—clubfooted)

P, I   Hooks, W. H. 1989. *The Three Little Pigs and the Fox.* New York: Macmillan. (Appalachian version of *The Three Little Pigs*)

P, I   Hopkinson, D. 1993. *Sweet Clara and the Freedom Quilt.* New York: Knopf. (Quilt story—different perspectives)

I   Hospital, J. T. 1987. *Dislocations.* Baton Rouge: Lousiana State University. (Immigration)

I   Hotze, S. 1988. *A Circle Unbroken.* New York: Clarion. (Stereotying, prejudice, Native American history)

I   House, P. 1993. *It's Our World, Too!: Stories of Young People Who Are Making a Difference.* Boston: Little, Brown. (Social activism)

I   Howard, D. E. 1996. *India.* Chicago: Children's Press. (Indian history, culture, contributions)

I   Howard, E. 1987. *Her Own Song.* New York: Atheneum. (Adopted family—one Chinese and one American)

P   Howard, E. F. 1991. *Aunt Flossie Hats and Crab Cakes Later.* New York: Dutton. (African American family)

P   Howlett, B. 1993. *I'm New Here.* Boston: Houghton Mifflin. (Spanish language)

I   Hoyt-Goldsmith, D. 1992. *Arctic Hunter.* New York: Holiday House. (Inupiat family)

P, I   Hoyt-Goldsmith, D. 1994. *Celebrating Kwanzaa.* New York: Holiday House. (African American history)

P   Hoyt-Goldsmith, D. 1993. *Cherokee Summer.* New York: Holiday House. (Native American family)

I   Hoyt-Goldsmith, D. 1994. *Days of the Dead: A Mexican–American Celebration.* New York: Holiday House. (Mexican American holiday)

P, I Hoyt-Goldsmith, D. 1992. *Hoang Anh: A Vietnamese American Boy*. New York: Holiday House. (Vietnamese people, immigration)

I Hoyt-Goldsmith, D. 1996. *Migrant Worker: A Boy from the Rio Grande Valley*. New York: Holiday House. (Migrant worker, Hispanic family, social activism)

I Hoyt-Goldsmith, D. 1991. *Pueblo Storyteller*. New York: Holiday House. (Native American family)

P, I Hoyt-Goldsmith, D. 1990. *Totem Pole*. New York: Holiday House. (Tsimshian and Klallam Indians)

P, I Hubbard, J. 1994. *Shooting Back from the Reservation*. New York: New Press. (Photographs of Native American life taken by Native American youth)

P Hudson, C. W., & Ford, G. F. *Bright Eyes, Brown Skin*. Littleton, MA: Sundance. (Self-concept, African Americans)

I Hudson, J. 1990. *Sweetgrass*. New York: Philomel. (Blackfoot Indian history, Blackfoot Indian family)

I Hudson, K. E. 1994. *The Will and the Way: Paul R. Williams, Architect*. New York: Rizzoli. (Famous African American)

P, I Hudson, W. 1991. *Jamal's Busy Day*. Orange, NJ: Just Us Books. (African American family)

P, I Hudson, W. 1993. *Pass It On: African American Poetry for Children*. New York: Scholastic. (African American poetry)

I Huff, B. A. 1990. *Greening the City Streets: The Story of Community Gardens*. New York: Clarion. (Environment, social activism)

I Hughes, L. 1994. *The Dream Keeper*. New York: Knopf. (African American poems)

P Hughes, M. 1996. *A Handful of Seeds*. New York: Orchard. (Hispanic family; foods—different perspectives)

I Hurmence, F. 1982. *A Girl Called Boy*. New York: Clarion. (African Americans)

I Hurwitz, J. 1988. *Anne Frank: Life in Hiding*. Philadelphia: Jewish Publication Society. (Jewish history, World War II)

I Hurwitz, J. 1990. *Class President*. New York: Morrow. (Latinos)

P Hurwitz, J. 1993. *New Shoes for Sylvia*. New York: Morrow. (Hispanic family)

P Ikeda, D. 1992. *The Cherry Tree*. New York: Knopf. (Peace)

P Jackson, G. N. 1993. *Elijah McCoy, Inventor*. Cleveland: Modern Curriculum Press. (Famous African American)

P Jackson, M. 1995. *Homes around the World*. Austin: Steck-Vaughn. (Houses and homes)

P, I Jacobs, F. 1992. *The Tainos: The People Who Welcomed Columbus*. New York: Putnam. (Columbus)

P, I Jacobs, J. 1989. *Tattercoats*. New York: Putnam. (Translation of *Cinderella*)

P, I Jacobs, J., ed. 1994. *Indian Fairy*. New York: Dover. (Tales from India)

I   Jacobs, S. K. 1993. *The Boy Who Loved Morning.* Boston: Little, Brown. (Native Americans)

I   Jacobs, W. J. 1990. *Ellis Island: New Hope in a New Land.* New York: Scribner's. (Immigration)

I   Jaffe, N. 1993. *The Uninvited Guest and Other Jewish Holiday Tales.* New York: Scholastic. (Jewish holiday tales)

P   Jaffrey, M. 1997. *Robi Dobi: The Marvelous Adventures of an Indian Elephant.* New York: Dial. (Indian history, culture, contributions)

I   Jaffrey, M. 1985. *Seasons of Splendor: Tales, Myths, and Legends from India.* New York: Macmillan. (Tales from India)

I   James, B. 1994. *The Mud Family.* New York: Putnam. (Anasazi Indian family)

I   Janeczko, P. B., ed. 1995. *Wherever Home Begins: 100 Contemporary Poems.* New York: Orchard. (Poems, homes)

I   Japanese American Curriculum Project. 1985. *The Japanese American Journey.* San Mateo, CA: AACP. (Japanese American culture)

I   Jassem, K. 1978. *Sacajawea.* Mahwah, NJ: Troll. (Native Americans)

P, I   Jeffers, S. 1991. *Brother Eagle, Sister Sky.* New York: Scholastic. (Native Americans)

I   Jen, G. 1991. *Typical American.* Boston: Houghton Mifflin. (Chinese Americans)

I   Jenness, A. 1988. *Families: A Celebration of Diversity, Commitment, and Love.* Boston: Houghton Mifflin. (Family)

I   Jenness, A., & Rivers, A. 1989. *In Two Worlds: A Yup'ik Eskimo Family.* Boston: Houghton. (Eskimo family)

P   Jennings, P. 1992. *Strawberry Thanksgiving.* Cleveland: Modern Curriculum Press. (Tales, Native America)

P   Jensen, P. 1997. *The Legend of Sleepy Hollow.* Mahwah, NJ: Troll. (American tall tales)

P   Jensen, P. 1995. *Paul Bunyan and His Blue Ox.* Mahwah, NJ: Troll. (American tall tales)

P   Jensen, P., & Litzinger, R. 1995. *John Henry and His Mighty Hammer.* Mahwah, NJ: Troll. (American tall tales)

P   Johnson, A. 1993. *Do Like Kyla.* New York: Orchard. (African American family)

P   Johnson, A. 1990. *When I Am Old with You.* New York: Orchard. (Elderly)

P, I   Johnson, D. 1993. *Now Let Me Fly: The Story of a Slave Family.* New York: Macmillan. (African American, slavery)

P, I   Johnson, D. 1994. *Seminole Diary: Remembrance of a Slave.* New York: Macmillan. (Slavery)

P   Johnson, D. 1990. *What Will Mommy Do When I'm at School?* London: Collier Macmillan. (African American family)

I   Johnson, J. 1995. *Puerto Rico.* Minneapolis: Lerner. (Puerto Rican history, Puerto Rican culture)

P, I   Johnson, J. W. 1995. *Lift Ev'ry Voice and Sing.* New York: Scholastic. (African American songs)

P   Johnston, T. 1985. *The Quilt Story.* New York: Putnam. (Quilt stories—pioneer version)

P   Jones, K. 1994. *Happy Birthday, Dr. King!* New York: Simon & Schuster. (African Americans)

I   Jones, R. C. 1988. *The Believers.* New York: Arcade. (Family—adopted)

P   Joose, B. M. 1991. *Mama, Do You Love Me?* New York: Scholastic. (Native American/Eskimo—Inuit people)

I   Kadohata, C. 1989. *Floating World.* New York: Viking. (Japanese Americans)

I   Kalman, E. 1995. *Tchaikovsky Discovers America.* New York: Orchard. (Russian emigres)

P   Kalman, M. 1995. *Swami on Rye: Max in India.* New York: Viking. (Indian history, culture, contributions)

P   Katz, B. 1992. *A Family's Hanukkah.* New York: Random House. (Jewish traditions)

I   Katz, E. 1996. *India in Pictures.* Minneapolis: Lerner. (Indian history, culture, contributions)

I   Katz, W. L. 1995. *Black Women of the Old West.* New York: Atheneum. (African American history)

I   Katz, W. L., & Franklin, P. A. 1993. *Proudly Red and Black: Stories of African and Native Americans.* New York: Atheneum. (African American history, Native American history)

P   Keams, G. 1995. *Grandmother Spider Brings the Sun.* Flagstaff, AZ: Northland. (Cherokee creation story)

P   Keats, E. J. 1971. *Apt. 3.* New York: Macmillan. (African American)

P   Keats, E. J. 1987. *Goggles.* New York: Macmillan. (African Americans)

P, I   Keats, E. J. 1965. *John Henry.* New York: Pantheon. (African Americans)

P   Keats, E. J. 1968. *A Letter to Amy.* New York: Harper. (African American)

P   Keats, E. J. 1967. *Peter's Chair.* New York: HarperCollins. (Family, African Americans)

P   Keats, E. J. 1976. *The Snowy Day.* New York: Penguin. (African Americans)

I   Keegan, M. 1991. *Pueblo Boy: Growing Up in Two Worlds.* New York: Dutton. (Pueblo culture)

P   Keller, H. 1989. *The Best Present.* New York: Greenwillow. (Family, elderly)

P   Keller, H. 1994. *Grandfather's Dream.* New York: Greenwillow. (Elderly; Vietnamese history)

P   Kellogg, S. 1994. *Paul Bunyan.* New York: Mulberry Books. (American tall tales)

P Kellogg, S. 1992. *Pecos Bill.* New York: Mulberry Books. (American tall tales)

I Kendall, R. 1992. *Eskimo Boy: Life in an Inupiaq Village.* New York: Scholastic. (Eskimo culture)

Kent, Z. 1989. *The Story of Geronimo.* Chicago: Children's Press. (Native American history)

P Kessel, J. 1983. *Squanto and the First Thanksgiving.* Minneapolis: Carolrhoda. (Native Americans)

P, I Kid, D. 1991. *Onion Tears.* New York: Orchard. (Vietnamese people, immigration)

P Kimmel, E. 1988. *The Chanukkah Guest.* New York: Holiday House. (Jewish traditions)

P Kimmel, E. 1989. *Hershel and the Hanukkah Goblins.* New York: Holiday House. (Jewish tale)

P King, S. 1993. *Shannon: An Ojibway Dancer.* Minneapolis: Lerner. (Ojibway culture)

I Kinsley-Warcock, N. 1989. *The Canada Geese Quilt.* New York: Cobblehill. (Quilt—Canadian; family)

P, I Kipling, R. 1987. *The Jungle Book.* New York: Puffin. (Tales from India)

I Kipling, R. 1987. *The Jungle Book: The Mowgli Stories.* New York: Morrow. (Tales from India)

P Kipling, R. 1997. *Rikki-Tikki-Tavi.* New York: Morrow. (Tales from India)

P, I Kipling, R.; Ashachik, D.; & Hannon, H. 1992. *The Jungle Book.* Mahwah, NJ: Troll. (Tales from India)

P Kirk, D. 1994. *Miss Spider's Tea Party.* New York: Scholastic. (Self-concept)

I Kitano, H. H. L. 1995. *The Japanese Americans.* New York: Chelsea House. (Japanese American immigration)

I Klausner, J. 1993. *Sequoyah's Gift: A Portrait of the Cherokee Leader.* New York: HarperCollins. (Cherokee history)

I Knight, M. B. 1996. *Talking Walls.* Gardiner, MA: Tilbury. (Houses—different perspectives)

P Koch, M. 1993. *World Water Watch.* New York: Greenwillow. (Environment)

I Kodama, T. 1995. *Shin's Tricycle.* New York: Walker. (Hiroshima, Japanese history)

P Koeler, P. 1990. *The Day We Met You.* New York: Bradbury. (Family—adoption)

P Koltach, A. 1992. *The Jewish Child's First Book of Why?* New York: Jonathan David. (Jewish history, Jewish holidays)

P Kroll, S. 1993. *Queen of the May.* New York: Holiday House. (Variation of Cinderella story)

P Kroll, V. 1995. *Fireflies, Peach Pies, and Lullabies.* New York: Simon & Schuster. (Elderly)

P Kroll, V. 1994. *Pink Paper Swans.* Grand Rapids, MI: Eerdman. (Challenged—arthritis; Asian Americans)

I   Krull, K. 1994. *The Other Side: How Kids Live in a California Latino Neighborhood.* New York: Lodestar. (Latino American culture)

I   Krumgold, J. 1953. *And Now Miguel.* New York: Crowell. (Hispanic people)

I   Kudlinski, K. V. 1990. *Helen Keller: A Light for the Blind.* New York: Viking. (Challenged—blind and deaf)

P   Kuklin, S. 1992. *How My Family Lives in America.* New York: Bradbury. (African American, Hispanic, and Chinese American immigrant families)

P   Lacapa, K., & Lacapa, M. 1994. *Less Than Half, More Than Whole.* Flagstaff, AZ: Northland. (Differences and likenesses)

I   Landau, E. 1991. *We Survived the Holocaust.* New York: Watts. (World War II, Holocaust)

P, I   Lankford, M. D. 1992. *Hopscotch around the World.* New York: Morrow. (Differences and likenesses)

P   Larry, C. 1993. *Peboan and Seeqwun.* New York: Farrar, Straus, & Giroux. (Ojibway tale)

I   Larsen, R. J. 1989. *The Puerto Ricans in America.* Minneapolis: Lerner. (Puerto Rican immigration)

I   Lasky, K. 1994. *Days of the Dead.* New York: Hyperion. (Mexican family, holiday)

P, I   Lattimore, D. N. 1989. *Why There Is No Arguing in Heaven: A Mayan Myth.* New York: Harper. (Maya creation story)

I   Laure, J. 1992. *Bangladesh.* Chicago: Children's Press. (Indian history, culture, contributions)

P, I   Lawrence, J. 1993. *The Great Migration: An American Story.* New York: HarperCollins. (African American history, migration)

P   Lears, L. 1998. *Ian's Walk: A Story about Autism.* Morton Grove, IL: Albert Whitman. (Challenged—autism)

I   Leathers, N. L. 1991. *The Japanese in America.* Minneapolis: Lerner. (Japanese American history)

P, I   Lee, G. L. 1989. *Interesting People: Black American History Makers.* New York: Ballantine. (Famous African American women)

P   Lee, H. V. 1994. *At the Beach.* New York: Holt. (Mandarin Chinese language)

I   Lehrman, R. 1992. *The Store That Mama Built.* New York: Macmillan. (Jewish immigration)

P, I   Lester, H. 1994. *John Henry.* New York: Dial. (African American tall tale)

P   Lester, H. 1988. *Tacky the Penguin.* Boston: Houghton Mifflin. (Self-concept)

I   Lester, J. 1989. *How Many Spots Does a Leopard Have?: And Other Tales.* New York: Scholastic. (African- and Jewish-based tales)

I   Levine, E. 1995. *A Fence Away from Freedom: Japanese Americans and World War II.* New York: Putnam. (Internment camps)

I   Levine, E. 1993. *Freedom's Children: Young Civil Rights Activists Tell Their Own Stories.* New York: Putnam. (Social activism)

I   Levine, E. 1988. *If You Traveled on the Underground Railroad.* New York: Scholastic. (African Americans)

P   Levine, E. 1989. *I Hate English.* New York: Scholastic. (Chinese and English languages)

I   Leveitin, P. 1993. *Journey to America.* New York: Atheneum. (Jewish history, World War II, immigration)

I   Levison, N. S. 1990. *Christopher Columbus: Voyager to the Unknown.* New York: Lodestar. (Columbus—different perspectives)

P   Lewin, H. 1981. *Jafta.* Minneapolis: Carolrhoda. (African Americans)

I   Lewin, T. 1994. *The Reindeer People.* New York: Macmillan/Simon & Schuster. (Life of the Lapp people)

P, I   Lewis, B. A. 1995. *The Kid's Guide to Service Projects: Over 500 Service Ideas for Young People Who Want to Make a Difference.* Minneapolis: Free Spirit. (Volunteerism)

P   Lewis, J. P. 1994. *The Frog Princess.* New York: Dial. (Version of classic tale)

P, I   Lewis, R. 1991. *All of You Was Singing.* New York: Atheneum. (Aztec myth)

P   Lewis, T. 1995. *Sacred River.* New York: Clarion. (Indian history, culture, contributions)

P   Lindbergh, R. 1993. *Grandfather's Lovesong.* New York: Viking. (Family, elderly)

P, I   Lincoln, A. 1995. *The Gettysburg Address.* Boston: Houghton Mifflin. (Abraham Lincoln)

P   Lindsay, J. W. 1994. *Do I Have a Daddy?: Story about a Single-Parent Child.* Buena Vista, CA; Morning Glory Press. (Family—single parent)

P, I   Ling, M. 1991. *Eyewitness Juniors: Amazing Wolves, Dogs, & Foxes.* New York: Knopf. (True stories about wolves, dogs, and foxes)

I   Lingard, J. 1990. *Tug of War.* New York: Lodestar. (Immigration)

I   Liptak, K. 1991. *Indians of the Pacific Northwest.* New York: Facts on File. (Native American history)

I   Litchtveld, N. 1993. *I Lost My Arrow in a Kankan Tree.* New York: Lothrop, Lee & Shepard. (Surinam)

P, I   Littlechild, G. 1993. *This Land Is My Land.* Emeryville, CA: Children's Book Press. (Native Americans; Columbus—different perspectives)

P, I   Livingston, M. C. 1996. *Festivals.* New York: Holiday House. (Holidays in India)

P   Livingston, M. C. 1994. *Keep on Singing: A Ballad of Marian Anderson.* London: Anderson. (African American women)

P, I   Locker, T. 1991. *The Land of the Gray Wolf.* New York: Dial. (Native American history; environment)

P   Loh, M. 1987. *Tucking Mommy In.* New York: Orchard. (Family, Asian Americans)

P, I   London, J. 1993. *The Eyes of the Gray Wolf.* San Francisco: Chronicle. (True story about wolves)

P   London, J. 1996. *Red Wolf Country.* New York: Dutton. (Wolves—different perspectives)

P   Long, D. J. 1995. *I Wish I Were the Baby.* Nashville: Ideals. (Family)

I   Lord, B. B. 1984. *In the Year of the Boar and Jackie Robinson.* New York: Harper. (Chinese people and African Americans)

P   Lotz, K. E. 1993. *Can't Sit Still.* New York: Dutton. (Cycles, African Americans)

P, I   Louie, A. L. 1982. *Yeh-Shen: A Cinderella Story from China.* New York: Sandcastle. (Chinese version of *Cinderella*)

P, I   Lowell, S. 1992. *The Three Little Javelinas.* New York: Scholastic. (Southwestern version of *The Three Little Pigs*)

P, I   Lowrey, L. 1995. *Somebody Somewhere Knows My Name.* Minneapolis: Carolrhoda. (Abandoned children, homeless people)

I   Lowry, L. 1989. *Number of Stars.* Boston: Houghton Mifflin. (Jewish people, World War II)

I   Lowes, J. 1995. *Looking at Photographs.* San Francisco: Chronicle. (Differences and likenesses)

P, I   Luenn, N. 1990. *Nessa's Fish.* New York: Atheneum. (Family, elderly)

P, I   Lum, D. 1994. *The Golden Slipper: A Vietnamese Legend.* Mahwah, NJ: Troll. (Vietnamese version of *Cinderella*)

P   Lyon, G. E. 1993. *Dreamplace.* New York: Orchard. (Anasazi history)

P   Lyon, G. E. 1992. *Who Came Down That Road?* New York: Orchard. (Native American history; differences and likenesses)

I   Lyons, M. E. 1993. *Stitching Stars: The Story Quilts of Harriet Powers.* New York: Scribner's. (African American history, quilt story)

P   MacGill-Callahan, S. 1991. *And Still the Turtle Watched.* New York: Dial. (Environment)

I   Machado, A. M. 1995. *Exploration into Latin America.* New Discovery. (Latin American culture)

I   MacLachlin, P. 1985. *Sarah, Plain and Tall.* New York: Harper & Row. (Family)

I   MacMahon, P. 1993. *A Korean Girl.* Honesdale, PA: Boyds Mills Press. (Korean life)

P, I   Maestro, B. 1996. *Coming to America: The Story of Immigration.* New York: Scholastic. (Immigration)

I   Maestro, B., & Maestro, G. 1991. *The Discovery of the Americas.* New York: Lothrop. (Columbus—different perspectives)

P Mahy, M. 1990. *The Seven Chinese Brothers.* New York: Scholastic. (Chinese history)

P Malone, N. L. 1988. *A Home.* New York: Bradbury. (Houses and homes)

P Manning, M. 1994. *A Ruined House.* Cambridge, MA: Candlestick Press. (Houses and homes)

P Margolies, B. A. 1992. *Kanu of Kathmandu: A Journey in Nepal.* New York: Simon & Schuster. (Indian history, culture, contributions)

I Marie, D. 1988. *Tears for Ashan.* Memphis: Creative Press. (Africans)

P, I Markin, P. M. 1993. *The Little Painter of Sabana Grande.* New York: Bradbury. (Houses and homes)

P Marshall, J. 1988. *Goldilocks and the Three Bears.* New York: Scholastic. (Fairy tale)

I Martin, A. M. 1990. *Kristy and the Secret of Susan.* New York: Scholastic. (Challenged—autism)

P, I Martin, B., & Archambault, B. 1989. *Knots on a Counting Rope.* New York: Holt. (Elderly; African Americans)

P, I Martin, R. 1993. *The Boy Who Lived with the Seals.* New York: Putnam. (Chinook Indian tale)

P Martin, R. 1997. *The Monkey Bridge.* New York: Knopf. (Tale from India)

P, I Martin, R. 1992. *The Rough-Faced Girl.* New York: Putnam. (Native American version of *Cinderella*)

P Martin, R., & Anderson, B. 1998. *The Brave Little Parrot.* New York: Putnam. (Tale from India)

P, I Maruki, T. 1980. *Hiroshima No Pika.* New York: Lothrop. (Japanese history, Hiroshima)

I Marvin, I. R. 1991. *Bridge to Freedom.* Philadelphia: Jewish Publication Society. (World War II, Jewish people)

I Marx, T. 1994. *Echoes of World War II.* Minneapolis: Lerner. (World War II)

P Marzollo, J. 1993. *Happy Birthday, Martin Luther King, Jr.* New York: Scholastic. (African American history)

I Matas, C. 1993. *Daniel's Story.* New York: Scholastic. (Jewish people, Holocaust)

P Mathers, P. 1991. *Borreguita and the Coyote.* New York: Knopf. (Mexican tale)

P, I Mathis, S. B. 1975. *The Hundred Penny Book.* New York: Viking. (Elderly)

P, I Mattern, J. 1992. *Young Martin Luther King, Jr.: "I Have a Dream."* Mahwah, NJ: Troll. (African Americans)

P Mattox, C. W. 1989. *Shake It to the One That You Love the Best.* Nashville: Jig. (African American songs)

I Mayerson, E. W. 1990. *The Cat Who Escaped from Steerage: A Bubbemeiser.* New York: Scribner's. (Jewish history, immigration)

I   Mayo, G. 1988. *Earthmaker's Tales: North American Indian Stories about Earth's Happenings.* New York: Walker. (North American Indian tales)

P   Mayo, G. W. 1993. *Meet Tricky Coyote.* New York: Walker. (Native American tales)

I   McCurdy, M. 1994. *Escape from Slavery: The Boyhood of Frederick Douglass in His Own Words.* New York: Knopf. (African American history, slavery)

P   McDermott, G. M. 1972. *Anansi the Spider.* New York: Scholastic. (African American tale)

P   McDermott, G. M. 1993. *Raven: A Trickster Tale from the Pacific Northwest.* New York: Scholastic. (Native American tale)

P   McDonald, M. 1996. *My House Has Stars.* New York: Orchard. (Homes—different perspectives)

P   McGovern, A. 1986. *Stone Soup.* New York: Scholastic. (French folklore)

P   McKee, D. 1989. *Elmer.* New York: Lothrop. (Self-concept; differences and likenesses)

P, I   McKenna, N. D. 1986. *A Zulu Family.* Minneapolis: Lerner. (African American)

I   McKissack, P. 1984. *The Apache: A New True Book.* Chicago: Children's Press. (Native Americans)

I   McKissack, P. 1992. *The Dark Thirty: Southern Tales of the Supernatural.* New York: Knopf. (Southern tales)

P, I   McKissack, P. 1986. *Flossie and the Fox.* New York: Dial. (African American version of *The Three Little Pigs*)

I   McKissack, P. 1989. *Jesse Jackson: A Biography.* New York: Scholastic. (African American history, social activism)

McKissack, P., & McKissack, F. 1984. *African-American Inventors.* Brookfield, CT: Millbrook. (Famous African Americans)

I   McKissack, P., & McKissack, F. 1994. *Black Diamond: The Story of the Negro Baseball Leagues.* New York: Scholastic. (African American history)

I   McKissack, P., & McKissack, F. 1994. *Christmas in the Big House, Christmas in the Quarters.* New York: Scholastic. (African American history, Civil War, holidays)

I   McKissack, P., & McKissack, F. 1988. *A Long Hard Journey: The Story of the Pullman Porter.* New York: Walker. (Civil rights movement)

P, I   McKissack, P., & McKissack, F. 1993. *Madame C. J. Walker: Self-Made Millionaire.* Springfield, NJ: Enslow. (Famous African American women)

P, I   McKissack, P., & McKissack, F. 1991. *Mary McLeod: A Great Teacher.* Springfield, NJ: Enslow. (Famous African American women)

I   McKissack, P., & McKissack, F. 1996. *Red-Tails Angels: The Story of the Tuskegee Airmen of World War II.* New York: Walker. (African American history, famous African Americans)

P, I   McLerran, A. 1995. *The Ghost Dance.* New York: Clarion. (Native American history)

I   McNair. 1990. *India.* Chicago: Children's Press. (Indian history, culture, contributions; immigration)

I   Mederias, A. S. 1993. *Come This Far to Freedom: A History of African Americans.* New York: Atheneum. (African American history)

P   Mederias, A. S. 1991. *Dancing with the Indians.* New York: Holiday House. (African Americans and Native Americans)

P   Mederias, A. S. 1989. *Our People.* New York: Atheneum. (African American history, elderly)

I   Meltzer, M. 1984. *The Black Americans: A History of Their Own Times.* New York: HarperCollins. (African American history)

I   Meltzer, M. 1980. *The Chinese Americans.* New York: HarperCollins. (Chinese American history)

I   Meltzer, M. 1990. *Columbus and the World around Him.* New York: Watts. (Columbus—different perspectives)

I   Meltzer, M. 1982. *The Hispanic Americans.* New York: HarperCollins. (Latino history)

I   Meltzer, M. 1976. *Never to Forget: The Jews of the Holocaust.* New York: Harper & Row. (Jewish people, Holocaust)

I   Meltzer, M. 1976. *The Story of How Gentiles Saved Jews in the Holocaust.* New York: Harper & Row. (Holocaust—different perspectives)

I   Meltzer, M. 1989. *Voices from the Civil War: A Documentary of the Great American Conflict.* New York: Crowell. (Civil War, prejudice)

I   Meltzer, M. 1994. *Who Cares: Millions Do . . . : A Book about Altruism.* New York: Walker. (Social activism)

I   Mendez, A. 1994. *Cubans in America.* Minneapolis: Lerner. (Cuban American history)

I   Mendez, P. 1989. *The Black Snowman.* New York: Scholastic. (African Americans, prejudice, self-concept)

I   Mettger, Z. 1994. *The Victory Is Won: Black Soldiers in the Civil War.* New York: Lodestar. (African American history, Civil War)

P, I   Miles, C. 1993. *Calvin's Christmas Wish.* New York: Viking. (African American author)

P   Miles, M. 1971. *Annie and the Old One.* Boston: Little, Brown. (Elderly; Native Americans)

I   Miller, R. 1992. *Reflections of a Black Cowboy.* Morristown, NJ: Silver Burdett. (African American history)

P   Miller, W. 1994. *Zora Hurston and the Chinaberry Tree.* New York: Lee & Low. (Famous African American women)

P   Mills, L. 1991. *The Rag Coat.* Boston: Little, Brown. (Appalachian quilt story)

I   Minard, R. 1975. *Womenfolk and Fairy Tales.* Boston: Houghton Mifflin. (Gender equity)

P, I   Minters, F. 1994. *Cinder-elly.* New York: Viking/Penguin. (Modern version of *Cinderella*)

P   Mitchell, B. 1993. *Down Buttermilk Lane.* New York: Lothrop. (Amish family)

P, I   Mitchell, M. K. 1993. *Uncle Jed's Barber Shop.* New York: Simon & Schuster. (African American history)

P   Mitchell, R. P. 1993. *Hue Boy.* New York: Dial. (Self-concept)

P, I   Mochizuki, K. 1993. *Baseball Saved Us.* New York: Lee & Low. (Japanese American history)

P   Mochizuki, K. 1995. *Heroes.* New York: Lee & Low. (Japanese Americans, stereotyping)

P   Mohr, N. 1993. *All for the Better: A Story of El Barrio.* Austin: Raintree/Steck-Vaughn. (Puerto Rican contributions, social activism)

P, I   Mohr, N., & Martorell, A. 1995. *The Song of el Coqui and Other Tales of Puerto Rico.* New York: Viking. (Puerto Rican culture)

P   Monjo, F. N. 1970. *The Drinking Gourd.* New York: Harper & Row. (African Americans, slavery)

I   Monroe, J. G., & Williamson, R. A. 1993. *First Houses: Native American Homes and Sacred Structures.* Boston: Houghton Mifflin. (Houses and homes)

P   Montresor, B. 1991. *Little Red Riding Hood.* New York: Doubleday. (The classic story)

I   Moore, K. 1994. *If You Lived at the Time of the Civil War.* New York: Scholastic. (African American history, Civil War)

I   Moore, Y. 1991. *Freedom Songs.* New York: Orchard. (African American history)

P   Mora, P. 1992. *A Birthday Basket for Tia.* New York: Macmillan. (Hispanic family, holiday)

P   Mora, P. 1994. *Pablo's Tree.* New York: Macmillan. (Hispanic family)

I   Morey, J., & Dunn, W. 1989. *Famous Mexican Americans.* New York: Cobblehill Books. (Mexican American history)

P, I   Morimoto, J. 1987. *My Hiroshima.* New York: Viking. (Japanese American history)

P   Morris, A. 1989. *Bread, Bread, Bread.* New York: Lothrop, Lee & Shepard. (Differences and likenesses)

P   Morris, A. 1989. *Hats, Hats, Hats.* New York: Lothrop, Lee & Shepard. (Differences and likenesses)

P   Morris, A. 1990. *Houses and Homes.* New York: Lothrop, Lee & Shepard. (Differences and likenesses; houses and homes)

P   Morris, A. 1990. *Loving.* New York: Lothrop, Lee & Shepard. (Differences and likenesses)

P   Moss, M. 1994. *In America.* New York: Dutton. (Elderly, immigration from Lithuania)

P   Munsch, R. 1980. *The Paper Bag Princess.* Toronto: Annick Press. (Gender-equity tale)

P, I   Murphy, C. R. 1993. *The Prince and the Salmon People.* New York: Rizzoli. (Native American tale)

I   Murphy, J. 1993. *Across America on an Emigrant Train.* New York: Clarion. (Emigrants)

P, I   Myers, W. D. 1993. *Brown Angels: An Album of Pictures and Verse.* New York: HarperCollins. (African Americans)

I   Myers, W. D. 1995. *One More River to Cross: An African American Photograph Album.* San Diego: Harcourt Brace. (African American history)

I   Myers, W. D. 1988. *Won't Know Till I Get There.* New York: Puffin. (Family)

I   Namioka, L. 1995. *Yang the Third and Her Impossible Family.* Boston: Little, Brown. (Chinese American family)

I   Namioka, L. 1992. *Yang the Youngest and His Terrible Ear.* Boston: Little, Brown. (Chinese family, white family)

I   National Geographic Staff. 1988. *Adventures in Your National Parks.* Washington, DC: National Geographic Society. (Environment)

P   Nay, S. 1973. *Jo, Flo and Yolando.* Chapel Hill, NC: Lollipop Power Books. (African Americans)

P, I   Nelson, M. 1993. *Mayfield Crossing.* New York: Putnam. (Stereotyping)

P   Nelson, M. N. 1988. *Always Gramma.* New York: Putnam. (Elderly—nursing home)

I   Nelson, T. 1988. *And One for All.* New York: Dell. (Social activism)

I   Neuberger, A. E. 1995. *The Girl–Son.* Minneapolis: Lerner. (Deconstructing stereotypes)

P, I   Newton Chocolate, D. M. 1990. *Kwanzaa.* Chicago: Children's Press. (African American holiday)

P   Newton Chocolate, D. M. 1992. *My First Kwanzaa Book.* New York: Scholastic. (African American holiday)

I   Nez, R. T., as told to K. Wilder. 1995. *Forbidden Talent.* Flagstaff, AZ: Northland. (Navajo family, elderly)

I   Nhuong, H. Q. 1982. *The Land I Lost: Adventures of a Boy in Vietnam.* New York: Harper. (Vietnamese people)

P   Nieves, E. R. 1994. *Juan Bobo: Four Folktales from Puerto Rico.* New York: HarperCollins. (Puerto Rican folktales)

P Nikola-Lisa, W. 1995. *Being with You This Way*. New York: Lee & Low. (Differences and likenesses)

I Nodar, C. S. 1992. *Abuelita's Paradise*. Morton Grove, IL: Albert Whitman. (Puerto Rican family, elderly)

I Nolan, D. 1988. *Wolf Child*. New York: Macmillan. (Family—different perspectives)

P Nunes, S. M. 1995. *The Last Dragon*. New York: Clarion. (Chinese American culture)

P Nye, N. S. 1993. *Siti's Secrets*. New York: Simon & Schuster. (Elderly; Palestinian/Arab American family)

I Nye, N. S. 1995. *The Tree Is Older Than You Are: A Bilingual Gathering of Poems and Stories from Mexico with Paintings by Mexican Artists*. New York: Simon & Schuster. (Bilingual literature, Mexican poems, Mexican culture)

I O'Dell, S. 1983. *Island of the Blue Dolphins*. Boston: Houghton Mifflin. (Native Americans)

I O'Dell, S. 1989. *My Name Is Not Angelica*. Boston: Houghton Mifflin. (African American history, slavery)

I O'Dell, S., & Hall, E. 1992. *Thunder Rolling in the Mountains*. New York: Dell. (Nez Perce Indians)

P Onyefulu, I. 1993. *A Is for Africa*. New York: Cobblehill Books. (African history)

P, I Ortiz, S. 1988. *The People Shall Continue*. Emeryville, CA: Children's Book Press. (Native Americans)

P, I Osborne, M. P. 1991. *American Tall Tales*. New York: Knopf. (American tall tales)

P, I Osborne, M. P. 1993. *Mermaid Tales from around the World*. New York: Scholastic. (Tales—different perspectives)

I Osinski, A. 1992. *The Navajo: A New True Book*. Chicago: Children's Press. (Native Americans)

P, I Osofsky, A. 1992. *Dreamcatcher*. New York: Orchard. (Native American tale)

P Otey, M. 1990. *Daddy Has a Pair of Striped Shorts*. New York: Farrar, Straus, & Giroux. (Family, stereotyping)

P Oughton, J. 1992. *How the Stars Fell into the Sky*. Boston: Houghton Mifflin. (Navajo folktale)

P, I Oughton, J. 1994. *The Magic Weaver of Rugs: A Tale of the Navajo*. Boston: Houghton Mifflin. (Navajo tale)

I Padden, C., & Humphries, T. 1988. *Deaf in America: Voices from a Culture*. New York: Orchard. (Challenged—deaf)

I Panzer, N. 1994. *Celebrate America in Poetry and Art*. New York: Hyperion. (America's diversity)

I Parker, M. 1990. *What Is Martin Luther King Jr. Day?* Chicago: Children's Press. (African American history)

I   Parks, R., with J. Haskins. 1992. *Rosa Parks: My Story.* New York: Dial. (Famous African American women)

P, I   Patent, D. H. 1990. *Gray Wolf, Red Wolf.* New York: Clarion. (True story about wolves)

I   Paterson, K. 1989. *Park's Quest.* New York: Puffin. (Vietnamese war)

P   Patterson, C. 1989. *Marian Anderson.* New York: Watts. (African American women)

P, I   Paul, A. W. 1991. *Eight Hands Round: A Patchwork Alphabet.* New York: HarperCollins. (Quilt story—U.S. history)

I   Paulsen, G. 1993. *Night John.* New York: Bantam Doubleday Dell. (African American history, slavery)

P   Paulsen, G. 1995. *The Tortilla Factory.* San Diego: Harcourt Brace. (Food—different perspectives)

P   Paxton, T. 1990. *Belling the Cat and Other Aesop's Fables.* New York: Morrow. (American tall tales)

P   Payne, L. M. 1993. *Just Because I Am.* Minneapolis: Free Spirit. (Self-concept)

I   Pelta, K. 1991. *Discovering Christopher Columbus: How History Is Invented.* Minneapolis: Lerner. (Columbus—different perspectives)

P   Pena, S. C. 1987. *Kikiriki Stories and Poems in English and Spanish for Children.* Houston: Arte Publico. (Puerto Rican poems; Spanish and English languages)

I   Penner, L. R. 1994. *The Native American Feast.* New York: Macmillan/Simon & Schuster. (Native American cooking)

P, I   Pennington, D. 1994. *Itse Selu: Cherokee Harvest Festival.* Watertown, MA: Charlesbridge. (Cherokee festival)

I   *Peoples of North America.* New York: Chelsea House. (Series of fifty-one books about immigration, etc.)

I   Perez, N. A. 1988. *Breaker.* Boston: Houghton Mifflin. (Immigration, prejudice)

I   Perkins, M. 1993. *The Sunita Experiment.* Boston: Little, Brown. (Indian family, elderly)

I   Perl, L. 1994. *Issac Bashevis Singer: The Life of a Storyteller.* Philadelphia: Jewish Publication Society. (Famous Jewish American, immigration)

I   Peters, R. M. 1992. *Clambake: A Wampanoag Tradition.* Minneapolis: Lerner. (Wampanoag culture)

P   Peterson, J. 1994. *My Mamma Sings.* New York: HarperCollins. (African American family)

P, I   Peterson, P. 1993. *Inunguak the Little Greenlander.* New York: Lothrop. (Inuit legend)

P   Pfister, M. 1992. *Rainbow Fish.* New York: North–South. (Self-concept)

I   Phelps, E. J. 1981. *The Maid of the North: Feminist Folk Tales from around the World.* New York: Holt. (Gender-equity version of folktales)

I   Phillips, N. 1995. *The Illustrated Book of World Myths: Tales and Legends of the World.* New York: DK. (Tales from different cultures)

I   Phillips, N., ed. 1995. *Singing America: Poems That Define a Nation.* New York: Viking. (Pueblo and Sioux Indian songs)

P   Pico, F. 1994. *The Red Comb.* Mahwah, NJ: Bridgewater. (Puerto Rican slavery)

P   Pirner, C. W. 1991. *Even Little Kids Get Diabetes.* Morton Grove, IL: Albert Whitman. (Challenged—diabetes)

P, I   Polacco, P. 1993. *Babushka Baba Yaga.* New York: Philomel. (Russian tale)

P   Polacco, P. 1990. *Babushka's Doll.* New York: Simon & Schuster. (Russian family, elderly)

P   Polacco, P. 1992. *Chicken Sunday.* New York: Philomel. (Russian family, holiday)

P   Polacco, P. 1990. *Just Plain Fancy.* New York: Dell. (Amish family)

P   Polacco, P. 1988. *The Keeping Quilt.* New York: Simon & Schuster. (Family—quilt)

P   Polacco, P. 1992. *Mrs. Katz and Tush.* New York: Dell. (Elderly; Jewish people; African Americans)

P, I   Polacco, P. 1994. *Pink and Say.* New York: Philomel. (Civil War)

P   Polacco, P. 1988. *Rechenka's Eggs.* New York: Philomel. (Russian family, holiday)

P   Politi, L. 1994. *Three Stalks of Corn.* New York: Aladdin. (Food—Hispanic)

P   Pomerantz, C. 1989. *The Chalk Doll.* Philadelphia: Lippincott. (Jamaican)

I   Porter, A. P. 1992. *Jump at de Sun: The Story of Zora Neale Hurston.* Minneapolis: Carolrhoda. (Famous African American women)

P   Portnay, M. A. 1994. *Matzah Ball.* Rockville, MD: Kar-Ben Copies. (Food—Jewish; Jewish holiday)

I   Potok, C. 1967. *The Chosen: A Novel.* New York: Simon & Schuster. (Jewish history)

I   Potter, J. 1994. *African American Firsts: Famous, Little-Known, and Unsung Triumphs of Blacks in America.* New York: Pinto. (African American history)

P, I   Powell, E. S. 1991. *Daisy.* Minneapolis: Carolrhoda/First Avenue. (Family—child abuse)

I   Powers, T. J., & Galvin, J. L. 1989. *Champions of Change: Biographies of Famous Hispanic Americans.* Austin: Steck-Vaughn. (Hispanic history)

I   Presilla, M. E. 1994. *Feliz Nochebueño, Feliz Navidad: Christmas Feasts of the Hispanic Carribean.* New York: Holt. (Caribbean Christmas)

I   Presilla, M. E., & Soto, G. 1996. *Life around the Lake: Embroideries by the Women of Lake Patzcuaro.* New York: Holt. (Hispanic culture, environment)

I   Press, P. 1995. *Puerto Rican Americans.* New York: Benchmark. (Puerto Rican American culture)

I   Prior, K. 1997. *The history of Emigration from the Indian Subcontinent.* New York: Watts. (Indian history, immigration)

I   Provost, G., & Provost, G. L. 1988. *David and Max.* Philadelphia: Jewish Publication Society. (Jewish people, Holocaust)

P   Quinlan, P. 1994. *Tiger Flowers.* New York: Dial. (Family—AIDS; challenged)

P   Raczek, L. T. 1995. *The Night the Grandfathers Died.* Flagstaff, AZ: Northland. (Ute culture, elderly)

P   Raffi. 1994. *Like Me and You.* New York: Crown. (Differences and likenesses)

P   Rajpust, M. 1997. *The Peacock's Pride.* New York: Disney Press. (Tale from India)

P, I   Rand, G. 1992. *Prince William.* New York: Holt. (Environment, social activism)

I   Rappaport, D. 1991. *Escape from Slavery: Five Journeys to Freedom.* New York: HarperCollins. (African American history, slavery)

I   Rappoport, K. 1993. *Bobby Bonnilla.* New York: Walker. (Famous Puerto Rican American)

P, I   Rattigan, J. K. 1993. *Dumpling Soup.* Boston: Little, Brown. (Holiday, Hawaiian new year)

I   Ray, D. 1991. *Behind the Blue and Gray: The Soldier's Life in the Civil War.* New York: Lodestar. (Civil War)

P   Ray, M. L. 1994. *Shaker Boy.* San Diego, CA: Harcourt. (Civil War, Shaker family)

P, I   Regguinti, G. 1991. *The Sacred Harvest: Ojibway Wild Rice Gathering.* Minneapolis: Lerner. (Ojibway wild rice gathering)

P   Reddix, V. 1991. *Dragon Kite of Autumn Moon.* New York: Lothrop, Lee & Shepard. (Elderly, Chinese holiday)

P   Reiser, L. 1993. *Margaret and Margarita.* New York: Greenwillow. (Spanish and English languages)

I   Reiss, J. 1972. *The Upstairs Room.* New York: Crowell. (Jewish people)

I   Reit, S. 1988. *Behind Rebel Lines: The Incredible Story of Emma Edmonds, Civil War Spy.* New York: Gulliver/San Diego: Harcourt Brace Jovanovich. (Civil War)

P, I   Rhea, M. 1992. *An Ellis Island Christmas.* New York: Viking. (Immigration, holidays)

P   Ringgold, F. 1992. *Aunt Harriet's Underground Railroad.* New York: Crown. (African Americans)

P, I   Ringgold, F. 1993. *Dinner at Aunt Carrie's House.* New York: Hyperion. (African American women)

P   Ringgold, F. 1979. *Tar Beach.* New York: Crown. (Puerto Rican history)

I   Robinet, H. G. 1991. *Children of the Fire.* New York: Atheneum. (Slavery, Underground Railroad, social activism)

P   Robison, M. 1993. *Cock-a-Doodle-Doo!: What Does It Sound Like to You?* New York: Stewart, Tabori, & Chang. (Differences and likenesses, languages)

I   Rochelle, B. 1993. *Witnesses to Freedom: Young People Who Fought for Human Rights.* New York: Lodestar. (Social activism)

P   Roessel, M. 1993. *Kinaalda: A Navajo Girl Grows Up.* Minneapolis: Lerner. (Navajo culture)

I   Rogasky, B. 1988. *Smoke and Ashes: The Story of the Holocaust.* New York: Holiday House. (Jewish history, Holocaust)

P   Rogers, A. 1987. *Luke Has Asthma, Too.* Burlington, VT: Waterfont. (Challenged—asthma)

I   Rol, R. van der, & Verhoeven, R. 1993. *Anne Frank: Beyond the Diary.* New York: Viking. (World War II, Jewish history)

I   Roop, P., & Roop, C., eds. 1990. *I, Columbus: My Journal—1492–3.* New York: Walker. (Columbus—different perspectives)

I   Roseblum, R. 1989. *The Old Synagogue.* Philadelphia: Jewish Publication Society. (Jewish history, immigration)

P, I   Rosen, M. J. 1992. *Elijah's Angel.* San Diego: Harcourt Brace. (Jewish family, Christian holiday)

P, I   Rosen, M. J., ed. 1994. *The Greatest Table: A Banquet to Fight against Hunger.* San Diego: Harcourt Brace. (Hunger)

I   Rosen, M. J., ed. 1992. *Home: A Collaboration of Thirty Distinguished Authors and Illustrators of Children's Books to Aid the Homeless.* New York: HarperCollins. (Homeless people)

P, I   Rosen, M. J., ed. 1992. *South and North, East and West.* New York: Walker. (Multicultural tales)

P, I   Rowland, D. 1994. *Upside Down Tales: Little Red Riding Hood and The Wolf's Tale.* New York: Carol Publishing Group. (Classic and wolf's versions of *Little Red Riding Hood*)

P, I   Rubel, D. 1990. *Fannie Lou Hamer: From Sharecropping to Politics.* Englewood Cliffs, NJ: Silver Burdett. (Famous African American woman).

I   Ruby, L. 1994. *Steal Away Home.* New York: Macmillan/Simon & Schuster. (Underground Railroad)

P, I   Rucki, A. 1992. *Turkey's Gift to the People.* Flagstaff, AZ: Northland. (Native American tale)

P, I   Ryland, C. 1992. *An Angel for Solomon Singer.* New York: Orchard. (Homeless people)

P   Ryland, C. 1982. *When I Was Young in the Mountains.* New York: Puffin. (Appalachian family)

I   Sabin, L. 1992. *Roberto Clemente: Young Baseball Hero.* Mahwah, NJ: Troll. (Latino history)

I   Samuels, G. 1991. *Yours, Bret.* New York: Lodestar. (Family—foster care)

I   San Souci, R. D. 1995. *Larger Than Life: The Adventures of American Legendary Heroes.* New York: Doubleday. (American tall tales)

P, I   San Souci, R. D. 1994. *Sootface: An Ojibway Cinderella Story.* New York: Doubleday. (Native American version of *Cinderella*)

P, I San Souci, R. D. 1988. *The Talking Egg: A Folktale from the American South.* New York: Dial. (Creole version of *Cinderella*)

P Sánchez, I. 1991. *Mis Primeros . . . Números.* New York: Barron's. (Spanish language)

I Sanders, D. 1990. *Clover: A Novel.* Boston: G. K. Hall. (Interracial family)

I Sandler, M. W. 1995. *Immigrants.* New York: HarperCollins. (Immigration—people around the world)

I Santoli, A. 1988. *New Americans: An Oral History.* New York: Viking. (Immigrants)

I Santrey, L. 1983. *Young Frederick Douglass: Fight for Freedom.* Mahwah, NJ: Troll. (African American history)

I Savan, B. 1991. *Earthwatch: Earthcycles and Ecosystems.* Boston: Addison Wesley. (Environment)

P Say, A. 1982. *The Bicycle Man.* New York: Scholastic. (African Americans and Asian Americans)

P Say, A. 1993. *Grandfather's Journey.* Boston: Houghton Mifflin. (Japanese family)

P Say, A. 1991. *Tree of Cranes.* Boston: Houghton Mifflin. (Family—adoption; peace)

P Schermbruber, R. 1991. *Charlie's House.* New York: Viking. (South Africans; houses and homes)

P Schick, E. 1993. *I Have Another Language: The Language Is Dance.* Louisville, KY: American Printing House for the Blind. (Challenged, languages)

P, I Schlein, M. 1995. *The Year of the Panda.* New York: Crowell. (Environment)

I Schlissel, L. 1995. *Black Frontiers: A History of African American Heroes in the Old West.* New York: Simon & Schuster. (African American history)

P Schmid, E. 1992. *The Air around Us.* New York: North–South. (Environment)

I Schmidt, J. 1994. *In the Village of the Elephants.* New York: Walker. (Indian history, culture, contributions)

P, I Scholes, K. 1989. *Peace Begins with You.* San Francisco: Sierra Club. (Peace, social activism)

P Schotter, R. 1993. *The Fruit and Vegetable Man.* Boston: Little, Brown. (Hispanic people)

P Schotter, R. 1995. *Passover Magic.* Boston: Little, Brown. (Jewish holiday)

I Schnur, S. 1994. *The Shadow Children.* New York: Morrow. (World War II)

P, I Schnur, S. 1995. *The Tie Man's Miracle: A Chanukka Tale.* New York: Morrow. (Jewish tale, Jewish holiday)

I Schwartz, H., & Rush, B. 1991. *The Diamond Tree: Jewish Tales from around the World.* New York: HarperCollins. (Jewish tales)

P, I Schwartz, L. 1994. *How Can You Help?: Creative Volunteer Projects for Kids Who Care.* California: The Learning Works, Inc. (Social Action)

P, I Scieszka, J. 1991. *The Frog Prince: Continued.* New York: Viking. (Tales)

P, I   Scieszka, J. 1989. *The True Story of the 3 Little Pigs by A. Wolf.* New York: Viking. (The wolf's version of *The Three Little Pigs*)

P, I   Scieszka, J., & Smith, L. 1992. *The Stinky Cheese Man and Other Fairly Stupid Tales.* New York: Viking. (Humorous folktales and fairy tales)

P   Scott, A. H. 1992. *On Mother's Lap.* New York: Clarion. (Asian American family)

P   Scott, A. H. 1967. *Sam.* New York: McGraw-Hill. (African Americans)

P, I   Seeger, P. 1994. *Abiyoyo.* New York: Aladdin. (Modern African American tale)

P, I   Seuss, Dr. 1971. *The Lorax.* New York: Random House. (Environment)

P, I   Seuss, Dr. 1990. *Oh, the Places You'll Go.* New York: Random House. (Self-concept)

P, I   Sewall, M. 1990. *People of the Breaking Day.* New York: Atheneum. (Wampanoag Indians)

I   Sewall, M. 1995. *Thunder from a Clear Sky.* New York: Atheneum. (Pilgrims—different perspectives)

P   Seymour, T. V. N. 1993. *The Gift of the Changing Women.* New York: Holt. (Navajo culture)

P   Sharmat, M. W. 1980. *Gila Monsters Meet You at the Airport.* New York: Aladdin. (Stereotyping)

P   Shea, P. D. 1995. *The Whispering Cloth.* New York: Boyd's Mills Press. (Thai refugee camp)

P   Shefelman, J. 1992. *A Peddler's Dream.* Boston: Houghton Mifflin. (Immigration)

P   Shelby, A. 1995. *Homeplace.* New York: Orchard. (Home from 1819 to present)

P   Shepard, A. 1995. *The Gifts of Wali Dad: A Tale of India and Pakistan.* New York: Atheneum. (Tale from India)

P   Shepard, A. 1992. *Savitri: A Tale of Ancient India.* New York: Philomel. (Tale from India)

I   Sherman, E. 1990. *Independence Avenue.* Philadelphia: Jewish Publication Society. (Jewish history, Jewish immigration—Galveston movement)

P, I   Sherman, O., & Schwartz, L. S. *The Four Questions.* New York: Dial. (Passover story)

P, I   Shetterly, S. H. 1991. *Raven's Light: A Myth from the People of the Northwest Coast.* New York: Atheneum. (Native American creation myth)

P, I   Shorto, R. 1994. *The Untold Story of Cinderella: Upside Down Tales.* New York: Carol Publishing Group. (Classic and stepmother's versions of *Cinderella*)

P   Siebert, D. 1991. *Sierra.* New York: HarperCollins. (Environment)

P, I   Silverstein, S. 1964. *The Giving Tree.* New York: HarperCollins. (Environment)

P   Simon, N. 1975. *All Kinds of Families.* Morton Grove, IL: Albert Whitman. (Family—differences and likenesses)

I   Simon, N. 1976. *Roll of Thunder, Hear My Cry.* New York: Dial. (African Americans)

I   Simon, N. 1976. *Why Am I Different?* Morton Grove, IL: Albert Whitman. (African Americans)

P, I　Singer, M. 1994. *Family Reunion.* New York: Macmillan/Simon & Schuster. (Extended family)

P　Sis, P. 1991. *Follow the Dream: The Story of Christopher Columbus.* New York: Knopf. (Columbus—different perspectives)

I　Siskind, L. 1992. *The Hopscotch Tree.* New York: Bantam/Skylark. (Prejudice, Jewish people)

P　Skutch, R. 1995. *Who's in a Family?* Berkeley: Tricycle Press. (Families—differences and likenesses)

P　Smalls, I. 1992. *Jonathan and His Mommy.* Boston: Little, Brown. (African American family)

I　Smith, D. B. 1994. *Remember the Red-Shouldered Hawk.* New York: Putnam. (Family; challenged—Alzheimer's; elderly)

I　Smucker, B. 1977. *Runaway to Freedom.* New York: Harper. (African American history, slavery)

P, I　Snyder, D. 1988. *The Boy of the Three-Year Nap.* Boston: Houghton Mifflin. (Chinese American tale)

P　Sonneborn, R. 1970. *Friday Night Is Papa Night.* New York: Puffin. (Hispanic family)

I　Sorensen, V. 1983. *Plain Girl.* San Diego: Harcourt Brace. (Amish family)

I　Soto, G. 1992. *Neighbor Odes.* San Diego: Harcourt Brace Jovanovich. (Mexican American poems)

P　Soto, G. 1993. *Too Many Tamales.* New York: Putnam. (Food—Hispanic)

P　Souhami, J. 1997. *Rama and the Demon King: An Ancient Tale from India.* New York: DK. (Tale from India)

I　Speare, E. 1983. *The Sign of the Beaver.* Boston: Houghton Mifflin. (Native Americans)

I　Spiegel, B. 1992. *The Year They Walked: Rosa Parks and the Montgomery Bus Boycott.* New York: Simon & Schuster. (African Americans, social activism)

P, I　Spier, P. 1980. *People.* New York: Doubleday. (Differences and likenesses)

P　Spier, P. 1973. *The Star-Spangled Banner.* New York: Doubleday. (Song—national anthem picture book)

I　Springer, N. 1989. *They're Called Wildfire.* New York: Atheneum. (Stereotyping, African Americans)

I　Springer, M. 1991. *Colt.* New York: Dial. (Challenged—spina bifida)

P, I　Spurr, E. 1995. *Lupe & Me.* New York: Gulliver. (Mexican culture, immigration)

P　Stanek, M. 1990. *I Speak English for My Mom.* Morton Grove, IL: Albert Whitman. (Spanish language)

I　Stanley, J. 1994. *I Am an American: A True Story of Japanese Internment.* New York: Crown. (Japanese American history)

P　Steptoe, J. 1980. *Daddy Is a Monster . . . Sometimes.* New York: Harper. (Single-parent family)

P, I   Steptoe, J. 1987. *Mufaro's Beautiful Daughters: An African Tale.* New York: Lothrop, Lee & Shepard. (African American version of *Cinderella*)

I   Stern, J. 1990. *The Filipino Americans.* New York: Chelsea House. (Filipino American history)

I   Stevens, B. 1992. *Frank Thompson: Her Civil War Story.* New York: Macmillan. (Social activism)

P, I   Stevens, J. 1993. *Coyote Steals the Blanket.* New York: Holiday House. (Ute tale)

I   Stevens, J. R. 1993. *Carlos and the Cornfield.* Flagstaff, AZ: Northland. (Hispanic people, self-concept)

P   Stevens, J. R. 1993. *Carlos and the Squash Plant.* Flagstaff, AZ: Northland. (Hispanic family)

P, I   Stevenson, J. 1977. *"Could Be Worse."* New York: Mulberry Books. (Elderly version of "It Could Always Be Worse" tale).

I   Stile, D. 1990. *Water Pollution.* Chicago: Children's Press. (Environment)

P   Stoltz, M. 1991. *Storm in the Night.* New York: Harper. (Elderly; African American family)

P   Stoltz, M. 1991. *Go Fish.* New York: HarperCollins. (African American family, elderly)

I   Stoutenburg, A., & Powers, R. M. 1976. *American Tall Tales.* New York: Viking. (American tall tales)

P, I   Straight, S. 1990. *Aquaboogie.* Minneapolis, MN: Milkweed. (African American tale)

P, I   Stroud, V. A. 1994. *Doesn't Fall Off His Horse.* New York: Dial. (Life of a Kiowa boy in the 1890s)

P   Sun, C. F. 1994. *Mama Bear.* Boston: Houghton Mifflin. (Asian American family)

P   Surat, M. M. 1983. *Angel Child, Dragon Child.* New York: Scholastic. (Vietnamese American family, stereotyping)

I   Swentzell, R. 1992. *Children of the Clay: A Family of Pueblo Potters.* Minneapolis: Lerner. (Pueblo culture)

I   Takaki, R. 1994. *In the Heart of Filipino America: Immigrants from the Pacific Isles.* New York: Chelsea House. (Filipino American history, Filipino immigrants)

I   Taylor, E. E. 1990. *Thank You, Dr. Martin Luther King, Jr.!* New York: Watts. (African American family, African American history)

I   Taylor, M. D. 1980. *Mississippi Bridge.* New York: Dial. (Stereotyping)

I   Taylor, M. D. 1989. *The Road to Memphis.* New York: Dial. (Prejudice)

I   Taylor, M. D. 1976. *Roll of Thunder, Hear My Cry.* New York: Dial. (African American family, prejudice)

I   Taylor, M. D. 1995. *The Well: David's Story.* New York: Dial. (African American history)

P   Taylor, S. 1980. *Danny Loves a Holiday.* New York: Dutton. (Jewish holiday)

I   Temple, L., ed. 1993. *Dear World: How Children around the World Feel about Our Environment.* New York: Random House. (Environment)

P, I   Thomas, J. C. 1993. *Brown Honey in Broomwheat Tea.* New York: HarperCollins. (African American poems)

I   Thomas, J. C. 1992. *When the Nightingale Sings.* New York: HarperCollins. (Modern African American *Cinderella*-like story)

P   Thomas, J. R. 1994. *Lights on the River.* New York: Hyperion. (Migrant workers; Spanish and English languages)

P, I   Thompson, C. 1992. *The Paper Bag Prince.* New York: Knopf. (Environment)

P   Thompson, M. 1996. *Andy and His Yellow Frisbee.* Bethesda, MD: Woodbine House. (Challenged—autism)

I   Thomson, P. 1993. *City Kids in China.* New York: HarperCollins. (China)

I   Time-Life Books, Editors of. 1994. *Creative Fire: African American Voices of Triumph.* New York: Time-Life. (Famous African Americans)

I   Tobias, T. 1993. *Pot Luck.* New York: Lothrop. (Family, elderly)

P, I   Tokuda, W., & Hall, R. 1986. *Humphrey the Lost Whale.* Union City, CA: Herian International. (Environment)

I   Toll, N. S. 1993. *Behind the Secret Window: A Memoir of a Hidden Childhood during World War Two.* New York: Dial. (Jewish people, World War II)

I   Tomcheck, A. H. 1992. *The Hopi: A New True Book.* Chicago: Children's Press. (Native American history)

I   Tompert, A. 1990. *Grandfather Tang's Story.* New York: Crown. (Chinese family)

P   Tompert, A. 1994. *Will You Come Back for Me?* Morton Grove, IL: Albert Whitman. (Asian American family)

P   Tran, K. 1987. *The Little Weaver of Thai-Shen Village.* San Francisco: Children's Book Press. (Vietnamese American tale)

P, I   Trivias, E., & Oxenbury, H. 1993. *The Three Little Wolves and the Big Bad Pig.* New York: Margaret K. McElderry Books. (Humorous version of *The Three Little Pigs*)

P   Tsaitui, Y. 1988. *Anna in Charge.* New York: Viking. (Self-concept, Japanese family)

P, I   Turner, A. 1989. *Heron Street.* New York: Harper. (Environment)

I   Turner, A. 1987. *Nettie's Trip South.* New York: Macmillan. (Civil War, prejudice)

P   Turner, A. 1990. *Through Moon and Stars and Night Skies.* New York: HarperCollins. (Family—adoption)

I   Turner, G. 1989. *Take a Walk in Their Shoes.* New York: Cobblestone. (African American history, social activism)

I   Turner, R. M. 1992. *Faith Ringgold.* Boston: Little, Brown. (Famous African American women, quilts)

I   Twain, M. 1993. *Mark Twain: Short Stories and Tall Tales.* Courage Books. (American tall tales)

I   Uchida, Y. 1983. *The Best of a Bad Thing.* New York: Simon & Schuster. (Japanese Americans)

I   Uchida, Y. 1985. *Journey to Topaz: Story of the Japanese–American Evacuation.* New York: Scribner's. (Japanese American history)

P   Uchida, Y. 1993. *The Magic Purse.* New York: Margaret McElderry. (Japanese folktale)

I   Uchida, Y. 1987. *Picture Bride.* Flagstaff, AZ: Northland. (Japanese Americans)

I   Uchida, Y. 1985. *Samurai of Gold Hill.* San Francisco: Creative Arts Books. (Japanese Americans)

P   Uchida, Y. 1994. *The Wise Old Women.* New York: Margaret McElderry. (Japanese folktale)

P, I   Uchida, Y., & Yardley, J. 1993. *The Bracelet.* New York: Philomel. (Japanese American history)

P   Udry, J. M. 1966. *What May Jo Shared.* New York: Scholastic. (African American family)

P   Va, L. 1991. *A Letter to King.* New York: HarperCollins. (Chinese tale, Chinese and English languages)

P, I   Van Allsburg. 1990. *Just a Dream.* Boston: Houghton Mifflin. (Environment, social activism)

P   Van Laan, N. 1991. *The Legend of El Dorado: A Latin American Tale.* New York: Knopf. (Latin American tale)

P   Van Leeuwen, J. 1995. *across the Wide Dark Sea: The Mayflower Journey.* New York: Dial. (Pilgrimages, Pilgrims)

I   Van Raven, P. 1989. *Harpoon Island.* New York: Scribner's. (Stereotyping)

I   Vazauez, A. M., & Casas, R. E. 1987. *Cuba: Enchantment of the World.* Chicago: Children's Press. (Cuban history, Cuban culture)

P, I   Vigna, J. 1995. *My Two Uncles.* New York: Whitman. (Gay uncle)

        Vos, I. 1991. *Hide and Seek.* Boston: Houghton Mifflin. (World War II, Jewish people)

I   Vuong, L. D. 1993. *The Golden Carp and Other Tales of Vietnam.* New York: Lothrop. (Vietnamese tales)

I   Vuong, L. D. 1993. *Sky Legends from Vietnam.* New York: HarperCollins. (Vietnamese stories, poems, and a song)

P   Waber, B. 1966. *You Look Ridiculous: Said the Rhinoceros to the Hippopotamus.* Boston: Houghton Mifflin. (Self-concept)

P   Waddell, M. 1990. *My Great-Grandpa.* New York: Putnam. (Family, elderly)

P, I   Walker, A. 1991. *Finding the Green Stone.* London: Hodder & Stoughton. (Love)

P, I   Walker, A. 1967. *To Hell with Dying.* San Diego: Harcourt Brace Jovanovich. (Elderly)

I   Walker, P. R. 1993. *Big Men, Big Country: A Collection of American Tall Tales.* San Diego: Harcourt Brace. (American tall tales)

P   Wallace, I. 1984. *Chin Chiang and the Dragon's Dance.* New York: Atheneum/Macmillan. (Chinese people)

P, I   Wallner, A. 1992. *Since 1920.* New York: Doubleday. (Native American family; houses and homes)

I   Walter, M. P. 1995. *Kwanzaa: A Family Affair.* New York: Lothrop, Lee & Shepard. (African American holiday)

P   Walter, M. P. 1983. *My Mama Needs Me.* New York: Macmillan. (African American family)

P, I   Waters, K. 1996. *On the Mayflower: Voyage of the Ship's Apprentice & a Passenger Girl.* New York: Scholastic. (Pilgrimages—different perspectives)

P, I   Waters, K. 1989. *Samuel Easton: A Day in the Life of a Pilgrim Boy.* New York: Scholastic. (Pilgrims—different perspectives)

P, I   Waters, K. 1989. *Sarah Morton's Day: A Day in the Life of a Pilgrim Girl.* New York: Scholastic. (Pilgrims—different perspectives)

P, I   Waters, K. 1996. *Tamenum's Day: A Wampanoag Indian Boy in Pilgrim Times.* New York: Scholastic. (Pilgrims—different perspectives)

P   Waters, K., & Slvenz-Low, M. 1990. *Lion Dancer: Ernie Wan's Chinese New Year.* New York: Scholastic. (Chinese holiday)

P   Watson, E. 1996. *Talking to Angels.* San Diego: Harcourt Brace. (Challenged—autism)

P   Watson, P., & Watson, M. 1995. *The Market Lady and the Mango Tree.* New York: Tambourine Books. (Africans)

I   Weatherford, D. 1995. *Foreign and Female: Immigrant Women in America 1840–1930.* New York: Facts on File. (Immigration, gender equity)

P, I   Weeks, S. 1995. *Red Ribbon.* New York: HarperCollins. (Social activism—AIDS)

P, I   Weir, B., & Weir, W. 1991. *Panther Dream: A Story of the African Rainforest.* New York: Hyperion. (Environment)

P, I   Weisman, J. 1993. *The Storyteller.* New York: Rizzoli. (Native American family, elderly)

P   Weiss, N. 1992. *The First Night of Hanukkah.* New York: Putnam/Grosset & Dunlap. (Jewish holiday)

I   Werlin, M. 1996. *Are You Alone on Purpose?* Boston: Houghton Mifflin. (Challenged—autism)

P   Westcott, N. R. 1984. *The Emperor's New Clothes.* Boston: Little, Brown. (Classic fairy tale)

I   Westridge Young Writer's Workshop. 1992. *Kids Explore America's Hispanic Heritage.* Santa Fe, NM: John Muir. (Mexican American culture)

I   Whelan, G. 1991. *Hannah.* New York: Knopf. (Challenged—blind)

I   White, F. M. 1973. *Cesar Chavez: Man of Courage.* Champaign, IL: Garrard. (Hispanic history)

I   Whitehouse, B. 1994. *Sunpainters: Eclipse of the Navajo Sun.* Flagstaff, AZ: Northland. (Navajo culture)

I   Wier, E. 1992. *The Loner.* New York: Scholastic. (Homeless people, migrant workers)

P   Wild, M. 1993. *All the Better to See You With.* Morton Grove, IL: Albert Whitman. (Challenged—handicapped)

P   Wild, M. 1994. *Our Granny.* Boston: Houghton Mifflin. (Elderly)

P   Willhoite, M. 1990. *Daddy's Roommate.* Boston: Alyson Wonderland. (Family—gay)

I   Williams, G. R. 1988. *Blue Tights.* New York: Lodestar. (African Americans, self-concept)

P   Williams, K. 1990. *Galimoto.* New York: Lothrop, Lee & Shepard. (Africans)

P   Williams, S. A. 1992. *Working Cotton.* San Diego: Harcourt Brace Jovanovich. (African American history)

P   Williams, V. B. 1982. *A Chair for My Mother.* New York: Scholastic. (Hispanic people)

P   Williams, V. B. 1982. *Music, Music for Everyone.* New York: Mulberry Books. (Hispanic people)

P   Williams, V. B. 1982. *Something Special for Me.* New York: Mulberry Books. (Hispanic people)

I   Willis, P. 1991. *A Place to Call Home.* New York: Clarion. (Family—orphan)

P   Wilson, B. P. 1990. *Jenny.* New York: Macmillan. (African American family)

P   Winter, J. 1991. *Diego.* New York: Knopf. (Hispanic history)

P, I   Winter, J. 1992. *Follow the Drinking Gourd.* New York: Dragonfly/Knopf. (African American history, slavery)

I   Witherspoon, W. R. 1985. *Martin Luther King, Jr.: To the Mountaintop.* Champaign, IL: Garrard. (African American history, social activism)

P, I   Wolf, B. 1995. *Homeless.* New York: Orchard. (Homeless people)

P   Wolf, G. 1996. *The Very Hungry Lion: A Folktale.* Toronto: Annick Press. (Tale from India)

P, I   Wolfe, R. E. 1992. *Mary McLeod Bethune.* New York: Watts. (Famous African American woman)

I   Wolfson, E. 1993. *From the Earth to Beyond the Sky: Native American Medicine.* Boston: Houghton Mifflin. (Native American medicine men)

I   Wood, J. R. 1992. *The Man Who Loved Clowns.* Morton Grove, IL: Albert Whitman. (Challenged—Down syndrome)

I   Wood, J. R. 1995. *When Pigs Fly.* New York: Putnam. (Challenged—Down syndrome)

I   Wood, N. 1995. *Dancing Moons.* New York: Doubleday. (Native American poems)

I   Wood, N. 1993. *Spirit Walker.* New York: Bantam Doubleday Dell. (Native American poems)

I   Woodson, J. 1991. *The Dear One.* San Diego: Delacorte. (African American family)

I   Woodson, J. 1992. *Maizon at Blue Hill.* San Diego: Delacorte. (Prejudice)

I   Wrede, P. 1990. *Dealing with Dragons.* New York: Harcourt Brace. (Gender equity)

I   Wright, B. 1969. *Black Boy: A Record of Childhood and Youth.* New York: Harper & Row. (African Americans)

P   Wyndham, R. 1968. *Chinese Mother Goose Rhymes.* New York: Putnam. (Chinese rhymes)

P, I   Yannuzzi, D. A. 1996. *Zora Neale Hurston: Southern Storyteller.* Springfield, NJ: Enslow. (Famous African American woman)

P   Yarbrough, C. 1979. *Cornrows.* New York: Coward-McCann. (African Americans)

P   Yashima, T. 1979. *Crow Boy.* New York: Puffin. (Japanese people)

I   Yee, P. 1990. *Tales from Gold Mountains: Stories of the Chinese in the New World.* New York: Macmillan. (Immigration, migration)

I   Yep, L. 1988. *Child of the Owl.* New York: Harper & Row. (Chinese American family, elderly, Chinese American culture)

I   Yep, L. 1993. *Dragons Gate.* New York: Harper. (Chinese immigration)

I   Yep, L. 1975. *Dragonwings.* New York: Harper. (Chinese American family)

I   Yep, L. 1995. *Hiroshima: A Novella.* New York: Scholastic. (Japanese history—Hiroshima)

I   Yep, L. 1995. *Later, Gator.* New York: Hyperion. (Chinese American family)

I   Yep, L. 1989. *The Rainbow People.* New York: Holt. (Chinese American tales)

P, I   Yep, L. 1993. *The Shell Woman and the King: A Chinese Folktale.* New York: Dial. (Chinese folktale)

P, I   Ying, P. C. 1988. *Monkey Creates Havoc in Heaven.* New York: Viking. (Chinese tale)

P, I   Yolen, J. 1992. *Encounter.* San Diego: Harcourt Brace Jovanovich. (Columbus—different perspectives)

P, I   Yolen, J. 1986. *Favorite Folktales from Around the World.* New York: Pantheon. (Multicultural tales)

P   Yolen, J. 1987. *Owl Moon.* New York: Philomel. (Environment, family)

P, I   Yolen, J. *Sky Dogs.* San Diego: Harcourt Brace Jovanovich. (Blackfeet Indian tale)

P   Young, E. 1987. *I Wish I Were a Butterfly.* San Diego: Harcourt Brace. (Self-concept)

P   Young, E. 1989. *Lon Po Po.* New York: Philomel. (Chinese version of *Little Red Riding Hood*)

P   Young, E. 1995. *Night Visitors.* New York: Philomel. (Chinese folktale)

P   Young, E. 1992. *Seven Blind Mice.* New York: Philomel. (Tales—Indian; different perspectives)

P   Young, R. 1992. *Golden Bear.* New York: Viking. (African Americans)

P, I   Zak, M. 1994. *Save My Rainforest.* Volcano, CA: Volcano Press. (Environment, Mexicans, social activism)

I   Zapater, B. M. 1992. *Fiesta!* Cleveland: Modern Curriculum Press. (Latin American history, Latin American holidays)

P   Zolotow, C. 1992. *The Seashore Book.* New York: Harper. (Environment)

P   Zolotow, C. 1972. *William's Doll.* New York: Harper & Row. (Self-concept, gender equity)

NAME INDEX

Adams, M., 18
Anderson, R. C., 14, 17–19, 20, 22
Aronson, E., 9
Asher, S. P., 14–15
Atwell, N., 15
Au, K. H., 9, 23

Banks, C., 10
Banks, J. A., 3–11
Beck, I. L., 19, 22
Becker, J. M., 6
Berhoff, B., 14–16
Blackman, J. A., 6–7, 9
Bowman, B., 9
Boyer, E. L., 24
Braddock, J., 9
Brookover, W. B., 8
Brown, A. L., 15, 17, 20
Bullivant, B. M., 10

Calkins, L., 20
Cambourne, B., 21
Carter, M., 23–24
Clay, M. M., 23
Cohen, E. G., 9
Cooper, E., 14–21, 23
Cooper, J. D., 9
Cullihan, B., 16
Cummins, J., 10

Dalrymple, J. D., 23
Danielson, K. E., 16
Darling-Hammond, L., 23–24
Desai, L., 23–24
Donaldson, B., 8
Dorsey-Gaines, C., 14
Dressel, J. H., 14–16
Durkin, D., 22

Egawa, K., 14–16
Erickson, E., 8

Fader, 14–15
Feitelson, L. G., 14, 16
Ferguson, R. F., 7

Fielding, L. G., 14, 16
Frazier, L., 3
Fredricks, A. D., 23–24
Freebody, P., 19
Freepon, P., 18
Frye, B. J., 22

Galda, L., 16
Garcia, R. I., 3, 9
Gardner, H., 10
Gay, G., 6–9, 11
Goldstein, R. C., 14, 16
Gonzales, A., 9
Goodman, K., 14–24
Goodman, Y., 15, 17
Gordon, C., 17
Gould, S. J., 8
Grant, C. A., 3–7, 9–10
Graves, D. H., 19–20, 22, 24
Greaves, M., 22

Hall, N., 22
Halliday, M. A. K., 14, 16, 18
Hansen, J., 17, 22
Harste, J., 20
Haussler, M. M., 15
Heath, S. B., 10
Helper, S., 15, 17
Hennings, D. G., 14–16, 18–21, 23
Herman, P. A., 23
Herrings, G., 15, 22, 24
Hickman, J., 15, 17
Hiebert, E. H., 18, 20
Holdaway, 14, 19, 22
Huck, C. S., 15–17

Jenkins, C. B., 23

Karelitz, E. B., 20
Kawakami, A. J., 9, 23
Kiefer, B. Z., 18, 20, 23
Kita, B., 14, 16

LaBondy, J., 16
Levstik, L. S., 18, 20, 23

SUBJECT INDEX